HOW SOCIETIES
EMBRACE INFORMATION
TECHNOLOGY

HOW SOCIETIES EMBRACE INFORMATION TECHNOLOGY

Lessons for Management and the Rest of Us

JAMES W. CORTADA

A JOHN WILEY & SONS, INC., PUBLICATION

Published by John Wiley & Sons, Inc., Hoboken, New Jersey
Published simultaneously in Canada.

For general information on our other products and services please contact our Customer Care Department within the U.S. at 877-762-2974, outside the U.S. at 317-572-3993 or fax 317-572-4002.

Wiley also publishes its books in a variety of electronic formats. Some content that appears in print, however, may not be available in electronic format.

Library of Congress Cataloging-in-Publication Data:

978-0470-53498-4

Printed in the United States of America.

10 9 8 7 6 5 4 3 2 1

CONTENTS

PREFACE

Whether you live in a sub-Saharan city or in downtown London, in a small village in southern India or Vietnam, or in a Midwestern community in the United States, computers and digital technologies are at work. There are hundreds of millions of PCs and laptops; over two billion people use wireless phones; Apple has sold over one hundred million iPods in a half-decade; every car manufactured in the last three decades has dozens of computers under the hood; and, oh yes, over a third of the world's population uses the Internet. Computers and their digital technologies are almost ubiquitous around the world. No technology in the history of humankind has spread so fast to so many nations. In 1950, there were less than 100 computers in the world; a decade later, maybe 6000. Forty years later, there were probably a billion systems. We cannot arrive at a good estimate, because so many microprocessors have been embedded in industrial equipment, airplanes, weapons, and in such household goods as microwave ovens, television sets, and music systems such that it is now impossible to know. In preparing an earlier book in the late 1990s, *Making the Information Society,* I went around my middle class American home and counted what I thought were some 50 computer systems, most embedded in our two TVs, two automobiles, kitchen appliances, two PCs, a large array of stereo music devices (my two daughters were teenagers at the time), digital clocks, and other items.

All of these developments lead to the obvious conclusion that we have reached a point where in order to understand the makeup of modern society and to discuss how it might continue to evolve, one needs to understand the role of computers and their myriad digital technologies. There are many questions to answer, however. This book will begin addressing a few that I believe are some of the most important ones that we face at this time. To be sure there are many others to be answered, but here I deal with a few. For example, how did the technology spread so fast and so completely around the world? Because governments have encouraged this spread, we have to ask what roles they play in the diffusion of this technology. It is governments, after all, that today play a crucial role in the evolution of many aspects of modern society, ranging from how they deliver services to their citizens, to how they protect us from terrorists, enemies, and criminals, to what industries they encourage as a way of maintaining improving standards of living.

After addressing those two big questions, I turn to an equally important, yet tactical issue: How did individual managers in the private and public sectors and their organizations make decisions to acquire computers? Why? I believe the Internet is only one aspect of a bigger story about the role of information technology (IT), or digital technologies, but an important one nonetheless.

Because this book is focused on the needs of corporate management, public administrators, and those scientists and engineers who shape the technologies, these chapters offer insights about the role each could or, indeed I believe, should play in the diffusion of IT and how the technology can shape societies. Each community already has a symbiotic relationship that is pointing the way to specific strategies and actions for them, especially as they continue collaborating. It is an important topic because that relationship has spilled over into a global setting. For corporations, for example, it can mean dealing with scores of governments, each different and operating in unique societies; for public officials it involves engaging with firms that also have to contend with circumstances in many other nations.

Meanwhile, it is almost impossible to find any commentator on modern society who can resist the temptation to declare that we live in the Information Age. I have hundreds of books in my personal library with that phrase or something similar in their title, and we have all read many articles making the same declaration. So I ask, do we really live in the Information Age? More than a fun question to ponder, the issue helps us describe the extent to which digital technologies define and shape contemporary society. To answer the question, I rely on the methods and values of the historian to guide our discussion. I conclude by suggesting possible milestone markers to help societies, their governments, businesses, and their technical communities measure their collective march toward an information age.

Regardless of whether we live in such a brave new world, there is little doubt that societies will continue to evolve because of, and, indeed be shaped by, the continuing emergence of additional IT. So, what can we expect? How can we define emerging trends coming over the next decade or two? Predicting and forecasting are tenuous exercises, but we know a great deal about trends because one secret we are rarely told about the evolution of computing is how slowly it really changes. So we know a great deal about what is pending around the corner. What strategies and actions should senior officials and executives take that represent win–win situations for nations and firms, for economies and consumers, and for the health of the planet? I call out only a few that are already having positive effects. Finally, enough changes occur that we do need to keep up, so the short bibliographic essay is more a strategy than a catalog of my favorite books and articles.

This book is essentially a collection of essays on the common theme of the role of IT in modern societies and not a formal, rigorous academic monograph. I did not intend for it to be a thorough and comprehensive study of the issues discussed, because too much remains to be better understood before anyone can tell the story comprehensively enough. Scholars are still formulating theories of behavior, debating the issues involved, and much history has yet to be done to find out what has happened even just so far in humankind's use of these new technologies. Many have tried to be comprehensive, and others will later. My book is intended to be a small contribution to the discussion, a snapshot of patterns of activities and proposed actions as of this moment in history that I personally find relevant based on my work in the industry and as a student of the technology's uses. Because it is a book of essays on related themes, there inevitably will be some repetition of important themes from one chapter to another. In some instances, that is done on purpose; in other instances it cannot be helped. That circumstance, however, makes it possible for every chapter to stand on its own without requiring the reader to have read earlier ones to appreciate the dialogue underway. This approach does assume that readers have more than a casual interest in the various themes discussed as well, which saves me from increasing sharply the size of the book.

In the spirit of full disclosure, I should point out that I have written over two dozen books dealing with the topics addressed in this one. I have studied the way organizations, industries, governments, and whole societies use computers. A great deal of that work focused on the experience of the United States, but partially as well on European and Asian aspects. If the reader senses a heavy hand of American perspectives, or even an "IBM view" (something I rarely observed, since IBMers share as many diverse views as people outside the firm), they might be right despite my attempts to provide a more global perspective. I am a product of my times and experience. The sadder truth is that most of what we know about the past sixty years of information technologies comes from the North American experience and we have to start somewhere. In some instances I have written on contemporary managerial issues for those publications aimed directly at corporate managers, computer scientists, IT management, and government officials working with the technology. In other instances I have published formal histories that have demonstrated the business history aspect of the role of computing, arguing that there is more to the history of IT than the history of the technology relevant to our understanding of the role of computers. I was trained as an historian but spent over thirty years working at IBM in various sales, consulting, and managerial roles, perched at the nexus where technology, its use, and how society functions meet, granting me a front row seat to watch what was happening, the ability to document its features, and the opportunity to persuade an editor to publish my findings. I have also watched scientists and engineers invent new things. I have been in many intense meetings persuading customers and clients to spend millions of dollars on computers and software. I hope that combination of involvement in the use and deployment of the technology and also being a student of its use and history has given me the special insight I believe this book provides.

Normally, books on managerial or social aspects of computing tend to ignore the computer scientists and inventors of the technology for a variety of reasons that I discuss later in the book. Yet their role is important, both as creators of these technologies but also as advocates about how best they should be used. I have not ignored them; I devote a chapter to their role and encourage them to speak with a strong voice as societies all over the world become so influenced by their inventions.

I want to acknowledge *Historical Methods* for allowing me to muse about whether we live in the Information Age; I drew heavily on my work there for writing Chapter 5. I also want to thank the *IEEE Annals of the History of Computing* for allowing me to use an article published in that journal to serve as the base for my comments in Chapter Two.

Book writing is a team event; nobody does it without help. As this book came together, Alan Clements at the IEEE Computer Society, always watchful for its interests, suggested that I submit it to the society's press after reading an earlier draft. Simultaneously, he got me interested in supporting the educational activities of the Computer Society, and most specifically, those of the Computer Society Educational Activities Board. To that end, all royalties generated by this book will remain in the Computer Society to further that mission. I am delighted to have the opportunity to give back something to an organization that has been so good to tens of thousands of us in the industry. The editorial staff at IEEE CS Press has been wonderful to work with and I am particularly appreciative of the good work of Janet Wilson. The production team at John Wiley & Sons also did their always professional work as well. Anonymous reviewers were most helpful in pointing out the strengths of the book—so, hopefully I did not tinker with those-while suggesting specific ways that I could improve it, so many thanks to them. However, despite their help, this book of essays is of my own doing. It does not necessarily reflect the views of the IBM Corporation, or of any of its employees, or those of the Computer Society; they are solely mine. Failings and errors are the result of my weaknesses, for which I am responsible.

JAMES W. CORTADA

Madison, Wisconsin
July 2009

1

INTRODUCING THE BIG PICTURE

A new social form, the network society, is being constituted around the planet, albeit in a diversity of shapes, and with considerable differences in its consequences for people's lives, depending on history, culture, and institutions.
—MANUEL CASTELLS [1]

Information technologies have become important artifacts—indeed key features—of modern life around the world. This did not happen by the accident of miraculous technologies being continuously served up by engineers and computer scientists selling themselves, so to speak. Managers in companies and in governments made millions of individual decisions to use the technology in support of their work. Additionally, public officials in time came to realize that encouraging use of this class of technology offered an opportunity to improve the quality of life of its citizens, and to make their economies competitive in an increasingly integrated global economy. Aspirations of individuals and institutions changed in the process. Today, corporations and governments interact quite intensively in the grand process of infusing information technologies in all manner of work and activities of a society. Some of the most important and obvious features of that experience are discussed in this book. By its scope, one will see that I have not discussed the role of individual consumers—the purchasers of iPods and laptops, the users of social networking software and the Internet to find information—because I believe their activities would not be possible without the work of corporations, governments, computer scientists, and engineers that is described in this book. Furthermore, the activities of the consumer are already receiving considerable attention, making the need for the discussion presented in this book all the more urgent to provide balance in our understanding of how nations and their societies are embracing the use of digital technologies.

THE PRESENCE OF INFORMATION TECHNOLOGY

Today, all nations turn to various types of technologies with which to support their current standard of living, to improve their quality of life, and support such daily activities as work, transportation, and entertainment. This applies to both businesses and government agencies. The most obvious collections of technologies used for these purposes have been computers and telecommunications over the past six decades. The most visible current form of this collection of technologies is, of course, the Internet, which went from a narrowly used form of communication in the 1970s and 1980s to the point where today over a third of the world's population uses it, overwhelmingly for e-mail and to find information, but increasingly as well to conduct business transactions. Yet that specific use of information technology (IT)—the Internet—while remarkable, is only one type of computing in use. Every midsized to large business in the advancing and most advanced economies uses computers in support of every major work process. If one could measure the volume of activity going through those systems, we could quite possibly discover more activity than on the Internet. If we look at IT in smaller forms, such as the use of computer chips in various devices, we would discover other vast uses of computing, most notably in cell phones, which are now used by over one-third of the world's population. Interestingly, the fastest deployment of that technology is now occurring in underdeveloped economies, ensuring that in this small form of computing IT is spreading to all countries on earth.

Finally, microcomputing has been embedded in all manner of sophisticated equipment, from rockets and airplanes, to paper making machines, to every automobile made in the past quarter century in Asia, Western Europe, and North America, in digital music systems over the past two decades, and in today's flat screen television sets. Myriad other consumer electronics have computers embedded in them, such as digital cameras, which essentially destroyed the market for film-based photography in less than a decade; video games, which are now played by over a billion people; and various small consumer and job-related equipment, ranging from microwave ovens to GPS-dependent surveying equipment and mapping. Then there are the hundreds of millions of personal computers, laptops, Blackberries, and iPods, to mention yet other classes of smaller devices used both by workers as part of their on-the-job activities and in the private lives of people from children to senior citizens. So, the first perspective one should keep in mind is that humankind has massively embraced a large variety of computer-based tools and consumer goods.

The second realization—and one that will affect how we look at what comes down the road over the next couple of decades—is how fast these various forms of IT were embraced by humankind. Figure 1.1 illustrates how quickly some technologies have been adopted. Such lists appear often in various forms in histories of computers and consumer products, and the data on rate of speed varies, although not a great deal. It is crucial to see that the rate of adoption of IT increased over time for some of the most important innovations of our age. As the technologies became less expensive, or conversely, one received more functionality for each dollar or Euro of investment, the more demand increased for such

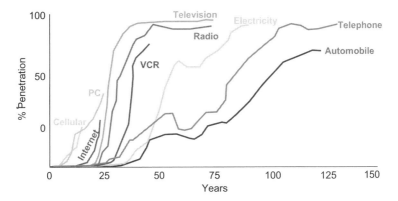

Figure 1.1. Adoptions of new technologies are taking hold at double or triple previous rates.

technologies. Additionally, over time three other technological features influenced in a positive manner the growth in demand: reliability of the technology increased, the number of things one could do with IT did too, and the forms it came in made the combination of functionality (what you could do with it) and cost proportional to potential buyers. What that means is that as the technology became less expensive or came in smaller packages (such as PCs instead of big room-sized computers), smaller organizations could afford to acquire and use them. Beginning in the late 1970s with PCs, the technology began to appear in smaller units, making it possible for individuals to acquire IT as well. By the end of the 1990s, a massive blending of the two classes of technology—big systems for companies and government agencies, and consumer-sized computing—bound together by computerized or computer-based telecommunications, made it possible for institutions and individuals to use IT in ways inconceivable and unaffordable even as late as the early 1970s.

It would be innocent to think that with all that hardware and software in use around the world that society would not be affected. Sociologist Manuel Castells has been looking at this issue for nearly three decades. As early as the 1980s, he began seeing a world networked closely together; that is to say, cities and countries interacted with each other by becoming increasingly dependent on telecommunications and computers. The massive adoption of the Internet by people living around the world, beginning in the late 1990s, reaffirmed his observation, allowing him to go so far as to declare that "the Internet is the fabric of our lives" [2]. While that might be an overstatement today and more true in the future, depending on which country one lives in, there is no denying the fact that its use is pervasive. More to the reality of our current circumstance, Castells concludes that, "If information technology is the present-day equivalent of electricity in the industrial era, in our age the Internet could be likened to both the electrical grid and the electric engine because of its ability to distribute the power of information throughout the entire realm of human activity" [3]. That comment leads to a third observation, that there is so much IT in use that how we work, play, and think of our world is now influenced profoundly by these various technologies. But, back to our first two points, it is more than just the Internet, it is the *combination* of all manner of computing technologies that have collectively begun to affect the way humans function.

There are limits, of course, although always stretched by thinking of ever greater possibilities. It has long been fashionable to think of computing as a replacement for the human mind, for instance. As early as 1948, a thoughtful manager in the insurance industry, Edmund C. Berkeley, wrote one of the first books on computers entitled *Giant Brains or, Brains that Think,* and on its cover was the picture of a human head with a transistor attached to it, suggesting it was augmenting people's intellectual capacities [4]. The previous year, MIT mathematician Norbert Wiener published his seminal book on the role of nervous systems, information, and the concept of feedback loops, which he entitled *Cybernetics; or Control and Communications in the Animal and the Machine* [5]. This kind of thinking launched a new field of academic research called artificial intelligence, or as it is more widely known, AI [6]. Over the next half-century, many commentators predicted the transformation of technology into forms so intelligent that either robots were going to take over the world, or humans would become partially mechanically and ever so much smarter [7]. As for us mortals, we are currently content to have spreadsheets that calculate mathematics correctly on our laptops; e-mail, of course; cell phones that are easy to use; video games and iPods to entertain us; and digital imaging in a doctor's office to let the medical profession see what is going on in our bodies.

It is important to account for the limits because there are so many new uses for computing that come along that we are tempted to overestimate what is realistic and practical to expect them to accomplish. For example, robots are used to paint automobiles, even to do all the welding of parts for those vehicles, but they do not look like humans, as in the movie *The Terminator* (1984). They appear more like metal boxes the size of a home refrigerator with an arm or two, and they can only do one or a few things. More sophisticated robots are just now being used to do delicate surgery for which a "steady hand" is intensively required, while Sony Corporation sells small gizmos with computer chips embedded in them that look like dogs and tiny people that are used for entertainment. Programmable vacuum cleaners and lawn mowers are proof that forecasts of future developments do come true. In the world of software, there are now programs that can determine who you really are, thus protecting your identity and your privacy from the user of that software, such as a government agency or a company. That is a wonderful development, since it is now essential to have trusted identification of people and things to prevent terrorism, to fight wars, and to provide the right services to an individual. We are nowhere near living in the computer-driven world of *Nineteen Eighty-Four* [8]. Nonetheless, we live in a world in which it seems most commentators about computing exaggerate the future to come or the present as it is.

So much is going on that this book cannot describe it all. Because of all this activity, it is at least worth giving a hint of its massiveness with some factoids. To begin with, all of humankind today spends over $3 trillion dollars annually just to acquire hardware, software, and digitally based consumer goods and services. About half of that is spent by organizations, such as companies and government agencies. They, in turn, spend an equal additional amount just using and maintaining what they acquired. It is not uncommon for an advanced national economy to spend between 6 and 16% of its gross domestic product (GDP) on this technology. In developing nations, it is largely spent on telecommunications such as wired telephony and, more often, on wireless phones [9]. In advanced economies we see that anywhere from half to two-thirds of the public uses the Internet or PCs on a regular basis; cell phone usage is now closer to 95%; worldwide, however, the total number of users had surpassed 2.4 billion by the start of 2007. It seems that only babies do not use cell phones in the most advanced economies. Consumers have acquired over 100 million iPods from Apple, and many tens of millions of similar devices from other firms. Today, the cost of the technology continues to decline or is packaged into smaller less expensive units, and we see Nicholas Negroponte at the Massachusetts Institute of Technology (MIT), Intel, and others selling laptops for use by schools that cost between $100 and $200 each. In the mid-1990s, a laptop cost nearly $2000 and there was no guarantee that one could access the Internet with it; the little $100 machines depend on that connection to work.

What are we to make of all this activity? The list of factoids presented above suggests that because there are so many developments underway, we have to be cautious about arriving at glib conclusions. For one thing, notice how many of the developments mentioned so far in this book, and others that will be discussed in succeeding pages, are interdependent on each other. Cell phones only work because of telecommunications and the availability of certain types of computer chips and batteries, the Internet is of value only if its voracious appetite for content is fed, and IT is only affordable if people find ways to pay for it. With so many things continuing to change that are outside the control of any one group, one has to be cautious about predictions. For example, scientists and engineers can transform technologies if someone can afford to pay their salaries; economic crises do lead to diminutions in research budgets. Also, political priorities in one country can lead to the deployment of much IT as an economic development strategy, whereas in another it may be curtailed due to national censorship policies. Import and export taxes influence the ebb and flow of components around the world, just as other taxes condition the movement of software development from one country to another. A war can spur developments and block routine usages. The list of variables affecting each other is nearly endless.

The one conclusion we can draw is that understanding this historically massive evolution in human society requires humility, caution, and the expectation that results will not always align with expectations. Our views will remain fragmented, not comprehensive. Always, things continue to remain in flux, with no visible end in sight. In short, the more we understand, the less certain we seem about our understanding. Yet it is that confluence of various IT activities underway that require that we form some appreciation of what is happening, since we still need to make decisions about our work and play and the role these technologies should have. That is why we next need to understand some broad patterns at work around the world.

MEGATRENDS AT WORK

There are many trends involving IT. These affect the work of managers, public officials, and their respective customers and citizens. Every student of the process has his or her own list. Mine is simple, short, and based on a considerable body of empirical evidence collected by myself and colleagues at IBM in the 2000s. Yet these are inclusive enough to support the contention that the big picture is in part painted by the various forms of currently used IT. There is no moral judgment involved here. Technology is not good or bad; only its uses apply here, to cure a disease or to make smart bombs, for instance. Some of it works very well, such as an iPod, whereas the operating system on a laptop can be intractable and infuriating. Large government agencies and corporations find that incrementally changing their software over the years leads to improved efficiencies and new services for citizens, but also that large projects implemented in big blocks can result in billions of dollars in unanticipated cost overruns and failures, particularly in the public sector, which historically always had the largest implementations of IT. The point is that technology is in use and has been long enough that it has affected profoundly the work and play of individuals. Several chapters, in particular, the fourth, explain how technology changes organizations, arguing that incremental changes in how work is done using computers accumulates change in a compound manner over time such that when one looks back a decade or so to contrast how things are done today as compared to that earlier period, one can easily conclude that they caused a revolution when, in fact, they evolved. This is an important insight for understanding how IT is changing our world and how decision makers will embrace future systems.

What are the trends one might keep in mind as one reads this book? On everyone's list in the early 2000s is globalization in its many forms. It seems every commentator has a unique definition of the word but they all have some common elements. The first that almost all observers agree on is the increase in cross-border trade. Wal-Mart in the United States is the world's largest importer of consumer goods made in China, bringing in more products than some nations import in total. The world's seven largest oil companies buy their crude from all over the world: Middle East, Latin America, the North Sea, Vietnam, Canada, and Nigeria. Indian software companies and call centers support retail, software, banking, insurance, and consumer goods firms around the world. The list is long. Globalization has many facets, however, and is not limited just to world trade, although that is an important feature. How important is that feature? One data point suggests the extent involved. In 1990, roughly 40% of all traded goods and services occurred in countries other than where they originated. By the end of 2005, that proportion had reached 60% [10]. The number of companies that operated in the global economy grew from some 35,000 in 1990 to over 70,000 in 2005, while the quantity of firms affiliated with these international companies as business partners increased fourfold [11].

That is merely the tip of the iceberg. At least 200 million people work or live in countries other than their own [12]. That number is expected to grow as workforces become increasingly mobile. Cases exist everywhere: massive migrations of young educated Poles to jobs in Ireland; Irish citizens returning to Ireland in larger numbers than those leaving—a first in the history of the country that occurred in the early 2000s; and millions of Mexican workers and their families moving legally or illegally into the United States, beginning in the 1980s. Again, the list of examples is long. One variant of this process worth pointing out is that there are internal migrations going on as well in response to the growing availability (or loss) of jobs often driven by international trade. This is occurring with millions of citizens moving from the countryside to fast growing industrializing cities in China, India, Brazil, and across Africa and parts of what used to be the Soviet Union. Internal migration within the enlarged European Union has also increased in the early 2000s. Sometime between when I started writing this book in 2007 and the time it was published, over half the world's population lived in cities—a first in humankind's history. These are now the people Manuel Castells is writing about and that are corporations' largest group of customers.

A subtrend of the globalized movement of people is the migration of talent. Talented, well-educated people with, in many instances, IT skills, are roving the world. New Zealand has become one of the major locations for making of movies that require extensive use of software and video game skills. It is where, for example, the *Lord of the Rings* movies were made. As recently as the early 1990s, many people associated New Zealand's economy more with mutton than with movies. South Korea and India are rapidly becoming the world's largest locales for the production of software, video games, design and manufacture of computer chips, and, in the specific case of South Korea, manufacture of chip-laden consumer electronics, such as digital cameras. As the dependence on IT to do one's work increased in the 1980s and 1990s, it became possible to work and live wherever one wanted. IBM employees around the world used to joke that they could live anywhere so long as they had nearby a fax machine and an airport. Thanks to telecommunications, the Internet, and laptops, they and so many others in thousands of firms no longer need either fax machines or airports to experience productive careers [13].

Another feature of globalization involves the international exchange of ideas and fashions, even culture. It is common today for senior public officials and private sector managers to speak English; scientists and engineers have for decades. In fact, English, Chinese, and Spanish are global languages, with English dominating in the worlds of politics, public administration, defense, academics, economics, business, ideas, media, and fashion. It is also not uncommon for these globe trotters to have attended the same universities or at least to have used the same textbooks in translation at school. Movies produced in the United States or European productions that win international prizes are seen all over the world; to be sure, it is an old story since Hollywood's productions have been one of the major exports of the United States since the dawn of the twentieth century. Major media companies in all fields of entertainment introduce their products around the world, creating shared experiences among their customers. It seems that we increasingly see the same movies in Europe and North America, read the same novels, and listen to similar, if not exactly the same, music. American-style Rap music is now played all over the world, whereas "fusion" music amalgamates flamenco, Rap, and Central European folk music.

Finally, globalization is extending to a variety of transnational public administrative functions. Before modern globalization, a large portion of governmental international activities largely involved diplomacy, war, law enforcement, and promoting trade. The international role of governments and other public institutions has been increasing since the 1980s. The creation of the World Trade Organization (WTO) in 1995 led to the almost instant establishment of a transnational institution that now describes and enforces rules under which global trade occurs. It did this in less than a decade and yet is still operationally in its childhood, so one can expect its role and power to increase. The World Health Organization (WHO) has increased its international influence due to the spread of various pandemic diseases in the 1990s and beyond, such as avian flu, which required a global response. Environmental groups have scaled up to deal with global warming, green issues, and other environmental concerns as both advocates for transnational responses and through assertion of their desire and effectiveness to lead where individual governments are not willing or able. Most recently, we have all seen a surge in collaboration by banking regulators all over the world in response to the crisis in their industry. It almost seems that the United Nations is being marginalized. But the trend goes further. The European Union (EU) has now taken the global lead in establishing many standards for safety of products that it imposes on the entire world because the rest of the world sells products to the EU. The U.S. Food and Drug Administration (FDA) long acted as the de facto global standards-setting body for drugs and medicines mimicked by many governments, although, even in this area of regulation, the EU is asserting its global influence when it disagrees with an action (or inaction) by the FDA.

IT technical standards boards are promoting open standards for software, about which we will have more to say in future chapters. All of these activities are facilitated by the fast and inexpensive flow of information through e-mail, telecommunications, and the Internet, and can be analyzed and leveraged using other forms of IT.

This increased transnational role of public officials and non-profit organizations (NPOs) and other nongovernment organizations (NGOs) is such a new development that it is not quite as obvious as it should be because corporations and small firms are not always as prepared as they need to be in dealing with this new wave of globalization. In fact, one of the messages from this book is that the private sector needs to be more engaged in the process than it has been in the past. There are emerging tasks senior management ought to undertake that are introduced in this book. In other words, private–public collaboration and confrontation is an emerging feature of globalization.

To summarize, globalization is a more complicated, nuanced phenomenon than we might have thought as recently as a decade ago [14]. Technology, trade, people, culture, and public administration have all gone global and all the evidence suggests this multifaceted trend is accelerating. A primary engine of that acceleration is the deployment of all manner of IT in communications, transportation, and in exchange of information, goods, and services.

Yet we can be too exuberant in our view that the world has gone or is going global. At the same time that many institutional–managerial infrastructures are globalizing, such as regulatory activities and transnational trade in goods and services, intense localization is also underway, a subject we cannot get into in any detail in this book. But this localization has very important implication for those concerned about technology, namely, that often technologies are embraced and funded differently from one nation to another. No more instructive example exists than cell phones. In the United States, one signs up for two years' worth of service at a fixed or variable cost, but with a contract, and then either buys or receives a telephone from the service provider. In Africa, users prepay for a certain number of minutes. In Europe and parts of Asia, service and the purchase of cell phones are separate transactions. In countries with the highest standards of living, people have their own personal mobile phone; in very poor countries, it could be the village as whole that owns one telephone. Uses also vary. Teenagers in the United States chat with friends, young Europeans text message a great deal, whereas farmers in India call in to find out the price of crops. The lesson is that although globalization in both how institutions and technologies work is increasing, localization remains vibrant and, one could argue, at a minimum makes possible the increased use of technologies in poor and developing economies. As managers, social commentators, and scientists we cannot ignore these countervailing winds of change.

A second megatrend, related to the first, but nonetheless distinctive in its own right, involves demographics. Managers and public officials should care about this one for two reasons. First, it is unfolding independent of what any individual organization does. Second, technology affects the role, work, and quality of life of people. We have already mentioned the global migration of employees and the massive international and internal migrations stimulating urbanization around the world, but there are other aspects involved in the megatrend of changing demographics that need to be recognized. Specifically, they involve ages of populations. In some countries, work forces and populations are aging rapidly. We are all familiar with accounts about aging populations in Italy, Germany, the United States (Boomers), Japan, and, increasingly, China. As they grow older, their medical needs will influence the development of IT-based medicine and procedures, ranging from more advanced forms of MRI scanners to computer-based development of new medicines, as occurs routinely in the pharmaceutical industry. These developments will, in turn, cause people to live longer, saddling corporate and governmental medical and pension programs with additional costs. Additionally, in the wealthiest economies, services to seniors by both the public and private sectors are increasingly delivered using IT. For example, citizens can apply for government services in many countries using the Internet, rather than going physically to some office and filling out paper forms. Government agencies in Western Europe are increasingly integrating the work of multiple agencies that work directly with citizens so that they have a total view of the needs and services provided to any particular individual. Trusted identity systems are just beginning to appear that will ensure that people get the services they really need and are really the individuals who should get the services they require and are qualified to receive. A similar process is underway in the delivery of goods and services to seniors: online ordering of medications delivered to one's home, integration of financial services into "one-stop shopping" formats, delivery of media and entertainment over the Internet to a variety of devices, and instruments (platforms) that will increasingly be more user friendly for the sight impaired or those with arthritis. In short, while most commentators focusing on aging populations concentrate on the rising costs of medical coverage and pensions, there is this other demographic trend unfolding involving a growing reliance on IT by aging communities of customers and citizens.

In other countries, the opposite demographic situation exists, in which populations are quite young. This situation that exists in many parts of Asia, Latin America, and across the African continent in some 54 countries. These people are not going away; in fact, many will go be around largely throughout this century and they are the most rapidly expanding cohort in the world's population. They are often poor, live in weak economies that have bad water and inadequate medical facilities, and whose societies invest less in educating their youth than the most advanced nations of the world. Issues and problems with younger populations manifest themselves in different ways, to be sure, but all share the reality that there is churn and change on the way. For example, in Saudi Arabia, a highly literate, well-educated male workforce is experiencing high levels of unemployment; in Brazil not enough children go to school; and the one characteristic shared by all countries with young populations is that children go to school fewer years than anywhere else. But public officials understand the problems and are addressing them. Negreponte sold 150,000 of his inexpensive laptops to Peru in 2007 to facilitate instruction of children in small villages. In Africa, the Internet is being used to transmit educational offerings to rural communities, while it seems that most elementary schools in the United States have formed alliances with elementary schools in other countries with large young populations. We can expect IT to be configured in ways that will help the young to do more than gain access to cell phones—they have these already all over the world—and instead acquire skills that will make it possible for many to thrive in the current century.

Corporations are playing a role as well. Many large corporations are collaborating with local governments in investing in training programs that result in a large pool of properly skilled workforces, especially in countries that have less expensive labor pools. Companies favor investing in those economies where workers already speak English or have higher levels of education than comparable economies. Developing specialized functions in a country is also popular: semiconductor and consumer electronics manufacturing in South Korea and China, software development and support in India and Russia, and extraction of minerals and other resources through the use of advanced technologies in Latin America and Sub-Saharan Africa are a few examples.

Yet another subtrend within demographics not fully appreciated around the world is the gender mismatch just becoming evident in China, but existing elsewhere too. With China's law making it possible for only one child to be born per couple in a nation that favors sons over daughters, there now exists a growing gender imbalance with more males than females. The implications are not well understood. Will men migrate out of China to find wives in other countries? If so, how will that change the culture of other nearby nations? Will that create wars? Will homosexuality increase? What will happen to levels of crime? Will women be "imported" into China? What will be the effects on the role of women? Will they assume more political and managerial leadership positions in China, a process that seems already to be underway? As China's population ages rapidly in the second half of the century with inadequate number of replacements, will the Chinese repeat the experiences the Germans and the Italians face today? All of these issues are slowly unfolding in a nation that has such environmental problems that one can also begin asking if there are some health-related megatrends that need to be accounted for too since China is home to nearly 15% of the world's human population. The follow-on questions these raise for managers with firms in China or dealing with Chinese enterprises, and for public officials in other countries, are complex, often new, and both disturbing (e.g., rising unrest and disruption of business operations) and potentially presenting positive opportunities (e.g., for sale of pollution control equipment).

So far, we have discussed two components of the big picture— accelerating globalization and changing demographics—each of which have been subtexts affected by the use of IT. But there are others to acknowledge.

During the late 1990s and into the next decade, it became increasingly apparent to scientists and public officials that there was something happening with respect to the world's environment.

Was it global warming, as many scientists were arguing? Were other factors at work? As the cost of oil and natural gas rose in the early 2000s and then sharply fluctuated wildly up and down, observers raised the question of carbon-based pollution and, just as serious, the possibility of running out of affordable fuels. Those are concerns of the industrialized economies and of the companies do business in them. Officials, scientists, and commentators all were worried that the consumption of oil was fundamentally damaging the environment. But these kinds of situations can reverse themselves as well. For example, take the situation in which the price of oil drops, generating some interesting implications for IT. In this situation, during the second half of 2008, the price of crude oil dropped from a high of over $100 a barrel to as low as $35–40 per barrel, and clearly remained below the $70 a barrel rate right into the new year. The reason $70 is important is because most oil-rich countries rely on that level of pricing to generate a volume of tax revenues necessary to run a government without having to tax its citizens. This is the case, for instance, in such varied economies as a U.S. state's (Alaska), Trinidad's, Venezuela's, Russia's, and, of course, of oil-producing Arab states. In the case of Trinidad, for instance, when oil dropped below $70, public officials decided to speed up economic development that involved industries outside the oil business, most notably software and other forms of IT. Of course, these strategies take years, if not decades, to implement, as the Irish learned in the 1980s and 1990s. But the point is, an activity in one industry—in this case the falling price of crude oil—can have important effects on the role and use of IT. What is most unnerving, however, is that such consequences of events are not all predictable, although to the credit of Trinidad's government, several years earlier it had already worked out the fundamental strategies necessary to move toward becoming an information society, learning from the experiences of such nations as the United States, Japan, Ireland, and Korea. And, of course, we are still left with the issue of consumption of oil, which remains to be addressed, also in part by the use of IT in protecting the environment.

Then there are the poor communities in India, China, and Africa more concerned with the lack of adequate supplies of clean drinking water, and, additionally in China, clean air. Collectively around the world, thoughtful individuals were again raising the question of how many people and how much human activity could the Earth sustain. Meanwhile, at international conferences attended by experts, corporate management, and senior public officials, one could hear pronouncements that there was enough water, gas, air, and oil, but in the wrong places, often in politically unstable societies, such as oil in Nigeria, or in underdeveloped economies, such as natural gas in nations bordering Russia to its east, its availability often driven more by political priorities in Moscow and elsewhere than by market demands [15]. Our discussion speaks to the very survival of humankind, to be sure, but also to other issues discussed in this book: economic development, public works, health and medical coverage, quality of life, and, in recent years, "green" issues in politics, social discourse, and business operations, all touched by IT as well.

What is clear is that a tipping point in the conversation occurred sometime in 2006–2008. Governments turned to the environmental issue in a substantive manner. Many corporations finally concluded that green operations could drive down expenses and create new market opportunities. Individual consumers in the most developed countries began to shrink their personal "carbon footprint." The poor in many African communities continued to suffer exposure to mercury and other substances as they dismantled retired personal computers and consumer electronics shipped to them from more advanced societies to recycle valuable components. To be sure, while the issue of environmental concerns exists, it is in a nascent stage of evolution. But already IT is part of the story. Governments are making their buildings greener to lower heating and cooling expenses driven up by the costs of fuel and gas in the early 2000s. Computers frequently manage and measure that effort. City and state governments are mandating less polluting cars, trucks, airplanes, and trains, while myriad digital devices are tracking pollution, sniffing car exhaust, and calculating a company's carbon expenditures. Companies are driving down the costs of heating and cooling their buildings, in using carbon-based fuels such as oil and coal, and in introducing products that are more environmentally "friendly." For many years, researchers working on pollution and global warming depended on data collection and analysis by computers, a use they will increase over time as new tools are developed or old ones simply used more extensively in more countries.

Finally, we should acknowledge what is either another megatrend that makes up part of the big picture, or is a byproduct of the other megatrends. It is becoming clearer that as part of the changing relationships of people, resources, and technologies that societal interactions are evolving and that some of these changes represent threats to social stability and normal business operations. This comment is far more comprehensive than the threats posed by terrorists in the Middle East, or violent political groupings in such disparate places as Pakistan, Kenya, borderlands next to Israel, and southern Mexico with its local Indian tribes. It is bigger than the narrower discussion about social networks or dating sites that seem to so captivate the press in many countries. In the past several years, we have seen North Africans riot in France, Moslem residents frustrated over their inability to integrate into the national social structures of Scandinavian countries or the Netherlands, people raised in Great Britain by Pakistani parents alienated to such a point that they blew up buses in London, while others of Arab citizenship did the same with a train in Madrid; the list of unrest and disturbance is long, active, dangerous, fundamental, and evident in well over a hundred nations.

This discussion is not intended to scare the reader, merely to point out that too many discussions about IT are too antiseptic, ignoring some fundamental megatrends—realities—that affect the users of computing and who, in turn, use the technology to support their personal priorities. Those evolving societal changes have in common with global economics the feature that in both instances relationships among groups, such as citizens with their governments and customers with their vendors, are changing, as expectations of citizens, consumers, public officials, and business management and employees evolve. Citizens are asking different things of their governments, for instance, for universal health care in the United States, lifetime job security and more generous pensions in Europe, jobs in China, clean water in India, and so forth. Many of these are new demands driven by rising expectations that improving economies stimulate, which IT contributes to by further diffusion of media showing "the good life" in other nations, or are triggered by rising levels of education and access to information. Consumers are better equipped with information about the quality of products and service and their relative worth and, hence, are demanding more and better value from their suppliers. As individuals become more affluent and aware of employment options, or are self-centered, they move around the world quickly to where they think they can fulfill their aspirations.

Although it is difficult to document adequately, and certainly will not be done in this book, regionalism seems to be on the rise too, along with allegiances to one's cultural heritage. There are several thousand provinces/states in the world functioning within national governments. They seem to be leading in the public administration of economic development, delivery of innovative services to citizens, control over environmental issues, and in local educational reforms. Some of these states are larger than nations, such as all of those in China, India, and even in the United States (California and Texas). Regionalist political aspirations are also high, as in the cases of the Catalans and the Basques in Spain, the Welsh in the United Kingdom, the Flemish, French enclaves in Canada, Palestinians in the Middle East, and myriad African tribes in over four dozen nations not limited to just Sub-Saharan countries. Similarly, ethnic groups are agitating for local control or recognition across large swaths of Asia, even in China (the Tibetans), and by Indian tribes in Brazil and elsewhere in Latin America. In short, unrest and challenges to the prevailing social and economic orders are numerous around the world. One almost has to go back to the experiences of nations in the middle of the nineteenth century to find a period of comparable uncertainty and unrest.

All of this is compounded and facilitated by digital technologies. Television coverage of riots and civil unrest in Paris in 2005 and again in 2007 by North African teenagers spurred others of similar ethnic backgrounds elsewhere in the country to do the same, protesting prejudice in education and lack of jobs. We know that Al-Qaeda operatives use cell phones and laptops as effectively as American and European military personnel, perhaps even more cleverly since they have to do it on the cheap. Arab terrorists leverage electronic press coverage on television and radio, often with better results than a highly paid advertising agency in New York. In short, technology has allowed people to become more aware of their surroundings and what other like-minded people are doing. To be sure, governments of all political stripes are responding by trying to impose controls over material coming from the Internet (China) and monitor telephone conversations (U.S.) [16]. These are all uncomfortable, disquieting features of modern society; though not caused by IT, they are certainly facilitated by use of the technology.

Corporations feel the brunt of these actions. For years eBay has been pressured, then ordered, by the French not to sell Nazi items in France, which has a law forbidding such sales. Yet the transactions can flow from anywhere in the world since eBay is global. How could it comply? Indeed, should it? Google has received similar pressure to report uses of its services to the Chinese government while the same government has been blocking the flow of content from media companies all over the world. How can a corporation function in a global economy with these kinds of issues affecting routine business operations? Many of these issues are new to the management teams of these corporations. eBay and Google, for instance, are essentially still being managed by their first-generation of managers. Even older firms, such as Microsoft, ran into antitrust problems with the European Union (E.U.) after wrestling with U.S. antitrust officials. Interspersed in all of this are the better known issues surrounding the protection, or lack thereof, of patents and copyrights, a problem that manifests itself all over the world in myriad forms and no more so than in anything that has digital features, such as DVDs, CDs, and music and films in digital forms available from computers and over the Internet.

Before exploring some of the implications of these nontechnological trends, because they are also affected by technologies far more today than even in the 1990s, we need to understand more thoroughly how IT is being used.

HOW SOCIETIES USE TECHNOLOGY TO SHAPE THEIR WORLD

The trends described are features of the big picture, the background against which the world's population goes about its business. The rest of this book discusses some of those IT activities which most affect the megatrends described earlier, showing in the process how key technology-related tasks are being carried out. We concentrate largely on the roles of businesses and government agencies, and offer recommendations on these. It is no longer enough to mention such things as "governments encourage the use of IT to further economic development," or that managers "must run globally integrated enterprises." We need a deeper understanding of their issues because so many people now participate in the adoption and use of computing with which to live out the megatrends. As mentioned in the Preface, there are many possible topics for discussion involving computing, but by limiting the focus to a few that are crucial to the way the world is shaping its immediate destiny managers and public officials can craft effective practices and strategies. However, this approach also means that much is left out but not dismissed as irrelevant. For example, I do not discuss the role of computers in modern warfare as I already did in a prior book [17]. Nor do I describe how computers are used in some 36 industries in the United States as I recently addressed those themes elsewhere too [18]. Rising above those narrower issues are those addressed below. They all share the common characteristic of being global in scope, not limited to the United States, the E.U., parts of India and China, or to interesting cities in Brazil and Eastern Europe.

To be sure, just like the megatrends manifest themselves in unique ways in each country, or even within provinces inside nations, so too what are described in the rest of this book manifest themselves in a unique fashion at four levels:

1. National
2. State/provincial
3. Industry (national and international)
4. Company or agency

That means consumers and individual users are not discussed here. Yet we will reaffirm variations in firms and nations. Every company is really different, so too is each industry, even common industries in different countries. The banking industry in the United States is not the same as that in Spain, for instance; Zara's department stores in Spain operate differently than Harrods of London, or the Sears chain in the United States. Some provinces have a great deal of industry and IT firms, while others are agricultural or low tech. The economies of Estonia, Brazil, China, United States, and Jamaica are quite different. But, in most instances, diffusion of IT is extensive, growing, and influential on the affairs of its users and societies. In short, there is a role for almost everyone in a leadership position or who influences affairs in this world of rising adoption of all manner of information technology.

To begin the discussion, it is helpful to understand how the technology spread so far so fast, which is the subject of the next chapter. In point of fact, there are eight discernable patterns of diffusion of IT. These are useful to describe because they demonstrate how diffusions of a technology are always tailored to the social, legal, economic, and historical proclivities of an individual nation. In a sense, this chapter reflects a form of the wisdom of crowds because these patterns of adoption are essentially the cumulative behavior of hundreds of thousands, if not a few million, business managers, public officials, IT users and their vendors and advisors around the world over the previous six decades. This discussion provides a proof point that it makes sense for each nation, region, company, or government to define its own path of adoption. The lesson is not limited just to computers and telecommunications, but applies to all manner of technologies which, in and of themselves, are flexible and can be shaped to meet the needs of an industry or society. IT is not the only technology humans will encounter in the twenty-first century, but it is a class of innovations that can be informative about subsequent ones. Next on the horizon is either nanotechnology (about tiny, even microscopic engines, for instance) or biotechnology, which involves programming living cells to cure diseases, provide healthy reengineered foods and medicines, or that can serve as new tools with which to do work (possibly bio-based computers). The chapter ends with some insights on what the various patterns teach us about the megatrends, lessons for managers and policy makers.

Armed with an overview of how IT spread around the world, we next move to the equally expansive question of how governments, also aware of the power of IT, are leveraging these technologies to improve the quality of their performance, the lives of their citizens, and the competitiveness of their economies. Governments at all levels have long been interested in leveraging existing local capabilities and emerging new markets and technologies to improve their economies. Research by many organizations clearly demonstrates that governments have been interested in doing many things with IT, at least since the 1970s [19]. Since the wide adoption of the Internet in the 1990s, and the even earlier manufacture of computer chips and PCs, public officials have been keen to promote the use of IT inside government and corporations, and by citizens at large. They have introduced computing into schools and supported curriculums that trained workers in IT-related skills. Today, the variety of initiatives undertaken by governments is so varied and extensive that one can begin to catalog them by type of economy, much as is done in the next chapter in describing types of deployment. Chapter three is tactical in that it assumes that the reader is a public official. This is done because readers influence what public officials do in many countries and can learn lessons about how best to use IT within their own companies and institutions. Although this chapter concentrates large-ly on public officials, because policy makers do not operate in iso-lation, there is much said about the role of private sector manage-ment as well. It ends with recommendations on how to proceed for both communities.

What is quite remarkable is how many governments and corpo-rations participate in the economic development process using IT. Even highly underdeveloped or poor economies seek to leverage the technology. Why? In the same countries, corporations also seek to leverage IT for their economic benefit. Why? Because, to-day economists know that IT can have a positive, indeed dramatic affect on the growth and improvement of a local, state, or national economy. In the 1990s, economists engaged in a major discussion about the "productivity paradox," in which they saw enormous investments being made in IT but could not tie those to any pro-ductivity gains of an economy at large. In earlier studies, I offered evidence to the effect that at the firm level benefits were accruing, some dating back to at least the 1960s in the case of the United States [20]. By the end of the 1990s, economists had been able to demonstrate the link between IT investments and national eco-nomic productivity across many economies [21]. Their finding was not lost on public officials, whose own economists were re-porting results, or on executives whose companies were also de-riving benefits from the technology. As a consequence, govern-ments pushed forward various initiatives that relied on IT in the early years of the 2000s. Those strategies are the subject of discus-sions later in the book.

Armed with information about what is happening on a global scale, we next turn our attention to the mundane, tactical, singular act of a business, technical, or government manager making a de-cision to do something new using IT. It is the millions and mil-lions of such decisions made in public and private institutions over many decades that, when added up, accounted for the ac-tions described in the first two chapters of this book. By looking at how such decisions are made and justified from an historical per-spective, one can see that the manner in which such decisions are made have not changed so much over many decades. Those pat-terns provide "lessons from history" applicable to decisions man-agers are making today. These apply to the adoption of large main-frame-based systems as well as to new uses of the Internet. These practices focus on institutional decision-making, not that of con-sumers, because the lion's share of acquisitions of computing over the past half-century were made by managers and IT professionals, not consumers buying iPods and laptops.

Having narrowed our view of IT issues as we move from one chapter to another, it then makes sense to step back and debate whether or not we now live in an information age. There are serious reasons to do so. For one thing, naming an age does set a tone and defines priorities; in other words, it helps shape a civilization or simply one's own society. For another, there are nations that have embraced notions of what they want their world to look like. The Japanese government, for instance, has many formal public programs and policies intended to make Japan an "information society." The South Koreans do too, but without giving it a label; they simply made their country the most broadband-intensive culture in the world and watched for consequences as individuals used their imagination, taste, and affordable IT to reshape aspects of their lives. Estonia and Finland have public policies to become some of the most Internet intensive nations on earth as a way to be highly competitive in the global economy. As early as the mid-1990s, President Bill Clinton wanted to give every classroom in America access to the Internet. For all practical purposes, and after investing billions of dollars, he succeeded; that it did not result in some miracle in education is another discussion we cannot address here [22]. The point is, however, that there is much intent and activity under way; hence, the discussion of what might otherwise seem some intellectual fancifulness is important to undertake.

Chapter six examines the historical and emerging role of computer scientists and engineers as the population increases around the world, suggesting a more activist agenda for them. This chapter is almost shamelessly propagandistic for me, but I did that to bring attention to an expanded role I believe the technical community can play, and make suggestions about the leadership role it can take.

The last chapter brings us back to a practical consideration of what we should do in light of any insights presented in this book. It is intended to answer several very blunt questions. The first is, So what? Next, Why do we care? Finally, What should one do next if either a public official or a corporate executive, a government or a company? It turns out that IT is not going away in anyone's lifetime; the technology is continuing to evolve. Most important, many of its effects on how societies and economies will be shaped in the twenty-first century are only just beginning to surface. Despite the enormous amount of hype about the Internet, for example, it has barely begun to influence societies to the extent that earlier technologies have but experts on the subject of the Internet are uniformally, absolutely confident it will shape the affairs of individuals, firms, governments, and nations and their economies. In very unprofessional English, the phrase "you ain't seen nothing yet" applies aptly to the Internet.

It also applies to other trends in the evolution and use of IT that are discernable, because there is a secret among technologists already noted earlier in this chapter not often shared widely outside their circle: technologies evolve very slowly, often taking 10 or 15 years to reach a point where they are mature enough to be used in public. Moreover, historical experience also illustrates that from the time someone announces the availability of some new software or hardware tools, to when they are widely used can range from 4 to 20 years. In short, one can begin to paint a picture of some of the uses and effects of IT that will unfold over the next twenty years with enough confidence that individuals can take actions based on such predictions. That is why this chapter alone could be worth the price of this book. By adding recommendations to the discussion based on proven ways and some others proposed initially here, one should expect to leverage trends and align corporate and public policies to the possible.

Each chapter is an independent essay that can be read and studied without reference to any of the others. However, as argued here, nothing operates in isolation; every discussion in this book is related to the others. That makes perspectives, lessons from history, and any forecast difficult to deal with but essential nonetheless. We are moving rapidly into a more highly integrated world, one in which the various points of connection are numerous, complex, and affect each other. Regardless of potential natural disasters, wars, and the inevitable emergence of positive surprises in the evolution of knowledge, science, and technology, IT is a glue that helps bind humankind together. It is, after all, the digital plumbing of modern times.

NOTES AND REFERENCES

1. Manuel Castells, *The Internet Galaxy: Reflections on the Internet, Business, and Society,* Oxford: Oxford University Press, 2001, p. 275.
2. Ibid., p. 1.
3. Ibid.

4. Edmund C. Berkeley, *Giant Brains or Machines that Think,* New York: Wiley, 1949.

5. Norbert Wiener, *Cybernetics: Or Control and Communication in the Animal and the Machine,* Cambridge, MA: MIT Press, 1948.

6. There is an encyclopedic history with a comprehensive bibliography: Margaret A. Boden, *Mind as Machine: A History of Cognitive Science,* 2 vols. Oxford: Clarendon Press, 2006.

7. Thoughtfully explored in a series of essays in Peter J. Denning and Robert M. Metcalfe (Eds.), *Beyond Calculation: The Next Fifty Years of Computing,* New York: Copernicus, 1997; for a more recent, extreme view, see Ray Kurzwell, *The Singularity Is Near: When Humans Transcend Biology,* New York: Viking, 2005.

8. *Nineteen Eighty-Four* is the name of a novel written by George Orwell, published in 1949, about life in a dictatorship.

9. James W. Cortada, Ashish M. Gupta, and Marc Le Noir, *How Nations Thrive in the Information Age,* Somers, NY: IBM Corporation, 2007, pp. 7–8.

10. Susanne Dirks, Mary Keeling, and Ronan Lyons, *Economic Development in a Rubik's Cube World: How To Turn Global Trends into Local Prosperity,* Somers, NY: IBM Corporation, 2008, pp. 3–4.

11. Ibid.

12. In fact, establishing an accurate count has proven difficult to accomplish because many migrants move illegally from one nation to another. The only substantive study of the issue and the role governments play in working with these workers and residents is Brian Lee-Archer, Chris Brailey, Marc Le Noir, and Oliver Ziehm, *For the Good of the Global Economy: Social Protection for the Migrant Worker,* Somers, NY: IBM Corporation, 2007. The United Nations has also published some statistics in *World Migration 2005,* Geneva: United Nations Publications, 2005.

13. This new creative class is described by Richard Florida, *The Flight of the Creative Class: The New Global Competition for Talent,* New York: HarperBusiness, 2005.

14. The first modern observer to make similar points was Robert Gilpin. Of his many books, see *The Challenge of Global Capitalism: The World Economy in the 21st Century,* Princeton, N.J.: Princeton University Press, 2000.

15. An example of the kind of gathering addressing these issues is the annual political risks conference hosted by the Royal Institute for International Affairs, which always draws senior public officials, experts from academia and think tanks, and managers from the private sector.

16. Nicholas Carr, *The Big Switch: Rewiring the World, From Edison to Google,* New York: W.W. Norton, 2008, pp. 179–184, 197–209.

17. James W. Cortada, *The Digital Hand,* vol. 3: *How Computers Changed the Work of American Public Sector Industries,* New York: Oxford University Press, 2008, pp. 49–102.

18. James W. Cortada, *The Digital Hand,* 3 vols., New York: Oxford University Press, 2004–2008.

19. The obvious ones include the European Union, OECD, U.S. General Services

Administration in the public sector, while many in the private sector also exist, such as IBM's Center for the Business of Government, or others run by this firm's competitors.

20. One of the key findings of Cortada, *The Digital Hand,* all 3 volumes.

21. For a very current update, not even published as of 2008, see Stephen D. Oliner, Daniel E. Sichel, and Kevin Stiroh, "Explaining a Productive Decade," Federal Reserve Board, August 2007.

22. Larry Cuban, *Oversold and Underused: Computers in the Classroom,* Cambridge, MA: Harvard University Press, 2001.

2

HOW COMPUTERS SPREAD AROUND THE WORLD SO FAST

> Many innovations require a lengthy period of many years from the time when they become available to the time when they are widely adopted.
>
> —EVERETT M. ROGERS [1]

It is obvious that the use of computers and reliance on computing technologies is now ubiquitous in many countries, from the large mainframes that support corporate and government applications and power the flow of much information through the Internet to the tiny Nano from Apple that plays music. Despite this massive dependence, we are still learning about how information technology (IT) is spreading around the world so quickly and intensively. Today, trackers are focusing increasingly on also understanding the percent of populations using such devices and applications, the percent with access to the Internet [2], and the extent of deployment of key IT-based devices and applications within whole national economies and industries. As a sign of changing circumstances, in the 1990s industry watchers monitored quality of access (high speed vs. dial-up); but with dial-up now almost a thing of the past, broadband can hardly be compared to any earlier form of transmission [3].

The spread of information technology, largely in the form of computer systems and their applications, reached the point at which the majority of the world's populations in advanced and rapidly developing economies rely on this class of technology to do their work, communicate, and be entertained. The whole process took place within a half century. Because it was a global process, we need a worldview of how the technology spread. Partial explanations exist, of course, for the experience of the United States, and to some extent we know about a few countries in Europe and barely anything about Japan—all advanced economies [4]. Africa and Latin America remain terra incognita regarding their experience with computers, yet today these regions are substantial users of cell phones. Large numbers of their citizens of all economic classes have increasingly gained access either to the Internet or to inexpensive laptops, such as Nicholas Negroponte's inexpensive laptops (One Laptop Per Child program) going into Peru [5].

We need this worldview for a number of reasons, and not just to satisfy the curiosity of historians and economists. Public officials are promoting the use of IT in their societies, as suggested in the previous chapter, and as described in some detail in this one and in the next chapter as well. So they need to know what models of diffusion there are and begin to form opinions about which ones have something to teach them about how best to proceed in their societies. Management in the private sector needs similar insight in order to place their bets on which societies to invest in—factories, capital, marketing, and sales—and which ones are most likely to yield attractive returns. Both classes of leaders and their organizations are thus dependent on each other. That codependence is also complicated by the global nature of the playing field on which both sets of managers play.

The general theme of technological diffusion has been the subject of over four thousand studies over the past half century, so these offer insights on methods for conducting the research needed to understand the experience with modern IT [6]. Here we will describe the many patterns of deployment of IT. The key message is that there were, and are, various ways in which societies embraced the computer. The one very important topic not taken up in this chapter is how information about computer science diffused around the world, a topic worthy of its own study.

To assist public administrators and business managers, this chapter will begin by clarifying definitions and issues related to diffusion, since much is said in print, at conferences, and in meeting rooms that mirror various meanings and agendas. Then we answer these fundamental questions: What are the ways in which firms, economies, and governments go about embracing IT in a society? Which ones work better than others and why? To be sure, each approach is worth a book, but here we will limit ourselves to a few pages to create the more useful overview that can point a leader toward a specific option. That chosen option then can lead to a more detailed set of actions they can take, depending on whether they are vendors, consumers, or government agencies. This chapter ends with a discussion of the implications for both the private and public sectors and a summary of historical experiences. The ultimate objective is to provide historical perspective, a context that can enrich the kinds of actions documented in the third chapter.

DEFINITIONS AND ISSUES

Discussions about the spread of technologies are often entangled in conversations concerning innovation, diffusion, deployment, and other topics. Currently, there is a heightened interest in the role of innovation in shaping modern economies and societies, and computers are seen as part of that mix of discussion points [7]. This interest exists in both the private and public sectors, and is evident in most countries. For our purposes, I will not discuss how innovations occur per se, although they are part of the diffusion/deployment process and because so many other commentators have done so over the past decade, and much of this material is familiar now to senior public officials and corporate executives. Fundamentally, an innovation is often born out of some need that, when met, eventually leads to its deployment. For instance, the innovation that came to be known as the browser in the early 1990s caused an explosive expansion in the use of the Internet by several billion people in less than 15 years [8].

Diffusion, as defined by its most eminent expert, Everett M. Rogers, is "the process in which an innovation is communicated through certain channels over time among the members of a social system" [9]. By that consensus definition, we would be concerned about which organizations promoted the use of computing. The role of the U.S. Government in the 1940s and 1950s in promoting such use in North America is a well-known story [10]. Today, we also understand better the role of industry associations in the United States in promoting use of computing through their support of the deployment of specific industry-centric applications, training, and publicity [11]. Western Europe's experience is now being investigated more intensely than ever [12]. Economists have long studied the economic incentives that motivated corporations and public institutions to integrate the technology into their daily work [13]. Yet, it is still unclear if Rogers' widely accepted definition applies to consumer electronics, such as iPods and cell phones, but perhaps it will be seen that way because corporations promote the sale of such products, while social conditions encourage their use, such as the desire for fashion accessories in Asia or peer pressure among young Americans.

Experts often distinguish diffusion from deployment. Deployment usually refers to tasks performed in order for a technology to be adopted. For example, the role of third- and fourth-generation programming languages, or technical standards, fits into discussions about deployment. For our purposes, thinking of the notions of diffusion and deployment as synonymous proves helpful in explaining macropatterns of adoption and use. One important principle is that one does not acquire a computer, or any innovation for that matter, without at least some idea of its purpose. For the most part, we can assume that if an organization acquires a computer, it uses it.

Path dependency is yet another paradigm by which to view the deployment of a technology. Economic, technology, and business historians, and economists in general are particularly enamored with this way of looking at how technologies, products, and practices become commonplace. Managers in government and business are seen as implementing it, but not knowing what it is that they are doing that is path dependent. In a phrase, path dependency accepts the notion that "history matters." Prior uses of technology, or existing practices and knowledge, limit options for novel uses of a new technology by limiting or forcing one to adopt something new that builds largely on existing circumstances. The exclusive use of Microsoft products, because Microsoft is the current technology standard in an organization, is perhaps today's most widely recognized example of path dependence in IT, as is the use of large IBM computers. Often, incrementally adding a new use or software is economically more attractive than a wholesale change to some new IT platform. The costs of disruption of migrating to a new technological platform can wipe out anticipated benefits.

Managers in many industries learned this lesson as early as the 1950s when computer systems were not compatibly upgradeable to new or larger models, making any migration painful, lengthy, and very expensive to accomplish. The introduction of IBM's System 360 family of five computers and over 140 other related products in 1964 was in direct response to this problem. Based on lessons learned about the expense of change, corporations for decades resisted moving off an IBM (or IBM-compatible) mainframe to competitors' platforms. The same reluctance usually held for users of non-IBM-compatible equipment until they had no choice, due, for instance, to the demise of a vendor or the inability of a supplier to continue providing ever newer and bigger systems. At the high end of supercomputing, CDC and Sun played similar roles until conventional mainframe computing power and cost advantages overtook these firms in the last quarter of the twentieth century. In short, adherence to technical standards can influence profoundly the nature and rate of deployment of any subsequent technologies [14]. It is a lesson worth remembering because issues concerning standards are very much with us today, with no expectation of that changing in the foreseeable future.

The language surrounding the issue of how some technology becomes accepted and used is diverse and laden with implied explanations of how adoption of IT occurs. But all attempts to address several basic issues can briefly be summarized in the form of several questions. How do the technical characteristics of some specific IT encourage or discourage adoption? How do costs and benefits—the economics of the issue—affect adoption? What organizations, institutions, and social structures encourage or impede adoption? How (or do) they vary by industry, type of firm, society, or economy? Why? What do the findings in response to such questions tell us about rates and speeds of adoption? If the whole world seems to be adopting IT so quickly, are there some homogenous factors at work shared by all?

What should be clear from these questions is that "feeds and speeds" of a computer (or software) alone do not provide a comprehensive view of how IT spreads. Technological features are only one class of inputs blended into the mix of explanations. Myriad considerations explain how IT diffuses around the world, and even these variables differ by country. A fully developed explanation of how computers spread around the world would look like a Rubik's Cube before anyone had attempted to align the squares. However, eight patterns of adoption are discernable; each can be briefly described (see Table 1.1). None addresses the conventional approach of discussing technological features; rather, all illustrate the more important nontechnical factors that control the

Table 1.1. Types of IT diffusion

Diffusion model type	Key features
Government Supported/ Private-Sector Driven	Initial government funding Relies on private sector to do work Shifts initiative to private sector
National-Champion Driven	National government drives National government invests in local firms Local firms become preferred suppliers
Asian Private-Sector Driven	Focuses initially on component manufacturing Government facilitates partnering with foreign firms Leverages foreign expertise and capital
Planned-Economy Driven	Centralizes control of IT development and manufacturing Centralizes ownership of manufacturing and distribution Largely a Soviet model
Industry Driven	Private sector vendors of IT create market demand Vendors develop IT, then sell and support it Governments invest only in high-risk R&D
Corporate Driven	Private firms (customers of IT) drive demand Private firms lead in implementation and use of IT IT used to drive down costs and create new sources of revenue
Application Driven	Compelling uses of IT stimulate diffusion Pushes vendors to develop new IT products Creates widely accepted standards
Technology Driven	Technical standards facilitate adoption and upgrades Increases cost-effectiveness of IT Path dependency propels adoption, constrains growth of alternative standards

scope and rate of adoption, suggesting that many individuals who are not IT experts play important roles in how a society or firm adopts computing.

GOVERNMENT-SUPPORTED/PRIVATE-SECTOR-DRIVEN MODEL

The most thoroughly examined case of IT's diffusion involves the experience of the United States. This story epitomizes our first model in which, at the dawn of the arrival of computer technology, the nation's government officials and scientists promoted its development and installation, then encouraged its movement into the private sector for deployment across the economy as commercially viable products. On a smaller scale and less intensively, the history of the use of computing in the United Kingdom paralleled this model of deployment in the same period of the 1940s through the 1960s, with residual support for IT R&D continuing right into the new century by both governments.

At the start of World War II in the United States, the army and navy services began sponsoring development of advanced electronics with the first major computing projects focusing on various military applications, most notably to decipher enemy encrypted communications, to prepare artillery and bombing firing tables, and later to perform calculations in the design of atomic weapons. All of the early computer projects of the 1940s and 1950s involved either government contracts or funding: ENIAC, BINAC, and UNIVAC to mention a few. By the late 1940s, there were already some 20-odd computer development projects underway, all funded by the American government. During the early 1950s, when government-sponsored scientific applications emerged, the Cold War and the Korean War motivated federal officials to support further technical developments in what clearly was still an expensive, complex, and unstable technology. They relied largely on academic institutions (such as MIT) and the private sector (such as IBM, National Cash Register, and General Electric) to do most of the actual work. By the mid-1950s, companies like Univac and IBM were transforming their government-supported machines into commercial products, proving so successful that within a decade the fastest growing and now largest market for this technology lay in the private sector. By the end of the 1970s, all major industries and large corporations in the United States had become extensive users of IT [15]. In fact, the private sector now provided the majority of the impetus and funding for further technological innovations for the rest of the century.

The Federal government also continued to meet its own IT needs through use of commercially available computers and software, while simultaneously developing tools needed for its own work, such as military weapons systems and, of course, the Internet. By the late 1990s, government officials were concerned that the private sector was transforming IT so quickly that they were losing control over its evolution and, indeed, were being forced to replace their own systems with newer ones appearing in the private sector sooner than they could comfortably acquire them.

The results emerging from this model of diffusion in the United States varied. From the 1940s through the 1960s, the massive infusion of funds exceeded any public investments in this technology outside that of the Soviet block. In addition, one needs to take into account the American market, which had a half-century of substantial use of information technologies (such as tabulating equipment, adding machines, and calculators) and had large firms prior to the arrival of computers, two circumstances that made attractive the reception for commercial computers. As a result, two realities played important roles: infusion of federal funds and existence of a potentially large commercial market, leading the technology to evolve most quickly in the United States [16]. Consequently, those firms most able to quickly convert this technology into commercial products operated in the United States. As knowledge of the continuously and rapidly evolving technology diffused across businesses, academic settings, and government agencies, American entrepreneurs were often some of the earliest in the world to exploit the situation. That is the story of Silicon Valley and of PC makers such as Apple, of PC software providers such as Microsoft, and, later, of firms that leveraged the Internet, for instance, eBay and Amazon.com [17].

Finally, we should recognize that early suppliers of commercial computers were often office appliance vendors who, by exercising considerable account control, had access to and the "ear" of potential customers of computers. They could direct them from old punch card and accounting machines to the new computer systems, many of which were designed to facilitate use of prior technologies as part of the migration to new platforms, such as reliance on punch cards for data entry and output (a use that continued until the late 1980s).

This model of diffusion was not limited to the United States. In Great Britain, engineers and others did more advanced work on the development of what is now called digital computing during World War II than anywhere else in the world. The Colossus systems built during the war were the most advanced processors at the time. These machines proved essential to the prosecution of the war by giving the Allies a nearly open-book view of Axis military communications [18]. Like the Americans, the British funded specific projects in the 1940s that involved almost every major computer initiative in the country, situating many of these projects in local universities, with some collaboration with the private sector [19]. By the end of the 1940s, even commercial firms began considering how to manufacture the technology, such as Lyons Teashops and, later, ICL [20]. However, with the partial exception of ICL, Lyons and the rest of the potential commercial suppliers of computing remained relatively minor players in both the British and European computer industries, unable to scale up or progress relative to the Americans.

In the 1950s, a combination of British military projects developed in parallel with the slow diffusion of commercial computers from such transnational firms as IBM, NCR, and Burroughs, and through local companies, such as ICL [21]. By the end of the 1970s, as in the United States and Canada, dominant users of computing resided in the private sector. By the end of the century, the extent of deployment of computing across the economy mirrored closely that of the United States. The British also embraced the Internet after European and American browsers made the technology easier to use. As in the American instance, initial support for all manner of computing came from government but later shifted to the private sector, particularly during Margaret Thatcher's leadership as prime minister (1979–1990), a time when senior public officials encouraged private entrepreneurship across all industries. Yet, the British private sector and public officials were not able to launch a successful domestic computer industry that could rival that of the Americans, largely due to the inability to create competitive firms through mergers and because of the smaller national economy in which to sell products [22].

This model of government-to-private-sector diffusion was not limited to the Anglo-Saxon world. It was also one of the most successful diffusion models as measured by the volume and speed with which computers spread in any given economy. This was evident in the United States, Netherlands, and Germany prior to the 1980s, and in Finland, Japan, and South Korea in subsequent years. In the case of South Korea in the 1990s, we see yet another variant of this model of diffusion at work. With the availability of the Internet spreading rapidly in the 1990s, South Korean public officials decided to make broadband access to the Internet a high priority for economic and social development. Regulatory and fiscal changes made the cost of the access and of PCs low enough to encourage the public to embrace the new access. The government simultaneously stimulated the growth and modernization of the private sector industries to deliver the service and to develop successful consumer electronics products [23]. By the early 2000s, use of computing in South Korea had become the most extensive in Asia, while broadband usage was the highest in the world, as measured by percent of population using it [24]. To a lesser extent, the Japanese in the 1990s and the Chinese in the 2000s adopted diffusion models similar to the Korean variant.

Each approach shared several similarities. National governments initiated the funding and even management in some cases of early projects. They had an indigenous technical base upon which they could rely to do the early work and later to convert the technology into commercial forms for local firms to sell in their regional economies. In each instance, there were electronics and office appliance firms and universities, and, to a lesser extent, some technical agencies, both civilian and military, with which to start diffusion.

The degree to which governments and private sectors exchanged responsibilities for deployment varied, of course. The American and British public officials were keen on having the private sector take over the lead in exploiting the technology as soon as possible. That happened when companies determined that a demand for such products was emerging fast enough to warrant the effort of offering such goods and services, and when they had enough confidence that they could pull it off technologically, economically, and operationally. The Koreans came decades later to the process but then too moved quickly in a similar manner. The Japanese also encouraged indigenous firms to take the lead, such as Amdahl and Hitachi, but also made the evolution of Japan into an "information society" (the government's phrase) a national priority at the highest level, with a cabinet department (Ministry of International Trade and Industry, better known as MITI) held largely responsible for driving economic aspects of the initiative, beginning in the 1980s [25]. The Chinese approach most closely paralleled that of the Japanese, but with a touch further of entrepreneurial activity that more closely paralleled the simultaneous experience of the Koreans.

NATIONAL CHAMPION MODEL

This model of diffusion became popular in the 1960s and extended into the 1980s, at which time it faded in popularity as its effectiveness waned. The textbook example of this approach to diffusion is that of France, although the British, the Italians, and the Dutch had tried it less aggressively. It is also normal to describe the French approach as failed, possibly a judgment historians will need to revise as they learn more about how computers spread in France [26]. Finally, we should point out that this approach was driven overwhelmingly by public officials, with the private sector playing a secondary role in implementing the strategies of the national government.

France had an indigenous office appliance company, Machines Bull, established in 1932, which, in the 1950s, sold successfully a computer product line called Gamma 3. The cost of developing its sequel (Gamma 60), however, nearly bankrupted the company, which led to its sale to the American firm GE in the 1960s when it was keen on developing into a global provider of computers. Meanwhile, the French government, under the leadership of Charles DeGaulle, had as national policy to challenge the growing economic and cultural influence of the United States in Western Europe. The successful introduction of the IBM S/360 family occurred in France as elsewhere in the mid-1960s, at a time for the French when their national government had barely invested in the development of a local computer industry. The De Gaulle administration announced its Plan Calcul which entailed creating a new firm supported and largely funded by the national government, Compagnie International de l'Informatique (Cii), a merger of two small firms, SEA and CEA. Other enterprises were established, also largely funded by the government: one to produce peripherals, a computer leasing company, and a national research institute. However, the introduction of yet another family of computers by IBM (S/370) within a few years pushed the market beyond that of France's newly reconstituted computer industry. GE sold Machines Bull to Honeywell and left the market. IBM immediately dominated the local computer industry [27].

The French government then tried to expand its failing national champion program by negotiating the establishment of a pan-European champion industry involving Siemens (Germany) and Philips (Netherlands) to go after IBM's growing market share in Europe, with the newly formed Unidata system. By 1975, the French government had to withdraw its untenable support for Unidata, after which Cii and Honewell-Bull merged into Cii-HB. But like most attempts around the world to merge computer firms, this too failed and could not prevail against IBM, even in the protected national economy of France [28]. In 1981, François Mitterand's government nationalized Cii-HB, taking a 42.5% ownership of the firm; the rest was shared with other companies, including the Japanese company NEC. Despite the investment of some $1 billion between 1983 and 1990, the initiative failed to become profitable, innovate sufficiently, or block the more entrenched American and, increasingly, Japanese firms.

The French effort to create a nationally rooted industry failed in the face of private sector competition that had more resources and technical innovations, and could bring them to market in the form of attractive products quickly enough to satisfy the needs of customers and that punished competitors. However, lost in that story is one significant consequence of the French experience. Beginning largely in the 1960s, the French economy was exposed to computers and embraced them so avidly that by the end of the century the largest enterprises and public agencies were using this technology for the same reasons evident in other economically advanced countries. By the turn of the century, France was routinely ranked by industry watchers as an extensive user of all manner of IT, ranging from an online telephone directory system to use of the Internet and cell phones [29]. By the early 2000s, like much of Western Europe, the French government had shifted from direct investment and control of the local computer industry to strategies more attuned to national economic development, and those always focused on uses, not simply on development of protected national industries [30].

The distinguishing feature of the national champion model is the creation of a national (local) computer industry protected aggressively and preferred through government policy and action. It is also a model that other European countries flirted with, including most of Central and Eastern Europe. In market-driven economies, however, the direct involvement of French officials and public funds in structuring and directing the activities of local firms proved unique because it was so extensive, in comparison, for example, to what happened in Italy, Germany, Great Britain, and Finland.

As business historian Alfred D. Chandler, Jr., observed of the futile French experience, "competitive organizational capabilities can rarely be achieved except through the creation of an integrated core enterprise that becomes a learning base through which new technologies are commercialized for world markets and in so doing create high barriers to entry that continue to protect that base." Those are the things IBM and Microsoft did well [31]. One might add, however, that at least during the period when General DeGaulle ruled, public policy was less about making an industry profitable and successful (although those were clearly objectives) and concentrated more on constraining the rising tide of U.S. influence in European affairs that was seen as an affront to French foreign policy objectives [32]. The political policy factor is one that always needs to be taken into account in describing any role of government in the deployment of IT.

What historians have yet to document adequately are the consequences of the French adoption of computers. Did their economy become as productive as that of other nations due to some role of computers? So far the focus has concentrated on simply documenting French productivity performance [33]. To what extent did computing change the nature of work and play in France? The current interest in the Internet and in mobile phones suggests that the French were less distinctive in their use of technology than their failed public policy of the 1960s and 1970s might suggest.

ASIAN PRIVATE-SECTOR-DRIVEN MODEL

Is there then no example of some sort of successful national champion model stimulated by national public policy? The question is normally asked in the context of understanding local computer industries—the supply side of the story. Rarely is the question answered with additional consideration of the demand side of the story—the extent to which computing from any source was ultimately implemented and used, and that led to economic and social results.

South Korea offers evidence of another model of the acquisition and, hence, diffusion of technology that proved highly successful. In this instance, the dominant pattern of behavior involves the government encouraging and supporting a local industry to acquire the necessary technical know-how to be competitive in a global market while at the same time allowing international partnerships with local firms to acquire the knowledge to reach new sources of capital investment and markets. There are numerous cases in South Korea, Taiwan, Singapore, Hong Kong, and Japan of that happening, as well as elsewhere in Asia, beginning in the 1970s and extending to the present [34].

The Asian diffusion model differs from others we have discussed in that the earliest manifestations of computer activities centered on the manufacture of components that went into the fabrication of computer systems designed in the United States and Western Europe. Rather than attempt initially to build whole new systems, or even retroengineer existing computers (something the Japanese did beginning in the 1970s), many Asian firms began by manufacturing components, such as semiconductors and actual frames in which parts were installed for other firms. This approach created a base of crucial knowledge about the manufacture and, later, design of semiconductors and myriad software/firmware components that could be transferred to the manufacture of such high-tech products as consumer electronics, PCs, mainframes, and peripherals. By looking at the role of component manufacturing, it is possible to describe this alternative approach to diffusion, moving first to the emergence of the semiconductor industry and then to consumer electronics. For purposes of describing the contours of this form of diffusion, we can focus on just the semiconductor industry.

Korean officials and local technology companies in the 1970s saw the positive effects that computer component manufacturing was having in Japan. In the mid-1980s, Korean companies invested extensively in acquiring know-how for manufacturing semiconductors, relying on American-trained management and technical staff and South Korea's relatively less expensive labor. A variety of cross-licensing agreements with American companies made possible the transfer of technical knowledge to the country and provided U.S. partners with new markets for their products. By 1986, the South Koreans were producing 1.2% of the world's supply of semiconductors; by 1993, they owned 5.2% of the market, with their share amounting to $4.77 billion in integrated circuits (ICs) [35].

Once they had the ability to manufacture semiconductors, next came the capability of designing new ICs, and the wherewithal to make products that relied on ICs and other forms of advanced electronics all through the 1990s. In turn, that combination of capabilities led to an expanded market for Korean made consumer electronics and computer-based components and final products in the country. In the process, thousands of South Korean workers and their families and friends became more technologically savvy consumers and users [36].

The Taiwanese underwent a similar experience. The local government encouraged and helped indigenous companies to seek foreign direct investments in their industry, normally from American and European companies. Taiwanese firms paid particular attention to acquiring technical knowledge through exchanges of engineering talent back and forth with the United States. In Taiwan's case, the import of capital investments and know-how made it possible for local firms both to manufacture (fabricate and assemble) and design ICs in the 1990s. This ramp-up proved quite successful, with annual growth rates in local revenues in the late 1980s and early 1990s often ranging from 20 to over 33% [37]. As in South Korea, the spillover of computing into the manufacture of all manner of industrial and consumer goods occurred in the 1990s and beyond, also making customers out of local citizens. As with the Koreans, annual consumption rates of IT, use of cell phones, broadband, and personal computers also rose [38].

This pattern was replicated across much of Asia and, indeed, continues today in the Philippines, Indonesia, and Vietnam. Public officials jumpstarted the process by encouraging indigenous firms to seek out and obtain foreign investments, know-how, and managerial talent, beginning in the 1970s, and they rapidly became global players. High-tech, inexpensive workforces emerged, trained both by schools and the firms themselves. As a result, local companies moved up the value chain from cheap manufacturing of components to the design and fabrication of sophisticated electronics, such as automotive parts, musical sound systems, PCs, and cell phones.

Asians began using technology in different ways than Americans and Europeans, yet another example of the localization discussed in the previous chapter. By the late 1990s, South Koreans became some of the most extensive players of online video games in the world, taking advantage of their access to high-speed broadband. Consumer electronics became fashion statements in this country as well, with consumers acquiring multiple iPods and cell phones in different colors to match or enhance the color of their suits and dresses [39]. Affluent Asian customers were some of the first to embrace computer-based products in the 1980s (e.g., PCs, CDs, cell phones, video games). As the costs of these items declined and their standard of living grew, these items diffused extensively across societies.

A similar process had occurred earlier in commercial enterprises, such as by manufacturing and banking companies, much as happened in North America and Western Europe, only beginning in the late 1970s. Because so many factories were new in the 1980s and 1990s, they also extensively incorporated state-of-the-art IT, as it was less expensive to do that than to retrofit old factories.

Additionally, as in the first diffusion model involving the United States and the United Kingdom, there was considerable dialogue and collaboration among public officials and private sector executives. This resulted in a successful allocation of responsibilities where they were mutually advantageous, from access to capital and international trade by officials to the private sector moving aggressively to assume responsibility for participating in an international market both with acumen and speed.

PLANNED ECONOMY: PUBLIC POLICY MODEL

Centrally controlled economies provide yet another variant of earlier models of diffusion of computers in more than two dozen national economies. This is the case of the Soviet bloc nations that operated for decades in an environment in which public officials created national economic policies that proved quite micro in scope and implementation. Public administrators determined which industries should be developed, set production and sales targets, and allocated capital and hiring authorizations. They also appointed the managers at various levels of state-owned enterprises. In short, it is difficult to think of a private sector existing in this model of diffusion. The model, which proved to be an unqualified disaster for running any national economy, also proved ineffective in diffusing computing throughout any society comparable to what occurred in market-driven economies, such as those in Western Europe, East Asia, and North America. Economic management and development was not effective in allowing the creative forces of innovation and competition to influence the features, costs, and rate of evolution of computing. Alan Greenspan, who chaired the American banking regulatory arm of the U.S. government (Federal Reserve Board) in the years when this model finally collapsed explained the problem this way: "Here there was no creative destruction, no impetus to build better tools." Greenspan observed further, "Missing is the ultimate consumer, who in a centrally planned economy is assumed to passively accept the goods planning agencies ordered produced. Even in the USSR, consumers didn't behave that way" [40].

Nowhere was this model more dramatically implemented than in the Soviet bloc. To be sure, a similar approach existed years ago in China (1950s–1980s), as, of course, it exists even today in Cuba, and appears to be emerging in Venezuela. The Soviet bloc of national economies was quite large, with their five-year economic plans spread from East Germany to the far eastern reaches of the Soviet Union in Central Asia, encompassing over a dozen republics, and almost all of Central and Eastern Europe [41].

Yet, there had been much activity behind the Iron Curtain with respect to computing. Publicly supported projects of the 1950s–1970s existed in Romania, Bulgaria, Estonia, Russia, Georgia, and East Germany to mention a few [42]. In short, in almost every Soviet Bloc European country and in Russia itself, national and state governments followed a pattern eerily similar to that of the United States in its early stages of computer development (1940s–1950s). National technology institutes and universities received public funding to invent and build computer systems. Although the full scope of those initiatives is not yet fully understood, all through the 1950s to the end of the 1970s governments sponsored R&D. This often happened for reasons similar to those stimulating the American government: for weapons systems in response to the Cold War, avionics for military and civilian use, weather forecasting, scientific research, and so forth. Systems emerged from these initiatives that incorporated local development, reliance on available technical literature from the West, and even a fairly extensive effort of retroengineering commercial products from the United States, such as IBM's computers. That latter activity was a surreptitious activity since American law forbade exportation of advanced technologies to those countries deemed by the U.S. government to be a threat to the military security of the United States. Yet, these were needed in order to retroengineer them [43].

Those industries deemed critical to the success of a Soviet bloc country were often early adopters of computers, beginning with the military (as happened in the United States), followed by large government agencies, and then by the late 1960s, on a limited basis, in state-managed manufacturing, chemical processing, and utilities [44]. There are yet no reliable statistics on the extent of deployment of computing within the economies of the Soviet Bloc. But, anecdotal evidence from Western companies attempting to sell their products in these economies suggests that diffusion remained quite limited. Where it had occurred, it often involved older generations of technologies than were in use in capitalist economies.

After the fall of the Berlin Wall in 1989, changes came quickly. New Russian regimes in the 1990s and early 2000s began privatizing what had previously been state-run factories and businesses. The gale forces of competition and innovation blew slowly through local industries, although large firms were often taken over quickly by members of elite classes, particularly in Russia. Again, there is a paucity of good data about diffusion in these years, but it would appear that as capital became attractive to invest in such places as the old East Germany, Poland, Estonia, Lithuania, and Russia in the 1990s, and restrictions lifted on the sale of current technologies by American firms to these countries, companies that survived began modernizing. Those efforts called for uses of computing already in widespread use across large parts of Western Europe and North America. By the early 2000s, consumer electronics were also in wide use, particularly in large urban centers, often in the form of digital sound systems and cell phones [45].

Internet use varied all over the area. Countries physically nearest to the West became the most extensive early users of the Internet, such as Estonia, where government officials effectively and aggressively sought to make their nation's telecommunications infrastructure modern. On the other hand, Internet use in Russia and in poorer East European countries progressed far slower, due more to the lack of effective infrastructure investments and poor economic conditions than perhaps from any public censorship.

State-driven diffusion of myriad IT-based devices and software varied widely, however. For example, in the case of China a combination of diffusion models emerged over time. Like the Soviets, the Chinese government sponsored limited state and academic managed R&D on computers in the 1950s and 1960s. As the national government and later state administrations began modernizing and expanding manufacturing and banking industries in the 1980s and 1990s, officials encouraged foreign investors to form alliances and partnerships with local firms, particularly in high-tech manufacturing. The Chinese learned from the Japanese and Korean experiences, mimicking them in areas in Eastern China designated as regions in which modern manufacturing should take place. Spillover effects of IT know-how occurred as computing spread to all manner of modern manufacturing of consumer products, consumer electronics, massively for the manufacture of PCs for almost every vendor around the world, and for IT peripherals. Along the way, Chinese officials began learning about the importance of property rights, issues that extended beyond the highly publicized pirating of CDs and DVDs, to how better to respect these as a condition for joining the World Trade Organization (WTO) [46].

In those areas of China in which IT became part of the local economy, the technology affected roughly a third of the country's population by the early 2000s. Diffusion occurred in a familiar way. As new factories were built, they incorporated use of computers, often relying on the experience of non-Chinese companies with whom partnerships and alliances had been formed [47]. As standards of living increased, so too did demand in China for modern consumer electronics.

Yet some 700 million Chinese still live in less prosperous circumstances. They work largely in agriculture, and have limited (or no) exposure to computing. An additional couple of hundred million workers and their families are dependent on low-wage First Industrial Revolution jobs, such as in the manufacture of clothing, plastic goods, and toys for export. In that sector of the economy, diffusion of computing is quite limited as inexpensive labor is often a cost-effective substitute for automation.

This pattern of variegated economic development within a nation exists to a similar extent in India. As a result, a similar pattern of consumer and industrial diffusion is currently playing out in cities that the national government has designated as high-tech centers, such as Bangalore, Hyderabad, and Mumbai [48]. It is no accident that these patterns are similar because public officials and an expanding cadre of private-sector managers were aware of each other's circumstances and policies and communicate through intragovernmental conversations, at international conferences on economic development, and through myriad surveys, studies, and consulting projects conducted by academics and consulting firms.

A third variant of this public-policy model emerged in Africa during the 1980s, almost entirely, however, focused on the diffusion of wireless telephone communications, particularly in Sub-Saharan countries. As a group, the continent's four-dozen national governments have generally been slow to adopt computers in the operation of public and private administrations, with notable exceptions in South Africa and somewhat along the Mediterranean rim, which had more advanced economies than those found in the heart of Africa. For vast reaches of Africa, the only computer-based diffusion has been the cell phone. However, there has been highly publicized but miniscule deployment of inexpensive laptops, just starting, for example, with Nicholas Negreponte's inexpensive laptops for children.

The Internet in Sub-Saharan Africa is, in particular, a development only just now underway, largely promoted by governments. Wireless telephony has largely been accomplished without extensive use of the Internet. E-government concepts are just now being explored in that middle section of the continent. Along the periphery of Africa, Internet usage increased in the early 2000s. Yet no country in Africa has comparable levels of use of the Internet as seen in Europe or North America [49]. Even good intentions of public officials to facilitate expanded use of the Internet have been stymied by social issues competing both for their time and financial resources, such as education, health, employment, and waging of regional wars. Deployment, thus, varied enormously. One United Nations study of the role of the Internet reported that in the early 2000s, "there is a big gap between the West African region and the Northern and Southern African regions. The Central and Eastern Africa regions are close in rankings, with Eastern Africa ranking slightly ahead," but when all is said and done, usage lagged the rest of the world [50].

Governments in many African countries focused their IT attention on creating telecommunications infrastructures, a priority for technology evident in almost every underdeveloped or developing economy in the world since the 1980s. By the early 1990s, wired telephone services had become too expensive when compared to wireless communications, largely because of the cost of stringing wire, often in areas where the cabling could also be stolen or damaged by warfare. As with other forms of information technology, the lower the GDP of a population, the smaller (hence less expensive) the technology must be. Additionally, wireless is also attractive where existing wired communications services are either weak or simply too expensive. Cell phone usage in African countries has been increasing over the past twenty years because national governments created sufficient infrastructure to support this, or formed alliances with foreign operators to provide the service. As the costs of cell phones declined, more people could use them. For example in the Democratic Republic of the Congo, by the end of the 1990s there were some 10,000 wired phones but 3 million cell phone users by the end of 2005. Nigeria had one million fixed phones but by the end of 2005 had 19 million cell phone users. A similar story could be told about Angola, Ghana, Kenya, Mali, Mauritania, Uganda, Tanzania, and other nations [51].

One can conclude that wireless communications was displacing or substituting for the traditional wired communications so evident in advanced economies. Additionally, payment schemes were introduced in line with the ability of local customers to pay for services, such as paying for use as consumed (e.g., a phone in one village, same in India and Algeria) [52], or extremely limited month-by-month plans, or others in which hundreds of individuals shared one phone [53].

What the historical evidence indicates is that the lower the per-capita GDP in a nation, the more likely it is that governments focus on diffusing modern telecommunications rather than computing, frequently while forming or encouraging alliances with manufacturers of high-tech components or products. It is a theme picked up again in the next chapter on the role of governments in leveraging IT in national economic development. Suffice it to point out here that as average per capita GDP rises, discretionary income makes it possible to acquire consumer electronics with ICs imbedded in them, while, slightly earlier and continuously, computing diffuses quickly into high-tech industries but slowly into the rest of an economy. The more industrialized an economy, the sooner governments using this model could afford to experiment with computing. However, in those economies that were state-driven, rather than competitive and capitalist, deployment of information technology of any kind remained severely limited throughout the second half of the twentieth century. Its most singular virtue, and hardly one at that, is that this model of deployment aligned nicely with the strategies implemented by public officials in the way they wanted to manage their economies as a whole across multiple industries.

INDUSTRY-DRIVEN MODEL

Not all diffusion of computing and other forms of IT in an economy is driven by public policy. The more IT became cost-effective for a company to use, and the more reliable and flexible the technology proved to be, the greater its deployment, especially in capitalist economies. Often, non-IT industry associations and task forces, along with consulting firms and computer vendors, disseminated information about the technology to end-user firms, which, in turn, then acquired and used the computing. As a particular technology became attractive for specific uses within an industry, such as ATMs in banking and point-of-sale (POS) terminals in retail, the more existing non-IT industry associations would report on the use and benefits of these to members of their industries. It would be difficult to overstate the importance of the role myriad industries played in facilitating the diffusion of technology, particularly those applications of IT used by government agencies, education, and corporations.

At the firm level, in this model a new technology is introduced into a company, often to a technical community, such as to engineers in the 1950s–1960s, or to IT staffs, as was commonly the operative case from the 1960s to the present. Niche suppliers of IT would routinely reach out to specific sets of users, such as engineers for high-performance terminals or CAD/CAM software, or to manufacturing managers with shop-floor and production-scheduling software tools. In early stages of adoption, internal task forces made (and still make) recommendations on how best to proceed and why, often developing early business cases for adoption. Later, IT departments acquired upgrades and more modern versions of the technology. In the past two decades, line management in divisions and departments outside of IT have been making decisions regarding adoption of newer forms of the technology. Associations, vendors, and customers thus created a virtuous circle of dialogue.

In the United States, for example, in every industry that became major users of computers, one could find an industry association that had explained the value, methods, and benefits of this technology. Normally, industry associations did this through their magazines and journals, such as the American Banking Association's *Banking*. A second popular approach involved a combination of hosting seminars, training sessions, and whole conferences devoted to IT, such as in the insurance industry by LOMA over the course of a half-century [54]. Often at such events, or through an industry's publications, vendors promoted their products, MIS management explained their experiences with IT, and consultants provided a great deal of "here's how you do it" information. These various forms of knowledge transfer aimed directly at managers and staffs in companies and government agencies facilitated implementation of computing.

Task forces also did the same. For instance, in the American grocery industry, the need to track all manner of inventory grew all through the 1950s and 1960s as the number of various products that could be offered to customers rose to such a point that by the early 1970s, a large supermarket could possibly have over 50,000 different products. Tracking that inventory, ordering more, and accounting for it was becoming expensive [55]. A task force consisting of a half-dozen grocery companies offered their industry the design of the universal product code (UPC), what we now know as the bar code, along with accompanying hardware and software. A pilot experiment conducted by one grocery store in Ohio provided the necessary proof of concept that scanning bar codes made economic and operational sense. Suppliers of boxed and canned goods were pressured by the industry into printing bar codes on their products per specifications of the grocery industry's technical committees [56].

Scanning led to the development of several generations of point-of-sale terminals for checkout, which, by the late 1980s, helped tie together in-store inventory systems in all retail industries. Meanwhile, use of bar codes spread rapidly to military and manufacturing firms, to libraries for tracking books, and even to hospitals and clinics, because bar codes made it possible to improve and automate tracking and movement of information about specific items [57].

Barcoding extended beyond the United States, spreading around the world, first across North America, next into Western Europe and East Asia. Deployment proved uneven in that the rate of adoption varied by national industries. A similar tale could be told about the experience banks had with ATMs, and government agencies with GIS applications. In each instance, the pattern of diffusion proved similar. An industry association would promote an application, facilitate education and adoption, and then encourage potential users, largely by reporting on how many firms or agencies were using a particular technology, while explaining the business rationale for the popularity of some device or software.

The important role of industry associations, publications, and task forces dates back to the time computers first became attractive to use in the private sector in the early 1950s. Yet, even before the dawn of commercial computing, communities had already established the pattern of coming together to discuss computers. Government officials and academics, who were the most extensive users of computers, acted in a similar way in that they would meet periodically at conferences to share experiences, or to teach each other at their universities about how to deploy a new digital innovation. The seminars famously held at various American universities immediately following World War II [58]; the establishment and growth of myriad computer associations, such as the Association for Computing Machinery (ACM) in 1947 and the Data Processing Management Association (DPMA) in 1949; and even an organization of IT associations, the American Federation of Information Processing Societies (AFIPS) in 1961, all mirrored the kinds of communal activities that became so evident both in the public and private sectors in subsequent decades.

In the 1940s–1980s, the majority of industry activities involved public institutions and, subsequently, companies. However, as configurations of digital technologies and software evolved into smaller devices available to consumers, such as personal computers in the late 1970s and their massive deployment around the world over the next quarter century, and later of such consumer electronics as Blackberries, cell phones, video games, iPods, and other digitally enhanced products, new associations and conventions appeared to support new communities of users and suppliers. Examples of such groups of users included those of early microcomputer owners in California in the late 1970s, video game aficionados in the 1980s, and consumer goods suppliers in the 1990s.

By the early 2000s, some of these user groups had become massive. For instance, today the largest annual product-centric convention in the world focuses on digital consumer goods. It is hosted by the Consumer Electronics Association (CEA) and called the Consumer Electronics Show. The first event, held in 1967, had 200 exhibitors and 17,500 individuals attended; an impressive 2,100 firms were members of CES that year. CES grew and in 2007, for instance, its annual conference had 2,700 exhibitors and 140,000 attendees [59]. Even in recession-filled 2009, 110,000 people attended its annual conference. It had rapidly grown into a major global business event with most of the key personalities of computing routinely appearing as keynote speakers over the years, such as Bill Gates and Steve Jobs. A similar tale could be told about video games as well. In short, as technologies evolved, new industry associations emerged, while preexisting ones transformed themselves in response to changing circumstances, proving continuously that this model of diffusion remained crucial to the story of how IT spread around the world.

CORPORATE DIFFUSION MODEL

So far, we have discussed diffusion models that were largely supply driven and overwhelmingly the consequence of actions taken by governments and whole industries. But as the last several pages demonstrated, even within these modes of diffusion, industries, companies within industries, and industry associations played aggressive roles in promoting the use of computing, while, simultaneously, within firms task forces and managers also made such decisions. To be sure, individual participants included public officials, but over time initiative spread to the private sector, which is what leads us to the concept of a corporate diffusion model. This was all about facilitating the creation and nurturing of a capability within an economy in which firms operated successfully in developing, selling, and installing IT. Closely tied to the deployment of IT was the work of organizations encouraging potential users to adopt a technology. In this model, one moves more fully to the demand side of the story, that is to say, to that of the user, the customer, and individual companies. The number of users of computers around the world always outnumbered the quantity of suppliers. IBM was one company, but throughout the past half-century it had tens of thousands of firms and agencies as customers, and millions of users of its products. The same held true for national champions in France, where a handful of firms supplied products to many more institutions and users than the vendors had as employees. Ultimately, customers—corporations from many industries and government agencies—for IT did more to diffuse the technology than any vendor or national economic policy.

It is almost impossible to speak purely about a demand-side (that is to say, end-user) model without intertwining the role of the supply side, such as that of vendors of computing. Suppliers introduced end users to IT as it continued to evolve, persuading them of the benefits of its use, while end users put pressure on vendors to drive down costs, increase reliability, capacity, and functionality of their products. It was common for all vendors and many users of IT to collaborate in the design and transformation of products, and to validate the applicability of a product to a set of customers.

There were several phases in the evolution of this diffusion model. Beginning as far back as the 1940s, when governments wanted to promote development of computers, they relied on companies and universities to provide the necessary technical talent. This was most pronounced in the United States, where office appliance firms, such as IBM, NCR, and Burroughs, played key, often collaborative roles with major universities and government agencies in the early development of computer systems. Others in electronics (e.g., GE) and weapons systems (e.g. McDonnell-Douglas) did the same, particularly after 1950. To a lesser extent, the same thing occurred in the United Kingdom, beginning in the 1940s, in Japan in the 1950s, and in various West European countries in the 1960s. We do not have evidence of this early form of behavior by the private sector in Soviet block countries, where companies were actually owned by the state and not necessarily given responsibility for development of a technology.

These activities outside the Soviet Bloc furthered appreciation for the potential uses of computers. Often, firms became early users of a technology in commercial applications, such as when GE installed a computer at the start of the 1950s in support of its manufacturing operations, defense contractors installed them to help in the fabrication of aircraft, and at the end of the decade, when Bank of America developed ERMA to process bank checks [60]. Vendors of IT products began convincing large enterprises to embrace the use of computing to automate existing processes in the 1950s and 1960s, and as these customers did that, they too learned about a technology's capabilities and went on to develop new uses, taking advantage of every new innovation in IT that came along. It is a pattern of adoption that has continued to the present, with firms around the world spending annually nearly two trillion dollars on the process by the early 2000s [61].

Large enterprises proved to be the most extensive consumers of IT. Obviously, having large populations of employees proved crucial in the equation. When a company implemented a common use of an application or technology, it routinely diffused it across the firm and often that use became standard across its industry. For example, it is common practice for a large company or government agency to make all its offices and retail outlets similar in look and feel and function for consistency in delivering goods and services. Thus, a McDonald's restaurant essentially looks the same around the world, IBM sales offices have been consistent with each other for a century, as were major banks' branches.

In various offices, manufacturing plants, and branches, organizations installed similar hardware and software. Thus, for instance, when senior IBM executives, in this case as consumers of IT, decided that all sales branch offices should start using e-mail at the start of the 1980s (PROFS), that led to the diffusion of the application across over 500 branches in the United States and to every other sales office around the world in that decade. The decision to diffuse around the world was made in Armonk, New York; the result was that in over 150 countries, business e-mail became ubiquitous in that one firm [62]. The implications are relatively obvious: what was learned at IBM was shared with customers as part of selling products, such as PROFS, and if IBM employees became managers in other firms, they brought with them their business practices to their new employer, such as e-mail. Their customers, in turn, also were exposed to new software tools and so the process of new uses of IT spread out across whole economies much like the ever-widening rings that one sees after throwing a pebble into a lake.

A similar story of diffusion could be told for nearly every major corporation in the world: Philips of the Netherlands, Sony of Japan, General Motors of the United States, and so forth. The largest enterprises had the financial wherewithal to implement such massive deployments of computing and they had the most extensive opportunities to gain economic and operational advantages from IT because of their huge employee populations. Over the past six decades, as various technologies dropped in relative costs and came packaged in ever varied sized configurations and costs, smaller enterprises and government agencies could afford the initial expense of deployment of the technology. This led to an ongoing diffusion of the technology to more diminutive enterprises and widely to departments, divisions and plants within firms, particularly beginning in the 1970s with minicomputers, then with even less expensive PCs in the 1980s.

The decline in relative costs led as well to deployment of newer applications, which replaced older systems and extended their uses to new functions and classes of users. Beginning in the early 1980s with massive diffusions of IBM PCs and compatible rivals, the availability of the PC in a commercial environment, in particular, meant that in advanced economies computing was now within the reach of all manner and size of organizations. In short, all through the past half-century IT spread first from the very largest organizations to the smallest, with diffusion driven largely by the demand and cost for these products as they appeared in the marketplace [63].

The largest organizations also spurred diffusion of IT around the world by forcing those who either supplied them with goods and services, or otherwise did business with them, also to use computing to conduct their interactions. For example, the three largest American automotive companies (GM, Ford, and Chrysler) compelled their suppliers to use computers beginning in the 1970s. They did this extensively by the end of the 1980s using highly computerized just-in-time supply chains, and later to participate digitally in the design of components and scheduling of deliveries and work. That caused many smaller enterprises around the world to acquire computers in order to be a supplier to these firms. Wal-Mart, the world's largest retailer, did the same with its suppliers from all over the world, most notably in China. Once a small firm had access to a computer for whatever original purpose, for instance, to sell to General Motors, it could (and did) use the technology to automate other functions and to engage with other large customers.

Governments followed suit. Many U.S. government agencies insisted that proposals and bills be presented electronically and that its tens of thousands of suppliers be able to accept payments electronically. Similar systems were established in some Asian nations and others within the European Union [64]. Citizens were also encouraged to seek out government information and forms via the Internet, to file online requests for permits, and to submit electronically their tax returns and applications. In turn, those activities increased the digital literacy of whole populations of citizens, encouraging them as well to use computing in other ways.

Thanks to historical research and the various tracking projects sponsored by government agencies, private foundations, and academic researchers, we understand how this process of diffusion occurred in the United States [65]. OECD and European Union studies, and those done by the Economist Intelligence Unit (EIU) and others, are beginning to reveal similar patterns of diffusion in Western Europe and also in those countries that were behind the Iron Curtain, the latter most notably since the early to mid-1990s [66]. Latin America and the experiences of Asia remain less known; yet, even in those cases, diffusion proved extensive within those sectors of an economy that relied on computing, especially in Asia. Thus, IBM offices in Beijing or Rio de Janeiro used the same computing tools as an IBM office in New York City; large national banks in almost all countries relied on computers to one extent or another. Local governments often pejoratively considered "primitive" or "backwards" by people in the most "advanced" economies also used some IT [67]. Unfortunately, there is insufficient reliable data available to say to what extent this is true.

Another feature of the pull strategy involved communities of end users. Particularly in the 1960s–1980s, manufacturing firms, engineering communities, and plant operations often acquired their own systems so that they could control and dedicate these to their needs. They were rebelling, in effect, against the centralized "glass house" data processing organizations that were under the control of the financial and accounting departments of a firm and more devoted to supporting accounting users than engineers and plant management. To gain sufficient wherewithal, many end-user communities embraced minicomputers, then PCs, and later their own mainframes and powerful desktop systems, such as those offered by Sun and DEC [68]. IBM and Burroughs aligned with the "glass house" firms; upstart vendors with large end-user communities. Engineers wrote their own software, shared this code with colleagues in other industries and firms, and, in many instances, these became software products sold to end-user customers. It was not uncommon by the end of the 1980s for these end users to have as much or more computing power than the centralized MIS (management information systems) establishment.

To be sure, the rate of diffusion varied widely by country, industry, and time. The biggest factor gating the rate of diffusion within an economy was more frequently the adaption practices of an industry's firms rather than public economic policy. The more extensively a form of IT supported an industry's core work, the greater the diffusion of IT within that industry's member companies. Those industries that had large bodies of common data and processed information and work in a highly repeatable manner were normally the earliest and consistently most extensive users of IT. Into this category one can place manufacturing, banking, insurance, and retailing companies. When technology could be configured into industry-specific forms, that event stimulated deployment as well. In this category, think of ATMs in banking, POS in retail, smart bombs for the military, GIS for governments, and, perhaps, Negreponte's laptops for students in impoverished nations.

Functions common to many industries also facilitated deployment of computing. The most obvious of these kinds of applications of IT included accounting, finance, inventory control (later, supply chain management), online account queries, e-mail, spreadsheets, and word processing. The history of these application diffusions became more complex as additional uses of a universal nature kept becoming available. To suggest a few, in the past two decades this occurred with consumer electronics that diffused all over the world: CDs, DVDs, video games, digital photography, wireless telephony, iPods, and social networking sites on the Internet.

APPLICATION DIFFUSION MODEL

This model of diffusion can be dispensed with quickly because it is a variant of the corporate model. Just suggested above was the deployment of common applications, such as accounting, made possible by the availability of software and hardware tools designed for these purposes. However, more subtle is the diffusion of the ways the work of businesses and agencies take place as a result of using IT. It is the influence, just now appearing, of how consumers use their technologies, such as social networking sites on the Internet, cell phones, and iPods.

Briefly described, as an individual or organization begins to use a particular technology in a certain way, that "certain way" of use, for instance, of a software tool, often defined by the vendor, becomes the way the technology is spread. For example, every time SAP sold a copy of one of its software products in the 1990s, it set in motion a process within customers' firms that had acquired its product to conform to SAP's way of processing and tracking financial and other data. As the number of SAP licenses spread around the world, so too did a common way—the SAP way—of handling certain types of financial and other operational data. As the number of people familiar with SAP increased and moved in and out of companies, they took with them the only way they knew how to do specific functions—the SAP way—with the result that whether using SAP products or a rival's in another firm, a common way of doing financial reporting emerged.

It is a phenomenon that IT executives and managers have understood for several decades. The process of standardizing work caused by the extensive use of certain types of IT-based applications has occurred in all industries, for all intents and purposes, since the early 1960s. We will discuss in more detail below the role of technological path dependency (i.e., role of standards and prior practices), but the point to make here is that standards emerged for how things were done, driven by the characteristics of specific software and hardware tools that spread around the world. One primary consequence is obvious: divisions within companies and whole firms could collaborate around the world, such as occurs routinely in the pharmaceutical, semiconductor, and automotive industries, and, increasingly, in banking, brokerage, and retailing [69].

We are just now beginning to see second-order consequences too. These are more fascinating in the standardization of work. Received orthodoxy from economists and political scientists holds that one of the unanticipated reasons for the speed-up of economic globalization has been the diffusion of the Internet and other forms of IT and transportation. Alan Greenspan observed that "these new technologies not only opened up a whole new vista of low-cost communications but also facilitated major advances in finance . . . a critical enabler of rapidly expanding globalization and prosperity" [70].

Another second-order unanticipated consequence involved governments. With increased harmonization of activities, government regulators have been able to collaborate transnationally in setting standards for such things as the flow of data in financial transactions around the world and safety standards for drugs, and, increasingly, for food, consumer goods, and environmental requirements. In part, they could do that because there was sufficient homogenization of products, services, and work activities to set expectations through law and practice. It would be difficult to imagine, for example, that the standards of the U.S. Food and Drug Administration (FDA), or those of either the European Union (EU), or the World Trade Organization (WTO) would be possible to implement if there were no second-order effects of IT on the work of individuals and their enterprises [71]. In other words, the intensification of social, economic, political, and regulatory globalization occurred in part due to many forms of IT diffusing across an economy, and not just as a result of the use of the Internet or cell phones.

An additional characteristic of an application diffusion model can be summarized as a use of a technology, in this instance, computing, becoming so compelling that it almost sells itself. To be sure, no technology actually "sells itself," but there are times in the life of a technology when some new use becomes so attractive that users are drawn to it, less because a community or some government policy compels them to, or as a result of some vendor's effective marketing efforts. History is replete with examples of this form of diffusion. Steam engine technology in the 1700s led to a massive transformation in the use of power in manufacturing over the course of some 150 years; electricity did the same in less than a half century. The cotton gin of the early 1800s transformed the agriculture of the American South, leading to the expansion of slavery and, one could argue, to key circumstances that led to the American Civil War.

In the twentieth century, information technologies led to new uses that proved profoundly compelling as well. Calculating equipment and tabulators made cost accounting perhaps the most important innovation to occur in bookkeeping in the twentieth century. Highly refined inventory control procedures became possible thanks to the availability of computers, beginning almost instantaneously and literally with the first installation of a computer in a company. "Must have" uses of computing continued arriving all through the second half of the twentieth century: mobile phones, word processing, e-mail, and, most recently, portable music downloaded one song at a time to iPods. Despite outstanding marketing by Apple, the reason that over 100 million people bought iPods within the first five and a half years of its introduction had more to do with the "must have" phenomenon than to the brilliant marketing efforts by Apple. These applications were often anticipated, their arrival even forecasted in some instances decades in advance of their arrival (e.g., wireless telephony and digital TV), but when they became available, they were so rapidly embraced that no one could reasonably conclude that one or a few suppliers compelled a market to emerge. That characteristic is what helped give the application-diffusion model its status as unique.

This model is not limited to consumer electronics such as mobile music systems or cell phones. As cost accounting and inventory control suggest, this model of diffusion exists within corporations, industries, and whole economies as well. It straddles consumer/corporate markets, for example, ATMs. Almost as quickly as a bank introduced this application, it became so popular with retail banking customers that within several years it became nearly impossible for any American or West European bank to be competitive without offering this service to its customers.

TECHNOLOGY-STANDARDS DIFFUSION MODEL

An underlying feature of a first-order result of diffusion is often the emergence and successful adoption of technical standards. This is as true for computers as for most classes of complex technologies. This form of diffusion has been the subject of extensive study by historians, economists, and technologists across many types of technologies ranging from electricity and telephony to automotive and air transport. As something became standardized, diffusion increased, even though people resisted any suggestion that they migrate to some new way of doing things.

The case of the typewriter is iconoclastically the best known example of standardization. Once the QWERTY-type keyboard of a typewriter was learned by typists (a difficult and time-consuming task), it made it virtually impossible to introduce a different layout of letters on a keyboard, because the transition would have taken individual months or years to accomplish for an insufficient increase in benefits. The typing standard established a century ago made it possible for people who typed to move easily and quickly from the typewriter to word processors, because PC makers did not change the layout of the keyboard [72]. Similarly, Microsoft's operating system became path-dependent for many users by the late 1980s because it had evolved into the dominant set of technical standards installed on 95% of all PCs around the world over the past quarter-century.

It is critical to realize that when a dominant technology or standard exists, as in the case of Microsoft's operating systems, path dependency comes very much into play. When an end user becomes familiar with Microsoft's products, the effort required to abandon them and to learn some other set of software tools is often greater than the anticipated benefits of such a move. Very few users of Microsoft have moved off that platform despite the fact that they often find much to criticize about this technology, such as its complexity, insufficient ease of use, or inadequate security protections [73].

A second effect of path dependency is that organizations will adopt the standard for similar reasons as individuals, imposing it across the entire enterprise. Thus, it is not uncommon for a government agency or a company to have a policy that says it will acquire and support Microsoft-compatible software and IBM-compatible PCs and peripherals. When a large firm is deploying an application to its factories, stores, or offices around the world, a technical standard is simultaneously being diffused. As with an application, once a standard is widely accepted, it causes users of that standard either to extend its deployment or to enhance use of it through incremental adoptions of new applications.

Another historically famous example of this type of technical diffusion at work involves IBM's mainframes [74]. The attraction of IBM's technical standard proved ultimately so great that some of its most serious competitors relied on IBM's technical standards and even operating systems software! These firms included RCA, Amdahl, Hitachi, and Futjitsu [75].

The pattern of dependency is also evident with video game consoles in the 1980s, extending to the present. Any history of the video game business of the 1990s, in particular, moves quickly to the battles among major providers of consoles because, just as with mainframes, what console a user had normally influenced what games they acquired without having to invest in yet another console. Also, as one learned to use that device and became comfortable with its "look and feel" and navigation of video games running on that digital machine, it became increasingly unattractive to move to another platform [76].

Experts from various disciplines are now exploring the power of technical standards in affecting how specific technologies and their applications evolved [77]. One has to conclude that deployment on the back of a shared technical standard is a key model of diffusion. This approach has the benefits of adding speed and ease to the process of acceptance and deployment, particularly for complex and expensive technologies such as those represented by the inner workings of consumer electronics and large computer systems. It is also one that is continuing to play out at all levels of computing, most notably with open source and open standards technologies, but also at the more mundane level of video games, digital movies, and digital photography [78].

PATTERNS, PRACTICES, AND IMPLICATIONS

The patterns and, indeed, styles of deployment of information technology reflect a variety of ways in which computing diffuses around many parts of the world. Eight approaches have been identified here but we have to keep in mind that none operated in isolation of others. Looked at over the course of six decades, it becomes evident that in practice no single nation's experience fits exactly any one or two models; rather, they generally describe a style, such as the French national champion model, which is one of the most well-defined of all models, but also evolved into other forms over time toward a more industry-driven approach. Despite the fluid nature of how diffusion takes place, or how long one dominates before evolving, a number of specific observations can be made.

First, no nation adopts one diffusion model to the exclusion of all others. Rather, they either begin consciously with one, such as centralized, state-run economic practices, or function as a de facto one due to various circumstances that historians give a name to after the fact. The first of several approaches described in this chapter had the shared feature that government officials primed the innovation process that made it possible to create the technology, get it deployed, and ultimately transferred initiative for diffusion to the private sector, specifically both to vendors and users. In fact, this pattern in the evolution of diffusion over time can be seen as nearly a megamodel of diffusion that transcends the eight approaches.

Second, in most national economies these eight models began when an economy had already reached a point of technical sophistication that made computing an attractive enhancement. That factor is also obvious. The Americans and the British had data processing issues in World War II; the Soviets began when the Cold War compelled them to act; Japan moved a decade later when it made sense for its economy; African nations began largely just in the past decade. Given the wide disparity of national GDPs, configuration of local industries and firms, and the availability of technically skilled workers in combination with adequate capital, one can conclude that there is no absolute minimum level of economic sophistication required to enter the world of computers. Just as historians have praised digital technology for being malleable, so too one can conclude that also was the case with a national economy facing the decision to adopt computing or not.

To be sure, the poorer an economy, the more necessary it became, indeed becomes, over time for national governments to sponsor adoption of computing. This proved evident in Asia in the 1950s–1970s and Eastern Europe in the 1960s–1980s, as it is today in Sub-Saharan Africa. Even within that circumstance, various approaches were and are possible. In the Asian private-sector model, actions were heavily primed by governments in the early years. Firms focused on manufacturing components, whereas in the United Kingdom they went straight to full computer systems. In the former instance, no indigenous knowledge existed about computers, whereas in Great Britain some of the leading engineers building computers in the world had been active there since the 1930s.

Third, in those countries where public officials assume commanding roles in shaping the use of computer technologies, their approaches prove both similar and dissimilar. In Soviet planned economies and with the French national champion model, political priorities drove decisions on how best to exploit this technology. The Soviets supported military objectives, whereas the French were concerned about potential American technological and market hegemony. Yet the approaches were dissimilar as well. The Soviets promoted diffusion of computing by using many of the same planned economic techniques and managerial practices they applied to other industries. The French and other European states sought to empower indigenous firms in the private market, even to the extent of investing in them, as did the French.

Fourth, no diffusion model remains static. They evolve over time. The French began with a national champion program but evolved into the American market-driven model. Central and Eastern Europe did the same, beginning in the 1990s. Some simply changed within the confines of their original forms, such as that in the United States, which remained capitalist and corporate driven but seems quite different today with the diffusion of so many high-tech consumer electronics from the mainframe centric forms it had been in the 1950s and 1960s. In the more capitalist-driven models (industry-, corporate-, and application-driven) all key participants in the private sector dominated the rate of innovation in technology, its form of adoption, and the speed with which that happened.

Next, we can ask if some approaches are more effective or unfolding faster. Given the fact that diffusion has been quite extensive over many parts of the world, one could easily conclude that they were all effective and worked very quickly. However, that conclusion would mask nuances in performance. Each model had prerequisites that made them work, for better or worse. For example, where alignment existed between a model and how a local economy worked, the results were better. In the United States, the system of government agencies outsourcing initial development to universities and to the private sector was compatible with how high-tech developments occurred in other parts of the economy. Linking that approach to the shift in responsibility to vendors and customers matched nicely with how the economy functioned anyway and, thus, facilitated rapid innovation in product development and acceptance.

In the case of the Soviets and East Europeans in the 1950s–1980s, these economies were so dependent on centralized managerial practices that extended even to establishing performance benchmarks and tying investments and budgets to these, that considering use of the American–British approach would not have worked. The fact that computing spread slower and not as effectively in these planned economies had less to do with the technology, or its possible uses, than to economy-wide managerial practices that simply proved, as Greenspan suggested, to be an utter failure. In short, diffusion's success or failure, speed, and effectiveness must be seen as linked to the broader performance of an economy and not rest simply on the merits of any particular technology.

Over time, the eight patterns of deployment merged to the point where one could begin arguing that their distinctiveness had all but disappeared, largely in those countries that had become extensive users of IT. In fact, one could take the position that this pattern of convergence reflects both a megapattern of the globalization of the world's economy and also the role information technologies and communications played in facilitating the massive integration of the planet's economic affairs. It is no accident that economic globalization and the diffusion of digital technologies occurred at the same time and continues to do so today. The historical evidence demonstrates that diffusion of the technology tends in general to homogenize into a global mode of deployment. In the process, this homogenization facilitated the spread of common operational practices, managerial beliefs, and even increasingly to shared social and cultural traits, such as the wide use of English as the language most used in business and government at the senior level. That set of by-products of diffusion conforms nicely to the already recognized shared patterns of such business practices as accounting, finance, manufacturing, logistics, and so forth becoming more similar around the world.

This discussion brings us back to the fundamental conclusion that, in combination, the eight approaches to the diffusion of IT facilitated the integration of the global economy and ever increasing reliance on worldwide technical and operational standards. Even a distinguished historian of world history not known for arguing that a digital hand manipulated events, Felipe Fernández-Armesto, attributed to technology a large portion of the responsibility for why "Global culture has scattered the world with lookalike styles and products," leading to "increasing interconnectedness," and "to increasing interdependence, which in turn demands new, ever-wider, ultimate worldwide 'frameworks' for action, transcending old nations, blocs, and civilizations" [79]. It is a good reason for why it is so important to understand the rich history of how computing spread around the world.

In the next chapter, we look more closely at what modern governments do in furtherance of the deployment of IT, a process that is continuing to integrate more closely the entire world along the lines described in our introduction to this book. I focus on the role of government officials and their practices, because as the eight-model diffusion discussion should have made quite evident, initial future deployments of IT will probably occur as a result of policies implemented by governments. Therefore, we need to understand what they are doing today now that we have reviewed prior experience.

NOTES AND REFERENCES

1. Everett M. Rogers, *Diffusion of Innovations. Fifth Edition,* New York: Free Press, 2003, p. 1.

2. In the United States, the largest ongoing study, with reports appearing every few weeks, is the "Pew Internet and American Life" project, http://www.pewinternet.org/ (last accessed 1/10/2007). For Europe, both the OECD and the Economist Intelligence Unit conduct similar, although less frequent, studies and surveys.

3. Since 2000, in particular, the EIU has conducted such studies; see, for example, Economist Intelligence Unit, *The 2008 e-Readiness Rankings,* London: Economist Intelligence Unit, 2008.

4. An important early attempt to address these issues can be found in a collection of papers discussing many countries: Richard Coopey (Ed.), *Information Technology Policy: An International History,* Oxford: Oxford University Press, 2004; Alan Siaroff and Lee Clement, "The State and Industrial Flowers: Japanese Versus French Computer Strategy, 1960s–1980s," *Journal of Public Policy* 17 (January–April 1997): 31–61.

5. For details of this initiative, see http://www.laptopgiving.org/en/vision.php (last accessed 1/8/2008).

6. Documented most recently by Everett M. Rogers in the fifth edition of his *Diffusion of Innovations,* New York: Free Press, 2003. But see also Eric von Hippel, *The Sources of Innovation,* New York: Oxford University Press, 1988. Historians have yet to develop comprehensive accounts of innovation in the

post-World War II period to the extent that experts in other disciplines have, such as Rogers and von Hippel.

7. Eric von Hippel, *Democratizing Innovation,* Cambridge, MA: MIT Press, 2005; Linsu Kim and Richard R. Nelson (Eds.), *Technology, Learning, and Innovation: Experiences of Newly Industrializing Economies,* Cambridge, UK: Cambridge University Press, 2000.

8. Tim Berners-Lee and Mark Fisschett, *Weaving the Web: The Original Design and Ultimate Destiny of the World Wide Web by Its Inventor,* New York: HarperCollins, 1999.

9. Rogers, *Diffusion of Innovations,* p. 474.

10. Best told by Kenneth Flamm, *Targeting the Computer: Government Support and International Competition,* Washington, DC: Brookings Institution, 1987; and in his *Creating the Computer: Government, Industry and High Technology,* Washington, DC: Brookings Institution, 1988.

11. I gave considerable attention to the role of such organizations in James W. Cortada, *The Digital Hand,* 3 vols., New York: Oxford University Press, 2004–2008.

12. In late 2008, a dozen historians in Europe began to collaborate on just such a project, led by Gerard Alberts and James W. Cortada, examining the experience of Western Europe since the end of World War II.

13. The literature is vast, but for an introduction to global issues see Dale W. Jorgenson, Mun S. Ho, and Kevin J. Stiroh, *Productivity,* 3 vols., Cambridge, MA: MIT Press, 1995–2005.

14. Kim and Nelson, *Technology, Learning, and Innovation,* pp. 113–116.

15. A key finding of Cortada, *The Digital Hand,* 3 vols.

16. One might also add that the availability of a large community of appropriately trained electrical engineers and scientists, resident in universities or had acquired skills in advanced electronics during World War II, was a factor that facilitated the rapid advance of computer technology in the United States.

17. Christophe Lécuyer, *Making Silicon Valley: Innovation and the Growth of High Tech, 1930–1970,* Cambridge, MA: MIT Press, 2006; Martin Kenny and John Seely-Brown (Eds.), *Understanding Silicon Valley: The Anatomy of an Entrepreneurial Region,* Stanford, CA: Stanford University Press, 2000.

18. Stephen Budiansky, *Battle of Wits: The Complete Story of Codebreaking in World War II,* New York: Free Press, 2000; Anthony E. Sale, "The Colossus of Bletchley Park—The German Cipher System," in Raúl Rojas and Ulf Hashagen (Eds.), *The First Computers: History and Architecture* (Cambridge, UK: Cambridge University Press, 2000, pp. 351–364.

19. Coopey, *Information Technology Policy,* pp. 144–157; Frank Verdon and Mike Wells, "Computing in British Universities: The Computer Board 1966–1991," *The Computer Journal* 38, 10 (1995): 822–830.

20. Georgina Ferry, *A Computer Called Leo: Lyons Teashops and the World's First Office Computer,* London: 4th Estate, 2003.

21. John Agar, *The Government Machine: A Revolutionary History of the Computer,* Cambridge, MA: MIT Press, 2003, takes the story back into the 19th

century but is the essential source along with Martin Campbell-Kelly, *ICL: A Business and Technical History,* Oxford: Oxford University Press, 1989; and John Hendry, *Innovating for Failure: Government Policy and the Early British Computer Industry,* Cambridge, MA: MIT Press, 1989.

22. The key issue discussed by Hendry, *Innovating for Failure.*

23. Kong Rae Lee, "Technological Learning and Entries of User Firms for Capital Goods in Korea," in Kim and Nelson, *Technology, Learning, and Innovation,* pp. 170–192.

24. On the relative IT prowess of Korea, see James W. Cortada, Ashish M. Gupta, and Marc Le Noir, *How Nations Thrive in the Information Age,* Somers, NY: IBM Corporation, 2007.

25. Martin Fransman, *The Market and Beyond:Cooperation and Competition in Information Technology in the Japanese System,* Cambridge, UK: Cambridge University Press, 1990, pp. 177–242.

26. Pierre E. Mounier, *Le Comité national du CNRS et l'émergence de nouvelles disciplines au CNRS : Le cas de l'informatique, 1946–1976,* Paris: Centre Science, Technologie et Societe, CNAM,1987. Also see his "Sur L'Histoire de L'Informatique en France," *Engineering Science and Education Journal* 3, 1 (February 1995): 37–40.

27. Jacques Maisonrouge, *Inside IBM: A Personal Story,* New York: McGraw-Hill, 1985, pp. 150–158; for an economic explanation on the role of innovation, see Barry Eichengreen, *The European Economy Since 1945: Coordinated Capitalism and Beyond,* Princeton, NJ: Princeton University Press, 2007, pp. 257–263.

28. Alfred D. Chandler, Jr., *Inventing the Electronic Century: The Epic Story of the Consumer Electronics and Computer Industries,* Cambridge, MA: Harvard University Press, 2005, pp. 181–183.

29. EIU, *The 2008 e-Readiness Ranking,* 2008.

30. Eichengreen, *The European Economy Since 1945,* pp. 400–406.

31. Chandler, *Inventing the Electronic Century,* p. 183.

32. Use of the private sector in support of public policy continues. Russian president Vladimir Putin was routinely accused of using his local oil and gas industries as tools to promote Russian foreign policy objectives in Poland and Germany, for example.

33. See, for example, Jorgenson, *Productivity,* vol. 2, pp. 242–244.

34. Kenneth Kraemer, J. Dedrick, T.C. Tu, C.Y. Hwang, and C.S. Yap, "Entrepreneurship, Flexibility and Policy Coordination: Taiwan's Computer Industry," *Information Society* 12, 3 (1996): 215–249; K.Y. Tam, "Analysis of Firm-Level Computer Investments: A Comparative Study of Three Pacific-Rim Economies," *IEEE Transactions on Energy Management* 45, 3 (1998): 276–286; Jan Vang and Bjorn Asheim, "Regions, Absorptive Capacity sand Strategic Coupling with High-Tech TNC: Lessons from India and China," *Science Technology and Society* 11 (2006): 39–66.

35. Richard N. Langlois and W. Edward Steinmueller, "The Evolution of Competitive Advantage in the Worldwide Semiconductor Industry, 1947–1996," in David C. Mowery and Richard R. Nelson (Eds.), *Sources of Industrial*

Leadership: Studies of Seven Industries, Cambridge, UK: Cambridge University Press, 1999, pp. 55–56.

36. John A. Mathews and Dong-Sung Cho, *Tiger Technology: The Creation of a Semiconductor Industry in East Asia,* Cambridge, UK: Cambridge University Press, 2000; Won-Young Lee, "The Role of Science and Technology Policy in Korea's Industrial Development," in Kim and Nelson, *Technology, Learning, and Innovation,* pp. 291–303.

37. Ibid., 56-57.

38. Recently studied for Japan; see Mizuko Ito, Daisuke Okabe, and Misa Matsuda (Eds.), *Personal, Portable, Pedestrian: Mobile Phones in Japanese Life,* Cambridge, MA: MIT Press, 2005.

39. Radha Chadha and Paul Husband, *The Cult of the Luxury Brand: Inside Asia's Love Affair with Luxury,* London: Nicholas Brealey, 2006, p. 287.

40. Alan Greenspan, *The Age of Turbulence: Adventures in a New World,* New York: Penguin, 2007, p. 127.

41. Eichengreen, *The European Economy Since 1945,* pp. 131–162, 294–334.

42. G. Banse, Langenbach, C.J., and Machleidt, P. (Eds.), *Towards the Information Society: The Case of Central and Eastern European Countries,* New York: Springer, 2000.

43. It is a topic that is hardly mentioned in any publication and remains shrouded in secrecy. When I worked in IBM sales, I personally witnessed several attempts in the 1970s and early 1980s of state-of-the-art computers moving from my customers through France and Mexico to destinations that I suspected would ultimately be behind the Iron Curtain. France, in particular, seemed to be a popular pass-through to Eastern Europe for American technology in these years. See also, Frank Cain, "Computers and the Cold War: United States Restrictions on the Export of Computers to the Soviet Union and Communist China," *Journal of Contemporary History* 40 (2005): 131–147.

44. Described in part by Slava Gerovitch, *From Newspeak to Cyberspeak: A History of Soviet Cybernetics,* Cambridge, MA: MIT Press, 2002.

45. The variety of inexpensive products made this situation possible. For descriptions of many, see Nicholas D. Evans, *Consumer Gadgets,* Upper Saddle River, NJ: Financial Times/Prentice-Hall, 2003.

46. Ernest J. Wilson III, *The Information Revolution and Developing Countries,* Cambridge, MA: MIT Press, 2004, pp. 223–297; James M. Popkin and Partha Lyengar, *IT and the East: How China and India Are Altering the Future of Technology and Innovation,* Boston, MA: Harvard University Press, 2007, pp. 11–69; Cyrill Eltschinger, *Source Code China: The New Global Hub of IT Outsourcing,* New York: Wiley, 2007, pp. 33–59.

47. Zhijun Ling and Martha Avery, *The Lenovo Affair: The Growth of China's Computer Giant and Its Takeover of IBM-PC,* New York: Wiley, 2006.

48. Popkin and Lyengar, *IT and the East,* pp. 73–125.

49. United Nations, *UN E-Government Survey 2008,* New York: United Nations, 2008, p. 20.

50. Ibid., p. 21.

51. From International Telecommunications Union, http://www.itu.int/net (last accessed 1/10/2007).

52. Cassell Bryan-Low, "New Frontiers for Cellphone Service," *Wall Street Journal,* February 13, 2007, p. B5.

53. Manuel Castells, Mireia Fernández-Ardèvol, Jack Linchuan Qiu, and Araba Sey, *Mobile Communication and Society: A Global Perspective,* Cambridge, MA: MIT Press, 2007, pp. 231–239.

54. Cortada, *The Digital Hand,* vol. 2, p. 120.

55. Widely read at the time was John Buchan, *Scientific Inventory Management,* Englewood Cliffs, NJ: Prentice-Hall, 1963.

56. Stephen A. Brown, *Revolution at the Checkout Counter: The Explosion of the Bar Code,* Cambridge, MA: Harvard University Press, 1997, pp. 139–173.

57. Ibid.

58. Martin Campbell-Kelly and William Aspray, *Computer: A History of the Information Machine,* New York: Basic Books, 1996, pp. 97–99. The role of these associations was profound and has not been methodically studied.

59. "2008 International CES: CES Fact sheet," http://www.cesweb.org/about_ces/fact_sheet.asp (last accessed 1/15/2008).

60. James L. McKenney, *Waves of Change: Business Evolution through Information Technology,* Boston, MA: Harvard Business School Press, 1995, pp. 41–95.

61. IBM market analysis.

62. Carl Shapiro and Hal R. Varian, *Information Rules: A Strategic Guide to the Network Economy,* Boston, MA: Harvard Business School Press, 1999, pp. 13–14, 183–184.

63. One of the main findings of Cortada, *The Digital Hand,* 3 vols.

64. This is increasingly becoming the subject of studies by the Economist Intelligence Unit, IBM Institute for Business Value, and others, but there are no contemporary major surveys available documenting the full range of public-sector applications. The closest is on the United States: Cortada, *The Digital Hand,* vol. 3.

65. For instance, U.S. Department of Commerce and the Pew Foundation.

66. Documented in the annual EIU's *E-Readiness Ranking* reports published every spring.

67. While there is a paucity of information about computing in Africa, there is activity there; see Wilson, *The Information Revolution and Developing Countries,* pp. 173–221.

68. This is the essence of DEC's story: engineers selling computers to fellow engineers or, conversely, engineers buying computers from other engineers; see Edgar H. Schein, *DEC Is Dead, Long Live DEC: The Lasting Legacy of Digital Equipment Corporation,* San Francisco, CA: Berrett-Koehler, 2004, pp. 42–45.

69. A theme recently studied in a very broad context by Yochai Benkler, *The Wealth of Networks: How Social Production Transforms Markets and Freedom,* New Haven, CT: Yale University Press, 2006.

70. Greenspan, *The Age of Turbulence,* pp. 11–12.

71. As part of my responsibilities at IBM, I met with European and American regulators between 2000 and the present who made these points to me regarding these specific industries.

72. The phenomenon is described in one of the most famous articles ever published on path dependency and technology: Paul David, "Clio and the Economics of QWERTY," *American Economic Review Papers and Proceedings* 75, 2 (1985): 332–337.

73. Most famously by Thomas K. Landauer, *The Trouble With Computers: Usefulness, Usability, and Productivity,* Cambridge, MA: MIT Press, 1995, pp. 76–78, 141–203.

74. Charles J. Bashe, Lyle R. Johnson, John H. Palmer, and Emerson W. Pugh, *IBM's Early Computers,* Cambridge, MA: MIT Press, 1986; and Emerson W. Pugh, Lyle R. Johnson, and John H. Palmer, *IBM's 360 and Early 370 Systems,* Cambridge, MA: MIT Press, 1991.

75. Chandler, *Inventing the Electronic Century,* pp. 110–117.

76. Melissa A. Schilling, "Technological Leapfrogging: Lessons From the U.S. Video Game Console Industry," *California Management Review* 45, 3 (Spring 2003): 6–32.

77. See, for example, Agatha C. Hughes and Thomas R. Hughes (Eds.), *Systems, Experts, and Computers,* Cambridge, MA: MIT Press, 2000.

78. Steven Weber, *The Success of Open Source,* Cambridge, MA: Harvard University Press, 2004.

79. Felipe Fernández-Armesto, *Civilizations: Culture, Ambition, and the Transformation of Nature,* New York: Free Press, 2001, p. 464.

3

HOW GOVERNMENTS LEVERAGE INFORMATION TECHNOLOGY TO IMPROVE THEIR NATIONAL ECONOMIES

This speaks to the international reputation that Bermuda has as an e-business and technology jurisdiction and the sophistication of Bermuda's technology environment.

—MICHAEL SCOTT,
Minister of Telecommunications and E-Commerce,
April, 2006 [1]

Most national, state, and local governments around the world have long played active roles in nurturing the use of information technologies (IT) to stimulate economic development. In recent years, nearly all the OECD countries and others as well have integrated IT into their national economic development strategies. Governments see IT as a way to improve the quality of life of their citizens. The extent of activity on the part of public officials in leveraging IT has increased in volume and intensity over the past half-dozen years or more in all countries, driven by a broad variety of considerations ranging from expanded use of the Internet and consumer electronics to globalization of significant portions of many nations' economic activities [2]. Although many useful policy practices of prior decades are relevant to today's initiatives, new ones are also emerging in response to current realities. A challenge for public officials, therefore, is to understand today's trends and apply effective instruments for creating and implementing policies that optimize the role of IT in their societies. These strategies are often novel, a result of the spread of relatively new technologies such as the Internet, wireless telephony with many innovative functions (such as access to the Internet, viewing movies, and e-mailing), and open source software and digital content (Linux, games, and information, for example). These developments also mean that government officials need to choose wisely among the variety of known policies and strategies being implemented today. In short, notions of "one size fits all" do not work well in the current environment. This reality parallels the diverse experiences in the deployment of IT described in the previous chapter.

The first issue often facing public officials is to determine what IT strategies to develop. What makes sense for their societies? How does one know if one's approach aligns well with what economists and technologists know works, or does not? Given the numerous changes in technology itself, what effects do such innovations have on economic policy? These are questions that senior public officials are increasingly asking, even those with formal training in economics and technologies, if for no other reason than because, though they may understand developmental economics, for example, they might not appreciate the information technology factor in the equation. A key purpose of this chapter is to provide an overview of current practices in leveraging technology as a way of beginning to answer these basic questions, addressing an interest that has a long history, as evidenced in the previous chapter.

There is also an important role to be played by the private sector in this process. In recent years, public officials, business leaders, and economic experts have increasingly collaborated on such matters. While this chapter focuses on the role of governments because they are driving forward economic development processes, it also includes comments on the role of the private sector and, just as it summarizes key practices for senior public officials, it does so for business leaders as well.

A BRIEF HISTORICAL REMINDER

As described in the previous chapter, governments' proactive interest in IT dates back to the 1940s when the United States Government supported the initial development of digital computing to the point where the technology became the basis of the American commercial computer industry in the 1950s. The practice of initially supporting R&D in the technology existed in countries as disparate as Japan, the Soviet Union, Bulgaria, the United States, and the United Kingdom, many beginning their initiatives in the 1950s. With the wide adoption of computing in many economies beginning in the 1970s and, particularly, consumer-based digital products starting in the 1980s, largely with personal computers, government officials reformulated the role they played in influencing the position of IT in their local economies and societies.

Their consequent ongoing need to react to emerging technologies took on a greater sense of urgency after the mid-1990s as the Internet spread rapidly, which quickly affected patterns of trade and business behavior and political discourse, what sociologist Manuel Castells called the "Internet Galaxy" [3]. Public officials widely recognized that within a decade, hundreds of millions of users of the Internet were actively changing the way they worked and played, the nature of the goods and services their firms offered, and their personal social lives [4]. New issues emerged: the need for broadband connections; how best to address the flow of information on the Internet, such as pornography (United States), misrepresentations of product data (Europe), and even political censorship (China); and the role of public agencies that had responsibility for providing telephone services, setting prices that either encouraged or discouraged use of online services, and so forth.

How did governments react to the surge in the demand for IT brought about by declining costs of telecommunications, improved specific Internet capabilities, and the effective merger of personal computers, communications, digital consumer goods (such as digital cameras and cell phones), and, of course, the Internet as a whole? The latter, for instance, respected no local borders and became increasingly a worldwide network. Information gathered by various public agencies, and, most specifically in the United States, by the United Nations (UN) and the European Commission (EC) on the one hand, and private researchers, such as the Economist Intelligence Unit (EIU), academics, and the World Economic Forum, on the other, demonstrate clearly that most national governments continued to play an active role in encouraging further use of IT while influencing the scope of its effects on national economies and political behavior [5].

Experiences of public officials between 2000 and 2010 not only reaffirms the historic role governments play in affecting the deployment of IT but, more dramatically, that IT is considered to be a major component of a national economic development policy. Today, no nation with what many like to call an "advanced economy" dares ignore the issue. International surveys on its use and role make that overwhelmingly clear [6]. Computing and communications have become so embedded in so many national economies that IT now is at least as important an economic development component as such traditional considerations as agricultural support mechanisms, promotion of heavy and light industry, expansion of financial services, or extensions of increasing amounts education to a country's population at large. This enhanced importance of IT is a result of the technological developments of the 1990s and, most notably, improvements in technical performance and resultant declines in their costs to firms and individuals. Increased economic rents to a growing number of many diverse industries from financial to consumer products also proved influential. While the massive expansion of the Internet played a central role, it is the increased importance of all manner of IT in their current highly networked forms that is now the relatively new circumstance in the economic development activities of the public sector. This is a development that is attracting renewed attention to the theme of technology and economic public policy by economists and public policy experts [7]. This reality is made more intense by the fact that the percent of people and firms reliant on IT to go about their work and private lives has increased sharply over the past quarter-century.

What are the emerging patterns of "good" and "bad" IT-centered economic development policies? How do these experiences compare to what experts noted were effective practices in prior times? [8] Now that IT and the Internet are increasingly seen as "public goods," similar to clean air, good and accessible roads, and national security, how are governments treating the new technology and what are the lessons for public officials? Answers are emerging that point to practices that either build on successful prior ones that rely on earlier forms of IT or other technologies and advanced practices in public and private administration applicable to the current set of IT and existing economic and political realities. For example, education in the use of contemporary technologies and laws and regulations in support of the application of those across an economy are now evident around the world.

The description presented here is compounded by the complexity of the topic, making it impossible to declare universal truths because of the wide variety of circumstances facing public officials and local business leaders, not the least of which is the reality that no two nations are alike in their economic structures, the health and vitality of their populations, or the nature of their political lives and cultures. Although those realities ensure that the discussion will seem complicated, perhaps too varied, and certainly not specific enough for some, one can discern some common considerations and identify emerging patterns of behavior on the part of public officials that are informative for other policy makers and other participants in their local economies.

ECONOMIC DEVELOPMENT IN A CONNECTED WORLD: THE BIG PICTURE

Public officials employ two fundamental strategies to promote use of IT in ways advantageous to their societies. Both strategies are implemented incrementally, yet simultaneously, with deployment affecting subsequent actions of public officials and the citizens who they serve or rule. A country needs both sets of strategic initiatives to optimize the effectiveness of IT in their society. Those nations that have the most advanced uses of computing and communications tend to have both sets of strategies in play. They also tend to have some of the highest standards of living and most vigorous economies in the world, as measured by such traditional benchmarks as per-capita GNP, a nation's GDP, or labor and capital productivity and yields [9]. So, what are these strategies?

Simply put, one strategic trajectory is the effective use of IT by government agencies themselves to improve their internal productivity (such as in lowering costs of existing tasks) or to enhance their ability to serve citizens (as in providing 24 × 7 service or greater access to information). Those uses of IT by governments promote directly the adoption of certain types of IT by individuals and firms at large. For example, by giving citizens convenient access to information around the clock over the Internet, a government encourages citizens to access public services, data, and application forms using PCs and the Internet. In turn, that action strengthens the knowledge citizens have of how to use the Internet and, by inference, encourages them to leverage that technology in other ways in their private and professional lives. Another popular tactic is to require suppliers to bid on, bill, and be paid for goods and services using online procurement systems, because, in addition to helping lower the costs of acquiring these by a government, it forces suppliers to start using the Internet and related technologies in an "e-business" environment [10].

Practicing what one preaches is a painful and difficult exercise for governments, yet necessary, as it can lead to restructuring and optimization of agencies and departments, much as is beginning to happen in Western Europe with social services, in Australia and the United States as well, and in the American and British governments, whose law enforcement agencies are in the process of merging internally closer together. This should be of no surprise because that is exactly what occurred, and continues to happen, in the private sector where the traditional hierarchical style of organization is beginning to give way to, as yet not fully defined, new forms. These are often characterized as being flatter or taking the form of more integrated partnerships across multiple companies. Governments in the past have followed many such transformations that first emerged in the private sector and it appears that the pattern is continuing.

The second set of strategies involves promoting use of IT by governments within their societies, external to the internal operations of public administration. These initiatives are the ones we normally hear the most about: funding installations of the Internet in classrooms, passing copyright laws to protect digital forms of media content, implementing regulations that govern monthly costs of telephony, wireless communications, government-to-business transactions, use of the Internet, and so forth. I will have more to say about these later. This second set of initiatives, policies, and programs have two key features. First, they tend to be facilitative; that is to say, they are designed to create the technical, social, political, and regulatory environments and infrastructures that make it more attractive for firms and individuals to use such technology in economically and socially attractive ways. This is an elegant way of saying that these are the actions taken by governments today to make their economies more competitive and their societies more attractive to live in. For instance, the Chinese have created many jobs in the manufacture of computer chips and components, an example of making an economy more competitive. On the other hand, making available high-speed broadband connections and providing local tax incentives are popular strategies for regional economic development, as we have seen in the United States in Raleigh, North Carolina, and in Austin, Texas. This pattern is repeating itself with the promotion of biotech firms in Wisconsin, Michigan, and California, among other regions. Of course, the trend of creating technology corridors is not limited to the United States. The instances of South Korea, eastern China, and Singapore in Asia, and Ireland and Netherlands in Europe are some of the most obvious examples of an unfolding global process at work.

At the moment, are there areas of particular interest to governments with respect to the use of IT? Within public agencies, several are prominent. First, internal security, involving the tracking of people moving in and out of a country, and even within it, is of particular interest as new technologies appear for surveillance and identity management. Border management applications, such as passports with computer chips and digital fingerprinting for visitors, accompanied by concerns about privacy, are common at the moment. A second area of interest is the reengineering of a wide range of social services, including medical coverage, pension administration, welfare, and the reorganization of whole agencies. These are made possible by the greater use of Internet-based delivery of services integrated and tailored to individual citizen's needs yet originating from multiple agencies. Third, the military in NATO nations are continuing to invest extensively in more integrated, data-intensive supply chains (logistics) and, additionally, in what are variously called "electronic battlefields" and "networked centric operations." Many other areas of governmental operations are infusing new generations of technology into their operations, but these three represent the most extensive currently in evidence.

Governments are also encouraging their citizens to deploy computing as well, and that is the subject of the bulk of this chapter. Finally, there are the special issues to examine that resulted from the widespread economic downturn that gripped so many parts of the world, starting in 2008, because they have much to teach us about how public officials are leveraging IT today.

HOW GOVERNMENTS USE IT TO ENCOURAGE ECONOMIC DEVELOPMENT

A half-dozen strategies are currently in use by governments to facilitate economic development by leveraging information and communications technologies. The extent of their deployment varies, of course, from one country to another in terms of emphasis, features, and effectiveness. Nonetheless, they are visible in one form or another in scores of nations.

Facilitating Expanded Connectivity and Technological Infrastructure

Having established the notion that to make a society and its economy more IT effective one needs progress along a variety of dimensions, let us begin our discussion with a technology-centric one. In recent years connectivity has been all about making it possible for individuals, firms, and institutions to access mobile (wireless) networks and the Internet. In the 1980s and 1990s, connectivity largely concentrated on wired telecommunications. Today, it also means gaining access to services provided over the Internet, such as placing an order for a product or filing a request for information or service from a government agency. Officials focus on extending deployment of these sets of technologies and services across their society. Additionally, governments all over the world measure the number of users, extent of use, and so forth to determine what volume of activity is occurring. Relative costs of these services to individuals and organizations in comparison to those in other nations are also monitored increasingly as yet another way of assessing the attractiveness of any one of the myriad services and activities within any economy. For example, today it is nearly impossible to attract software programmers, video game creators, and even film and music producers to any particular community or nation that lacks extensive and modern communication infrastructures. These have to include wireless Internet service available all over a city, for instance. For many communities, making such facilities available has become a high priority, particularly in mid-sized North and South American cities and in large urban centers across Europe and East Asia. Where tech-savvy people come together in smaller communities, the same is true, as is happening, for example, with American tourists in Costa Rica or Honduras checking their e-mail, German and English vacationers doing so along the Spanish Costa Brava or participating in conference calls with their home offices, or foreign residents conducting the same kinds of Internet-based transactions as they did in their home countries.

In South Korea, for instance, it had long been government policy to encourage the nation's public and private telephony and telecommunications organizations to make available broadband connections. The result is that today its citizens are the most extensive users in the world of broadband applications and, obviously, some of its most intensive users of the Internet [11]. Pricing strategies for Internet connections have proven to be some of the most effective levers countries have relied upon to increase or decrease use of telephony and communications. The OECD and the EU noticed this in the early 1990s when their economists and officials observed that charging Europeans by the minute for time spent on the Internet (through long distance phone charges) discouraged such use. People tried to conduct the minimum amount of business online to keep charges low. By contrast, in the United States users were charged a flat monthly fee, which encouraged them to spend as much time online as they wanted, with the result that they rapidly became extensive early users of the technology. In the late 1990s, therefore, those governments that wanted to encourage use of the Internet by its citizens and, indirectly, expansion of communications offerings by their local telecommunications industries, began altering the terms, conditions, and billing practices of online access services through regulatory practices [12].

Nurturing Business Environments Conducive to the Use of Modern IT

This is a broad topic that encompasses many circumstances, laws, and regulations. For public officials, the issue largely turns on the extent to which they facilitate trading and performing transactions, and, second, attracting investments to local enterprises from other nations. These investments can consist of capital, skilled labor, families moving into a country, and other assets. Success in this sphere requires:

- A stable political environment
- A healthy local economic environment (e.g., inflation is under control, availability of appropriately skilled labor with competitive salaries)
- Existence of complimentary industries (e.g., those needed to supply goods and services to a particular industry)

- Opportunities for sales (e.g., demand existing for specific goods and services)
- Protection of private property
- Friendly foreign investment practices
- Competitive taxes
- Availability of capital, especially for new businesses
- Social infrastructures (e.g., housing, schools, health care, shopping, and parks)

These items have been on public officials' lists of necessary topics to be addressed since at least the 1930s and, thus, do not represent new findings. However, because they are requirements of a "high-tech" society, they continue to be addressed.

Thus, for example, having a workforce skilled in the use of modern equipment (which often has IT components), PCs, and the Internet are prerequisites for many jobs. Possessing a labor force that does not have a reputation for going on strike or having higher than average absentee rates than those of other nations was and continues to be crucial as well to the successful functioning of a modern economy. Failure to be competitive leads to rapid outsourcing of jobs and work. Many countries recognize the importance of skills and are betting their economic future success on improving those. In this category one can include India, China, Estonia, Lithuania, Malaysia, and Brazil—not always the obvious countries one thinks of when pondering who is very IT-savvy. Additionally, changing requirements in skills for IT are causing governments to change their educational offerings, such as the United States, Australia, and Singapore [13].

Political scientist Susanne Berger in her study on how firms compete in the global economy observed that "because of the preponderance of resources that remain at home—even under globalization—home-country institutions and policies do continue to have an important shaping role" [14]. She notes further that local realities often mean "devising and re-forming policies that contribute to the future productivity and innovative capacity of the home society" [15]. Increasingly, research results are reaffirming that these policies are promoting and must continue to promote openness, encouraging

- Use of open-source software and open standards to invigorate technical platforms that lead to innovations [16]

- Education policies and programs that create needed emerging skills, both technical and work-related (e.g., the ability to work in teams or speak the right languages)
- Others policies that foster the continuing innovation of firms and industries

One reason American firms did so well in the twentieth century was because they operated in an environment in which they could transform whole businesses and industries (not just invent new goods or technologies) and bring to market new products and services with less government restrictions than found in other countries. As business and economic historian Richard Coopey and his colleagues noted in documenting the recent history of government policies to encourage expansion of information technology, the strategies and paths officials took varied, in part as a function of local economic realities but also of indigenous culture, all of which makes it difficult to generalize on best practices [17]. What so many countries shared was the fact that they did take action in overt ways to promote the use of IT as a national priority, from the French support of "national champions" to Japan's "Fifth Generation" initiatives, to the American "Internet in every classroom" investments.

Encouraging Consumer and Business Adoptions

Between the mid-1990s and the present, several fundamental trends in economic and public administration manifested themselves to a greater extent than before concerning this dimension. First, the Internet became a viable technology, facilitating the work of small enterprises that could not otherwise reach out to customers, with communications tools available all over the world. Second, firms and agencies used the technology to reduce internal operating expenses and the cost of interacting with their customers and citizens. Third, the proportion of GDP coming from service industries (as opposed to Second Industrial Revolution manufacturing industries) increased, particularly in the most advanced economies, but now also increasingly in those most rapidly transforming, such as in Ireland, New Zealand, and Taiwan. These trends illustrate the growing importance to an economy of making it possible for individuals, firms, and public agencies to use various IT tools to thrive. Widely embraced strategies involve passing laws and implementing regulations that make it affordable for citizens and organizations to use information and communications technologies, and that promote such use through regulatory and tax laws incentives. They also facilitated the establishment of e-based businesses. In the United States, for example, that meant not charging sales taxes for transactions conducted over the Internet, whereas retail sales are subject to such taxes. Metrics of success normally include percent of consumer spending on IT, especially for digital products (e.g., software), for communications (e.g., Internet and broadband access, cell phone services), and percent of a nation's online transactions (today up to 10% is not out of the ordinary in the most advanced economies). Governments can measure their own e-performance as well [18].

Establishing Legal and Policy Environments Friendly to High-Tech Applications

Economists and public officials have long recognized the value of maintaining economies and societies that are politically and economically stable on the one hand and, on the other, transparency in their transactions and support for property rights and legal and contractual activities. Thus, governments decide increasingly to support competition across most, if not all, industries; protect private property; promote trade; encourage external and internal investments in their local economy; and provide open and transparent, yet fair and predictable, enforcement of laws and regulations. The United States has historically done extremely well in each of these categories. In recent years, Ireland did a spectacular job in creating stability and transparency in its economy with the result that it was recognized as a model for other countries to follow, the "Celtic Tiger," despite the fact it could not escape the economic downturn that involved most of the world beginning in 2008. But Ireland was not alone in its economic transformation to a competitive modern society; high on almost anyone's list would also be Hong Kong, Great Britain, Chile, Denmark, Australia, New Zealand, Netherlands, and Singapore, all of which shared the common features of nurturing economies that provide property protection, encouraging foreign investment, and creating sustained stable economies and societies [19].

Of particular interest over the past twenty years has been the requirement to modernize the protections needed for innovation resulting from new forms of IT. Governments all over the world have had to update copyright, patent, and property protection laws to account for the existence of software products, proprietary data (including music, electronic publications, and videos), and to accommodate the execution of Internet-based transactions. It is a process still in its early stages and the subject of much debate, occurring as use of digital files and the Internet continue to diffuse into new forms, applications, and across ever-larger communities of users. However, just as property and transactions had to be protected in the pre-Internet era, when people and things, not online communications, dominated business and social activities, and governments created whole bodies of laws and regulations to protect and guide them. These have worked reasonably well for the last two centuries and, drawing upon that experience, there is movement to incorporate new technologies and activities.

The issue today is less about what or how to legislate, although there is much passion about that, particularly at the moment for recorded music and software, than how quickly or slowly governments are creating the necessary legal and regulatory infrastructures to facilitate the ability of their economies to connect into the global economy, while stimulating improvements in the competitiveness and attraction of their own domestic economy. In other words, implementing policies that facilitate the competitive performance of a national economy in the broader globalized economy is crucial. Perhaps France's Finance Minister, Christine Lagarde, put it best in August, 2007, when she said "that globalization is not something that we can deny or challenge," and "is something you have to cope with and for which you have to be prepared" [20].

Governments have increasingly focused on digital records and use of the Internet over the past decade. They also are still working through issues concerning copyright and patent legislation for software. At the same time, the open-software movement swirls about them and the way people make money over the Internet continues to evolve. So far, the most effective legislation and legal infrastructures are those that facilitate Internet-based commerce, and offer protection and management of digital rights and intellectual property. What has hardly been addressed yet, however, is the need to curb abuses in transactions (e.g., false advertising and not fulfilling orders after collecting fees for these), and the shifting of ownership rights caused by the open-source movement and its innovative contractual terms, all of which remain uncertain and fluid, if not problematic. Additionally, governments and regional organizations are only just beginning to work on how to block noncompetitive behavior that otherwise affects the extent to which consumers are protected. The complex, often innovative, activities of the European Union over the past decade suggest fruitful directions that can be taken by all governments [21]. Where there has been positive action taken, businesses and individuals are able to create new online businesses quickly, and that makes it possible to change these (including their work forces) more rapidly than in the past. These circumstances have helped North America and Singapore, for instance, to evolve rapidly and to benefit economically from every new evolution in IT that appeared over the past decade. In short, effective practices are emerging, along with thoughtful strategies and informative examples, leading to the conclusion that the greater issue at hand is now how quickly can other nations adapt.

Constantly in the forefront of much policy making is the delicate issue of censorship, which keeps coming up in discussions about IT. From a purely economic perspective—not from any moral, legal, or philosophical points of view—censorship slows, or blocks, the flow of information, which, in turn, either makes a society less attractive to well-educated consumers, or constrains product development and trade, not to mention those noneconomic activities that normally attract press coverage, such as politics and freedom of expression. China is normally cited as the exemplar of censorship and blockage of its citizens' access to information over the Internet. But, as mentioned in the previous chapter, the problem exists in various forms in other countries as well, both overtly as public policy, say, in an authoritarian society, or as a moral issue in others. It is quite significant within the context of economic development and so warrants additional comments. Economists argue that economic activity is facilitated when information about goods, services, and transactions are transparent, free flowing, and move about quickly and easily. That position has not changed with the arrival of digital products or the Internet [22].

The issue facing public officials who want to constrain access to certain types of information in digital form is what to allow that facilitates economic activity, and what not to permit. It remains a thorny issue, even in countries that claim to be open societies. For example, the French do not want people to buy Nazi memorabilia from eBay, yet, otherwise, it is a society that allows the free flow of ideas and expression. Americans are very concerned about child pornography and the sale of sexually explicit products and services over the Internet, but does not prohibit the sale of Nazi memorabilia. So far, the French government has blocked sales of what its laws call objectionable materials, whereas the Americans have no intention of implementing additional laws with respect to child pornography, choosing instead to rely on preexisting laws, for instance, those which govern inappropriate sexual behavior and publication. As a general observation, however, governments are increasingly allowing their citizens access to digital data and transactions, extending preexisting consumer protections of a traditional bricks-and-mortar type to the Internet. Such protections and laws either sustain pre-Internet era levels of censorship or open access over the Internet [23].

Protecting and Expanding Social and Cultural Environments

There now exists a vast body of literature on modern social and cultural environments in the age of the computer, the Internet, and so forth, and attention to the subject shows no signs of slowing down. Sociologists and media experts in particular are prolific. Richard Florida talks about creative, highly educated workforces migrating to nations that have good broadband and Internet access, whereas sociologist Manuel Castells describes networked societies [24]. *The World is Flat* by Thomas Friedman became a best seller in 2006, indeed "must" reading for many public officials and senior executives in the private sector on how the world is becoming globalized and connected [25]. Although all of this makes for interesting reading, there are some fundamental features of modern society that public officials understand constitute the basic infrastructure that makes it possible to leverage IT for their country's competitive advantage. None is more essential and obvious than education.

The evidence from the past decade alone indicates that those societies that are the most extensive users of IT are also the ones that have the most educated citizenry, as measured by number of years of schooling (see Table 3.1). Additionally, the same holds true for populations that are most familiar, hence, educated/trained, in the use of IT, such as PCs and the Internet. A by-product is the degree to which such a community is receptive to the idea of using tech-

Table 3.1. Mean years of schooling by type of economy and sample nations

Type of economy	Years of schooling	Nations
Established leaders	9–10	Denmark, United States, Switzerland, Hong Kong
Rapid developers	6–7	Japan, Israel, Taiwan, Spain, Chile
Late entrants	3–4	Brazil, Argentina, Bulgaria, Turkey

For list of all countries by type and definitions of each category of country based on IBM–EIU ranking data, see James W. Cortada, Ashish M. Gupta, and Marc Le Noir, *How Nations Thrive in the Information Age* (Somers, NY: IBM Corporation, 2007); see also *Economist Intelligence Unit, The 2007 e-Readiness Rankings* (London: Economist Intelligence Unit, 2007).

nology, whereas familiarity with it breeds acceptance. There is debate on whether a general education makes a society more fit to adopt computing in its work force (often said of the English or American school systems) or whether a more vocationally oriented system is better suited (as Germany's is often cited) [26]. Regardless in which camp a public official resides, education of all types is an essential element, something public officials in all advancing economies manage or pay attention to as part of their economic development policies. To enhance skills and knowledge of IT, governments make IT tools available to schools in the belief that such familiarity will result in a more skilled workforce and a society better able to adopt and adapt technology in effective ways. Their actions range from providing Internet access and terminals in classrooms to funding technical training. Progress is measured by tracking years of education and literacy (even levels of IT literacy and use of the Internet) and the indirect spillover results, such as the number of high-tech startups, technical degrees awarded, and so forth. That focus on education has spread in the early 2000s, and shows no signs of abatement.

If we accept the notion that knowledge of technology and the acceptance and diffusion of its use affects the social and cultural features of a society, then one would expect to see public officials use and track the use of IT and leverage that data to adjust public policies. This is happening. For example, public officials are finding that if they use increasing amounts of IT they help diffuse benefits and knowledge of the technology. This varies from giving laptops to cabinet officials (Estonia) and to state legislators (United States), to using the Internet to deliver social services (Scandinavian countries), to even offering its citizens e-mail services (Finland). Governments track progress economically by such means as the number of patents awarded, new product introductions, number of new businesses established (hence the need for fast permit processes), and number, size, and growth rates of industries that depend extensively on well-educated workforces and on IT. Today, the most aggressive public policies incorporate each of these elements into their incremental or comprehensive economic development strategies. Often, the key differentiators between those economies that are aggressively leveraging IT and others that are not center around social and cultural issues underpinned in a supportive manner by IT.

Encouraging Emergence of New High-Tech Services

In those economies that are most reliant on IT today, high-tech services has emerged as a significant new trend. It even appears in some less developed economies as well as a strategic area of economic development, such as software and IT services in India, which evolved in large part due to the encouragement of the national government and not simply as a result of entrepreneurship. So far, much of the thinking about how to expand a nation's ability to provide IT services has focused on extending the same policies and practices that led to the expanded deployment and sale of IT hardware and software. India, for example, is now set on a path to extend IT services as a new component of its economy, focusing on expanding educational offerings to train the next generation of service providers. Second, it is beginning to invest in additional infrastructures—in this case in such mundane yet essential elements as bridges, highways, seaports, and electricity—while other countries are focused more on educational and other infrastructures in support of related industries, such as telecommunications and media. A third strategy evident in some nations is the practice of funding and protecting firms that are innovating services industries, normally through patent and copyright legislation [27].

Experts who have looked at various efforts by governments to promote high-tech economic development have studied many examples: the cotton textile industry during the First Industrial Revolution, the iron industry in the late 1700s to early 1800s, the chemical industry of the late 1800s to early 1900s, the twentieth century's automotive industry, and, most recently, the informa-

tion technology and telecommunications industries of the twentieth century. There are common patterns of successful public policy, and they should be of no surprise, indeed, should be reassur-
ing. To quote a leading scholar of the evidence, Espen Moe, "The
role of the state is one of creating conditions that are conducive to
unlocking the creative potential of the population, to stimulating
and diffusing knowledge and innovation, and promoting the
growth of new and promising industries" [28]. In the most effective instances, governments are very stable and simultaneously
also able to prevent sclerosis of any particular industry or vested
interests blocking the emergence of new industries that have the
potential of creating a Schumpeterian "creative destruction" of an
incumbent industry or set of firms. The latter point—preventing
vested interests from blocking emergence of innovation in technologies, products, and firms—is the core macropolicy initiative
that governments must succeed at if they are to exploit IT as an
economic lever. That is the central lesson of the historical experience.

Are the variables at play different in any given country? Yes. Do
they carry different weights of importance? Again, yes. Furthermore, the reality is that they vary in importance from country to
country. The evidence in support of the absolute answers to these
questions are emerging from various measures and ranking of the
behavior of economies and societies. Economists conducting surveys and establishing rankings are providing more formal models
of desired performance, often converting their tacit knowledge of
developmental economics into score cards. This may appear as ar-
bitrary, but one can argue that these are helpful to public officials
who want to appreciate their own *relative* economic progress
when compared either to some absolute standard required by an
international organization, such as the EU or WTO, or as a way to
understand the attractiveness of their economy and society to
their citizens and firms, and to people living in other nations. In
short, rankings are important because they are convenient benchmarks of economic realities.

One example will have to suffice to illustrate scoring as a tool
useful to officials. Using the EIU, which has been ranking the
economies of nations for many years, and has focused on the specific e-readiness of nations since 2000, demonstrates the process.
In the early years, the EIU weighted connectivity as an extremely
important variable in its economic model, diminishing the per-

cent of weight this variable had on a nation's overall score only after connectivity became relatively ubiquitous. That ranking stimulated dialogue among officials regarding what to do and what to defend (or brag about). As various types of connectivity increased, scores narrowed as if the proverbial "everyone" now had a cell phone, broadband, or access to the Internet. Over time, the EIU's economists modified their model to decrease the percent of weight of such variables. They also changed what they comprised, moving, for example, from cell phones to wireless Internet, from dial-up access to the Internet, to broadband adoption, and so forth. With this technology so variable in its forms and uses, it ended up only accounting for between 20 and 25% of the total scoring over time, in recognition of the fact that other dimensions were either of equal impact or nearly as important to the performance of a modern economy. Business, social, and cultural environmental factors, and the role of government policy and vision each were weighted the same, normally between 15 and 20%. However, over many years, consumer and business adoption of telecommunications mirrored the importance of connectivity and technology infrastructure. (see Figure 3.1)

There is one fundamental change, however, that officials need to keep in mind. All during the 1990s and early 2000s, governments, economists, and consultants focused largely on the extent of adoption, in other words, on how many people and organizations had access to the technology. They did this in the belief that one could not expect positive results accruing to an economy from the use of IT unless people were already using it. By 2006–2007, however, the percent of businesses, agencies, and individuals with access to various types of modern IT and, thus, reporting using it, had passed through a tipping point, in many cases to over 50–60%. That meant that simply measuring how many people had access to any established form of IT was no longer useful as a significant differentiator. Analysts then started to shift to harder measures, namely, measuring results of use, a process still in an immature stage of development. It is a transition that public officials need to understand and embrace. If the majority of their citizens and institutions have access to the Internet, then availability is no longer a competitive differentiator. The next phase of development has to be on what it needs to be used for (e.g., electronic delivery of public services or for e-commerce) and, for the most advanced economies, understanding

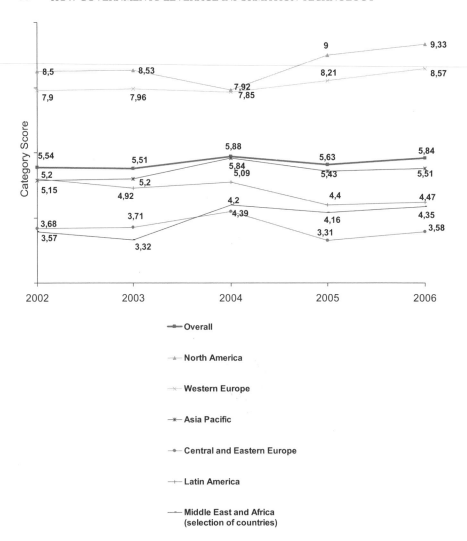

Figure 3.1. Consumer and business adoption of telecommunications and the Internet, 2002–2006. Source: IBM Institute for Business Value and Economist Intelligence Unit. Data are ranking scores of over 60 countries in their adoption of telecommunications.

what effects these uses are having on GNP, GDP, labor and capital productivity, quality of life, health standards, and so forth. Those who study the role of technology and economics increasingly see the shift to how IT and communications are used as critical to the competitiveness of nations as destinations for more economic and social activity [29].

Finally, an unstated characteristic of the most successful economies that most economic surveys and rankings do not always point out, but which become obvious when looking at any list, is the role of political stability, mentioned earlier in our discussion of Moe's findings. The most politically stable countries (governments) have done the best job of leveraging technology to enhance their economies and the relative global competitiveness of their local industries. As you work your way down the rankings of countries, you quickly see that political turmoil is increasingly a feature of ever-lower ranking countries either at the present time or in recent decades. At the bottom of any list we see nations plagued with civil wars, political unrest, lawlessness, and corruption, as evident in the nations that made up the old Yugoslavia, parts of the ex-Soviet Union, some countries in Latin America, and across large swaths of Saharan and Sub-Saharan Africa [30].

WHAT MOTIVATES GOVERNMENTS TO ENCOURAGE THEIR CITIZENS AND ECONOMIES TO USE IT?

Since the late 1990s, governments around the world have become extremely active in implementing policies and practices that are directly focused on communications, such as broadband and use of the Internet, but also wireless and cell phone communications and transactions. The range of actions they are taking is quite broad, yet very consistent with what economists have long believed to be appropriate for economic development. Economists at the EIU and IT experts at the IBM Institute for Business Value have identified six dimensions that characterize current behavior of national economies and the activities of both public- and private-sector agencies and firms that inform public strategies for economic development worth discussing. These six consist of:

1. Initiatives concerned with connectivity and technological infrastructures
2. Nurturing business environments conducive to the use of modern IT (or its production, such as cell phones in Finland or consumer electronics in South Korea)
3. Encouraging consumer and business adoptions (such as elimination of U.S. sales taxes for transactions done over the Internet, or government e-procurement practices)

4. Establishing legal and policy environments friendly to high-tech applications

5. Protecting and expanding social and cultural environments that attract the kinds of creative skills a society wants (such as video game developers in New Zealand and the United States)

6. Emergence of new high-tech service industries and offerings (such as those supporting e-commerce) [31]

These dimensions reaffirm the importance that economists, sociologists, and political scientists have long placed on the totality of initiatives that a society engages in as it moves from one technologically based economy to another. The megatransitions are of nations moving into and beyond the First and Second Industrial Revolutions over the past three centuries, and possibly now into the early stages of something new, variously called the Information Age, the New Economy, and so forth, about which more will be said in a subsequent chapter [32]. What is very evident, however, is that actions taken by governments are as broad-based, varied, and on the same dimensions as implemented by public officials in prior decades [33]. The central pervasive feature of government actions characterizing their support of IT is their creation of supporting institutions (or political, social, and economic environments) in which individuals and firms can exercise their initiative to promote their personal and institutional well-being.

To a large extent, the economies of the world are market-based. To be sure there are still extensive state interventions in China, Cuba, and Venezuela; even Russia's use of energy as a diplomatic tool. Nonetheless, as a general statement, most countries are market-driven, or capitalist, and their policy makers see it as part of their role to create environments in which their economies thrive, and not just local elites. Strategies are often aimed at helping specific industry sectors and, increasingly, these are IT in nature, such as IT-centered services (e.g., consulting) and IT telecommunications (e.g., cell phones and broadband availability) in highly advanced economies. This is also true of investment in state-of-the-art communications in rapidly evolving economies, such as Chile, Latvia, Taiwan, and Israel [34]. To be sure, however, the promotion of IT is also not done in isolation. For instance, governments are also prioritizing the development of energy (e.g., Russia and Nigeria) and their defense industries (e.g., North Korea and

Iran), both of which are not IT in nature. During times of great economic crises, such as the one the world entered in 2008, governments intervene in the functioning of an economy to such an extent that some citizens begin to question whether capitalism is under siege by officials. In general, governments more often play supportive roles, and after a major crisis they tend to alter regulatory practices in response to perceived problems with the functioning of an industry, and revert back to precrisis levels of engagement with an economy.

A second feature of this role of government is the need to reconcile two seemingly contradictory circumstances facing public officials. They clearly recognize that the economy of the world is rapidly becoming more integrated and, thus, for many of their own citizens to prosper, they must find ways to adapt their economies to permit their country's participation in the global economy [35]. To accomplish that task one of the actions they have taken is to participate in broad international collaborative practices, such as those of the World Trade Organization (WTO), which is a relatively new entrant onto the global economic scene (established 1995), others promoted by the United Nations (UN) and the European Union (EU), and public agencies implementing the North American Free Trade Agreement (NAFTA), to mention a few. Conforming to the requirements of these organizations has led to reforms along the six dimensions mentioned above. In the case of those governments now operating in what used to be the old Soviet Union or its bloc, membership in these kinds of international communities is leading to the creation of many new laws (largely driven by the WTO and EU), reduction of national debts as a percent of a nation's GDP, and implementation of more rigorous fiscal and economic policies more evident in market-oriented capitalist economies (encouraged largely by the EU). In Latin America, many of the influences on policy are coming from the World Bank and the International Monetary Fund (IMF). No nation that became a member of the EU or the WTO, for example, has been immune from the process. How each one addresses their unique circumstances varies enormously. Of the nearly 70 nations we examined, not a single one attempted to integrate itself into the global economy by ignoring the developmental opportunities presented by IT. This even includes countries that one normally might not think of as concerned about IT, as evidenced by the epigram at the start of this chapter. In every instance, there were various government policies and programs aimed at facilitating integration of their economies into their local regions or into the world at large in many ways and, invariably, with IT playing some role in the process.

Following historic patterns of policy implementation, officials craft IT strategies that fit closely the peculiarities and priorities of their governments and societies, taking into account national aspirations and myriad constraints (e.g., technical capabilities and budgets), and preexisting economic realities. This set of considerations goes far to explain the rich variety of actions and priorities one encounters in looking at economic development practices involving IT. This also suggests strongly why one must be very careful before blithely embracing another country's practices without appreciating thoroughly local mitigating circumstances that affect expectations, implementation, and consequences.

In addition to wanting to take advantage of the larger markets potentially available to one's industries and their member firms, there is also the desire to make one's national economy competitive relative to others participating in the global economy. In fact, I have failed to find examples of governments willing to relinquish the ability to make their economy more competitive vis-à-vis those of other nations; that they were not always effective in doing so is another matter [36]. Economic rivalry among nations is a reality of modern life that has been around since time immemorial, a subtext to any discussion about the "global economy." What is different is that IT has led to intensified economic competition in new ways. This is specifically the case with high-quality communications and computing, and with a similarly fast, inexpensive, and reliable transportation network to move goods and people. For example, flower growers in the Netherlands battle for sales in the American market against Asian providers, dueling with marketing and pricing, and, of course, using high-speed airplanes and telecommunications that bring fresh products to market. For decades, semiconductor manufacturers resided in multiple nations and moved from one country to another as the technology and attractiveness of workforces changed over time [37]. Call centers in the past decade have migrated from high-cost labor markets in North America to Ireland, India, and now, increasingly, to English-speaking parts of Africa. Moving call centers has been made directly possible by new and emerging uses of IT and communications technologies. Movement of data entry around the world has occurred across the health, insurance, banking, and brokerage industries, to name a few. The extent to which any of these examples occurs is often directly a result of government policies and regulations as well.

The challenge for governments, then, is to balance two sets of initiatives and realities: the need to improve internal operations of public institutions themselves (to make it possible for their economies to integrate into the global economy and international life of its citizens) and yet to keep their nations economically competitive, socially attractive, and distinct in terms relevant to their citizens. As many observers acknowledge, the decisions made by public administrators have always been influenced profoundly by local political considerations and the values and points of view of their citizens. Thus, the influence of politics and social values weigh heavily on the decisions taken by officials rather than just on some explicit economic theory guiding the advice of the many economists and other experts who normally populate numerous senior positions in government today [38].

Economists who have looked at these difficult-to-define influences, such as Richard R. Nelson, acknowledge the ambiguity and imprecision of the process. Nelson explained that what is always needed involves the evolution of many facets of a society in order to make use of a technology that is economically effective and, conversely, that the creation of the kind of societies one wants is facilitated by effective application of IT. Let Nelson describe the complexity and breadth of the dilemmas for all the players in this drama:

> The evolution of institutions relevant to a technology or industry may be a very complex process involving not only the actions of private firms competing with each other in a market environment, but also organizations like industry associations, technical societies, universities, courts, government agencies, and legislatures. [39]

His main point, therefore, is that "to be effective with those technologies (fundamental technologies dominant in any era) a nation requires a set of institutions compatible with and supportive of them" [40]. Other economists have recently made a similar point, such as William J. Baumol and his colleagues [41].

Beginning largely in the period following World War I, and continuing to the present, governments were the most influential components of societies that could directly affect the creation, destruction, and transformation of institutions or the economic behavior of nations. It is a reality long recognized by public officials. So it should be of no surprise that they are so engaged in the half-dozen dimensions listed above. The core of their work can ultimately be described as either facilitative or, conversely, unconstructive and a hindrance. In general, they know that they are supposed to create and nurture environments that allow other parts of their society to transform and innovate in ways desirable to officials and citizens. And while this is not the place to discuss the role of "technology champions," such as France's attempt to implement in the 1960s policies to promote world class rivals to the computer industry of the United States, even such initiatives are part of the potential toolkit available to officials [42]. But, over the first few years of the twenty-first century, regarding technology and economic development, they focused largely on leveraging IT along these half-dozen dimensions.

Before reviewing aspects of these in more detail, note that many public officials who are implementing strategies for economic development involving a more IT-intensive environment understand that these cannot be implemented successfully just by playing a technology card. Rather, they know progress has to be made simultaneously along a variety of fronts since one reinforces another. Their reality is that progress occurs normally in an uneven fashion across all six dimensions. Local political, historical, economic, and social conditions affect the speed of innovation along these dimensions, which accounts for why one economy may be more IT-intensive than another.

EMERGING STRATEGIES FOR THE MOST ADVANCED NATIONS COMPARED TO RAPIDLY ADVANCING NATIONS

In a simple manner, Table 3.2 catalogs key strategies currently observable in two categories of countries. These strategies are also the ones that are routinely recommended to national governments since no one country is implementing each one listed at the same time. The first are those that rank high in all the major surveys on the extent of IT deployment inside government and across a society (and its economy). These countries comprise a community of about 20 to 25 nations, depending on whose list one uses, but these are re-

Table 3.2. Economic development strategies for most advanced and rapidly advancing nations

Most Advanced Economies	
Political Environment	**Economic Environment**
• Reduce or maintain product and labor market regulation at low levels to sustain economic growth • Government e-strategy to be better coordinated to provide a more consistent and integrated experience for all government services online • Market reforms to reduce the costs of new technology to facilitate access for people excluded due to high costs	• Focus on increasing cross-sector and cross-community linkages to enable sharing of best practices to help increase the overall effectiveness of ICT in the economy • Digital channels for governments and businesses need to be made more convenient and cost-effective to encourage higher adoption among consumers and citizens • Strengthen governance for e-commerce and internet security with industry to promote online trade.
Social Environment	**Technological Environment**
• Focus on improving quality of secondary and tertiary education and reduce school drop-out rates • Improve participation of minorities in the labor force and specific groups not represented adequately • Better sharing of demographic data across government agencies through integration and automation of systems	• Government vision for creating a strong ICT environment with a clearly articulated digital strategy to be implemented against measurable targets, e.g. governments target of ICT in NZ contributing 10% of GDP in 2012 up from 4.3% in 2003 • Formally coordinated government–industry programs to enable efficient rollout of new technologies • Develop efficient technology commercialization and transfer rules for faster diffusion
Rapidly Advancing Nations	
Political Environment	**Economic Environment**
• Establish coherent and far-reaching government "e-strategy" providing citizens with incentives to conduct online, government-related transactions • Reform product market regulation to enhance competition • Relax labor market legislation to make temporary and permanent employment contracting more flexible • Push public services like filing tax returns, car license renewal, and registration of new business online	• Promote the public–private approach to infrastructure development and roll-out • Provide more affordable and varied financing options to new start-ups to foster innovation • Reduce the lead time and simplify procedure for new business registration in the country • Subsidize consulting services and provide tax incentives to help firms put their businesses online

(continued)

Table 3.2. *Continued*

Rapidly Advancing Nations	
Social Environment	Technological Environment

• Increase linkages between the education system and the labor market to keep up with demand
   Technical training to facilitate up-skill of workforce to keep up with the demand of technically skilled labor
   Increase access to and improve quality of tertiary education attainment amongst population
• Improve transport and housing infrastructure to increase labor transfer toward areas with higher levels of employment and better-paid jobs
	• Need for community access programs to provide ICT access to people or enterprise with no access due to geographical constraints or affordability
	• Greater scope for experimentation for firms facilitated through low regulatory burdens may enable new ideas and innovation to emerge more rapidly, leading to faster technology diffusion
	• Improve trust in online payment systems using targeted legislation to promote online trade

markably similar. They include such nations as the United States, United Kingdom, all the Scandinavian countries, Japan, South Korea, and, normally, Australia as well, to mention a few of the most obvious ones. A second group comprises those that are rapidly adopting IT in the operations of government agencies, where a plethora of private-public alliances are forming, and where IT is diffusing rapidly throughout an economy. Typically, these are countries that are already extensive users of IT, have certainly embraced it at many levels, and are racing to meet EU or WTO standards, to compete against the most advanced economies, and in which old legal, economic, and technical infrastructures and practices are being updated to account for the new realities. They are leapfrogging the painful experiences of first-entrant advanced economies by relying on more modern IT as key tools for economic development, while leveraging the first users' experiences to avoid older problems. In this second group, there are somewhere between 40 and 50 nations, again depending on whose list one uses. Obvious members include Taiwan; Israel; Portugal; ex-Soviet Bloc members such as Estonia, Slovenia, Poland, and Hungary; and Chile and Mexico in Latin America. Both groups of nations have representation around the world, with the majority in Europe, North America, and along the East Asian rim.

These two lists beg the question, What about the other half of the world, the some 60 to 100 other nations? There is now considerable evidence of IT economic strategies at work in the majority, although to a far lesser extent than in the first two groups. Furthermore, as the most experienced public officials relying on IT as a strategic pillar for their economic development have clearly demonstrated over the past two decades and, in some cases, their agencies for as long as a half century, many nontechnologically oriented issues need resolution if IT is to become a comparative advantage, let alone an engine for economic and social development. These include creating appropriate legal and regulatory environments that nurture and protect use, investing in the education of both children and workers, and making available sufficient affordable capital for entrepreneurial initiatives. The strategies outlined in Table 3.2 also suggest that there is some overlap in the strategies deployed by these two types of nations, and that should be of no surprise since they all share some degrees of similarity.

A third group of nations tends to be the weakest in addressing these nontechnical issues. Thus, for example, Brazil, which aspires to have a high-tech modern economy, simply has not been investing effectively enough in the education of its young, and yet the country as a whole has a youthful population relative to many other nations. The lack of stable social and legal infrastructures is a chronic problem in many parts of Africa, across parts of the Middle East, Latin America, and Asia. In Asia, however, there are also spectacular pockets of private–public initiatives and effective public strategies designed to encourage IT-centered or IT-supported economic development, such as in eastern China, South Korea, Singapore, and in several cities in India. In Russia, some development initiatives of these kinds are underway, although they have been occurring only most recently more as a result of private initiative and current economic realities than through intentional public policy [43].

The strategies cataloged in Table 3.2 are being implemented on a country-by-country basis with specific initiatives tailored to the particular circumstances of that society. This is even the case where there are transnational guidelines or requirements that have to be met, such as those of the EU or WTO, and even where international firms are diffusing their own internal practices across their enterprises around the globe, such as IBM in information technology, Pfizer in pharmaceuticals, and Nissan in automotive manufacturing.

THE SPECIAL ROLE OF LABOR

The various actions and strategies implemented by governments around the world intended to promote use and sale of all manner of technologies, not just IT, are also influenced profoundly by local issues involving labor. The ultimate political reality concerning labor for all public officials in most countries is that they must implement policies that keep the majority of their adults employed throughout their working years and have to facilitate improvement in their quality of lives, especially now (2009) as various national economies were experiencing very difficult times. These goals are often accomplished by making it possible for a worker to increase his or her productivity per hour worked relative to other nations. Additionally, officials have to provide them with state-supported added-value amenities, such as pensions, health care, mandated vacation and holiday time, and so forth. In those societies where officials are elected to public office, or are fearful that revolt would topple them from power, paying attention to the economic welfare of their constituents is de rigueur for their personal success [44]. In short, of all the factors influencing policy makers, labor remains number one.

Of course, realities of labor considerations vary by country. In Europe, workers cannot move easily from one industry to another, that is to say, from a declining industry to some new high-tech one, as easily or quickly as occurs in the United States and in parts of East Asia. This is due largely to strong unions and work-practices legislation (among other factors). In Asia, the problem is often insufficient historical experience with high-technology products and industries comparable to what exists in the United States and, thus, in not having an adequate supply of properly trained individuals to populate either high-tech jobs in any chosen industry or to work in emerging high-tech markets, a situation, however, that has also been changing as skills are acquired to design, build, and sell goods and services, and to run large, complex, private high-tech firms. In some countries, there are other considerations that affect the work of labor, such as rising and falling interest rates in the United States, where the propensity remains high for its citizens to incur extraordinary levels of consumer debt and who save less per capita than in many countries. In yet others, governments, investors, and employers can channel available capital to business investments that occasionally have negative effects on high-tech employment. The dot-com bust of the early 2000s, for instance, reminded many public officials that high tech industries per se are not immune to the wider macroeconomic gales that blow across a nation's economy [45].

There are other labor-related realities that condition the rate and extent to which policy makers can move forward with any IT-centered policy or practice. For example, union work rules may constrict the ability of a company, or even a government agency, from automating internal operations, a problem that many U.S. firms faced in heavily unionized industries for decades, but that dissipated, albeit slowly, in the last three decades of the twentieth century. This factor takes a long time to work its way out in such a manner that IT can increasingly be used to improve labor productivity. Historically, governments in most nations lag the private sector in this form of labor productivity [46]. That lag is important because, as this chapter began with the observation that one of the two fundamental areas of IT-oriented economic development involved government agencies serving as leading and influential examples by using the technology itself, simply not implementing the second strategy of creating economic incentives makes little sense.

The realities of labor conditions in any nation affect profoundly the role of policy and practice in the implementation of IT-centered economic development strategies. It is a reminder to those who are enthusiastic proponents of transforming an economy into some kind of high-tech nirvana that a factor that has influenced national economic policies for centuries remains a powerful consideration as officials implement their economic development plans. It is why, in the category of lessons learned from the past and current experiences, creating and sustaining effective and skilled workforces with the right mix of capabilities in support of various uses of technology or its development and sale must go hand in hand with such other considerations, such as the availability of capital to fund internal and external innovations, an appropriate collection of property protections (both digital and physical), flexibility to encourage entrepreneurship, and policies that encourage specific technologies to improve and enhance a local economy. The latter is applicable in a wide range of circumstances, whether, for instance, consumer electronics in Asia, cell phones and MRI technologies in Europe, or software in the United States and in Germany.

GLOBAL RECESSION, TWENTY-FIRST CENTURY STYLE

As this book was being written in 2008 and 2009, large swaths of the advanced economies of the world were slipping into a serious economic recession, triggered initially by questionable business practices on the part of banks, largely tied to bad home mortgages but also to myriad investment products, soon followed by a sharp decline in the availability of credit for normal business transactions, reduced spending by individuals and firms, and, subsequently, by rising unemployment all over the world. There were several features of this particular recession that were relatively new when compared to those of the early 2000s, 1980s, 1970s, and, yes, even to the Great Depression of the 1930s. First, when the recessionary activities began in 2008 they picked up speed faster than earlier ones. Credit freezes occurred in weeks rather than months; consumer spending dropped by several percentage points per month; unemployment increased sharply by as much as two-tenths to four-tenths of a percent per month. While this may not sound like much, in the United States, for example, that meant that 600,000 or more additional people lost their jobs per month. China faced a newly unemployed population of over 50 million migrant workers, while many European countries experienced double-digit unemployment. Essentially, it only took from September 2008 to the end of that year to push many economies into recession.

In addition to the speed with which this recession flowered, was its scope. Economies were so tightly linked, so codependent on each other, that just as IT had made it possible to increase the globalization of world trade, so too bad events in one country could quickly create problems in other nations. For example, China's largest source of export business was to the American consumer. When the latter quickly cut back consumer spending, within weeks the Chinese economy felt the effects. Historians and economists will spend many years sorting through the causes of this intense, rapidly spreading recession that caused governments to respond in new ways.

For one thing, the G-20 nations almost immediately began collaborating on policy and regulatory actions to address first the banking crisis, followed by the larger problem of rising unemployment. Market-based economies received massive injections of public funding directed toward banks, insurance companies, taxpayers, and "shovel ready" public works projects to stabilize financial institutions, unblock credit freezes, and protect and create jobs while staunching the rise in home foreclosures. Regulators and senior public officials worked on weekends, held multinational economic summits, and passed massive spending laws. When compared to responses to earlier economic crises, officials moved at a remarkably quick speed, making decisions and passing laws in days and weeks rather than over periods of months and years.

Led by such government leaders as those of France and Britain, treasury and financial cabinet members worked closely to craft operating principles that could be implemented around the world. There was talk of creating global regulatory watchdog agencies, perhaps turning that responsibility over the International Monetary Fund (IMF) and equipping it with a "high-tech" set of tools and "dashboards" to monitor potential problems in an economy. Presidents and prime ministers spoke about implementing "harmonized" regulatory practices that were "transparent" to officials and citizens alike.

For the first time, there was significant IT content in all of the events. Many of the securitized loans that originally triggered the crisis could not have been turned into financial products without software to scoop up bits of various mortgages and other financial instruments and turn them into marketable offerings. Also, members of the IT industry came forward with specific recommendations about how they and their technologies could help mitigate the effects of the recession and lead to the creation of new jobs. We had never really witnessed this second feature of IT's role in prior recessions.

The Information Technology Innovation Institute, an influential IT think tank in Washington, DC, advocated that the Obama administration invest in IT R&D as a way to stimulate economic growth: "We estimate that spurring an additional $20 billion investment in research would create approximately 402,000 American jobs for one year" [47]. IBM's CEO, Samuel Palmisano, suggested to the American president that investing in all manner of IT projects could raise that number closer to a million, while modernizing electrical, communications, health, and transportation infrastructures [48]. The Business Software Alliance (BSA) called for more extensive patent reforms, training, preserving "technology-neutral principles in procurement and policy initiatives," while investing as well in critical infrastructures. BSA and others recommended fighting cyber crime, enhancing cyber security, and reforms in immigration practices to make it easier for IT professionals to migrate to jobs in the United States, for example [49]. Other observers in the industry argued that President Obama's government should "see IT not as a sideline issue, but as a key component of its domestic and foreign policy" [50].

Even in the pages of the Computer Society's publication, *Internet Computing,* there were calls for implementing "ten ideas for policymakers to drive digital progress." Though typical of what was appearing in print elsewhere, its list suggested the breadth of the economy that could now be affected by IT: managing traffic congestion; optimizing parking lots; controlling pollution; reducing administrative costs of healthcare through the use of electronic records; installing sensors in cars, trucks, and on roads and bridges to improve safety; increasing investments in R&D, expanding deployment of broadband Internet access in support of wireless computing; and moving from Second Industrial Revolution electric networks to "intelligent power grids" that promise more efficient transportation and effective use of electricity [51]. The governor of California in March, 2009, told IT to get green as well. This partial list is nearly breathtaking in its scope. Just focusing on electricity, health, and broadband uses of IT alone would allow us to declare that this recession had a profoundly IT feature to it beyond anything we had seen in the past. It seemed that every week another major set of recommendations regarding IT was landing on the desks of senior public officials all over North America, Europe, and Japan.

As this book was going to press in 2009, some responses were already emerging. Perhaps essential to observe is that public officials this time included IT as integral to their responses to the economic crisis, and largely addressed two problems: rising unemployment and the need for stimulus to do some refurbishing of parts of an economy in need of updating. Although this is not the place to have a detailed discussion of the topic, it is appropriate to suggest the scope of IT's new role. In both Europe and North

America, banking regulators began discussing new auditing and regulatory practices that could be implemented using new software tools. In the United States, in February 2009, the U.S. Congress passed a massive economic stimulus law that included billions of dollars to digitize health records. Additionally, Congress made funds available to invest in the deployment of broadband Internet connections and to start working on modernizing networks that supplied electricity to homes, businesses, and agencies. Battery research (largely for electric cars) also received financial support from governments in North America, Israel, Asia, and Europe, while private firms such as IBM increased their focus on the same topic. All of these were actions taken within months of the economic crisis erupting, while other initiatives were unfolding that would not generate results for more than a year: pollution control, greening of products and activities, and other initiatives such as additional grid digitization and the implementation of intelligent traffic management systems, the latter already underway before the crisis in such cities as Stockholm, Singapore, and London. It was expected that these would now accelerate in adoption by many other cities around the world.

During the Great Depression of the 1930s, governments collaborated with companies and communities to create jobs as a primary response to the economic woes of the day. Building roads and bridges, along with parks and other public spaces, proved effective in creating new jobs while upgrading older infrastructures. Today's response is remarkably similar, with "information highways" and electrical grids receiving additional attention. Of course, the challenges are different, too. In the 1930s, someone with a strong back could be given a shovel to work on road construction and the project foreman could be confident that that individual had the skills and experience to use the digging tool. To enhance or refurbish a telecommunications network today, or to clean up pollution, requires that the unemployed worker have IT skills or environmental management knowledge, something far more extensive than understanding how to use a shovel. But with so many knowledge workers out of work, perhaps there are available the necessary skills; time will tell. The concept of applying governmental funds to create jobs in building infrastructures has a positive history.

The conclusion we can reach almost immediately is that in future economic crises, governments and companies will turn increasingly to IT-centric solutions far more than in the past. Successful solutions will require a workforce more knowledgeable about IT than before, across more segments of a nation's population. The existence of a greater number of digital networks and infrastructures will be essential as well, whereas in prior years cement and metal dominated and sufficed.

IMPLICATIONS FOR PUBLIC OFFICIALS

With the certain understanding that economies all go through cycles of recession and prosperity, we can turn to a discussion of longer term implications that transcend specific ebbs and flows of economic activity. Economists have learned a great deal about the economic value of IT from the experiences of governments and firms of the 1990s and early 2000s. Perhaps one of the most important lessons is that investment in information technology alone only accounts for small increases in national economic productivity and, thus, many economists and public officials have concluded that this situation would continue for some time [52]. In the case of those nations with extensive IT industries, the positive impact on an economy of these kinds of companies is greater, as is the situation in the United States [53]. But what is most effective is when a technology is embedded into the processes and activities of a nation, creating the new digital style referred to earlier, or, in economic terms, contributing to total factor productivity (TFP) [54]. This is an elegant way of suggesting that labor and capital alone do not make up the total inputs to today's economic development, nor does the extended use of IT by itself; other inputs are needed as well, such as education and training, and, by extension, the various economic, legal, and social environmental factors discussed in this chapter.

Circumstances have varied by country. For example, the effect of IT has been most positive on GDP in wholesale and retail industries and in banking in the United States when judged over many decades. In Europe, communications industries have enjoyed substantial increases in productivity; however, this is also due to the implementation of relatively uniform technical product standards and the privatization of firms in the industry [55]. I have argued elsewhere that in highly advanced economies, work has become so integrated with IT that whole economies are entering a new era

in which the use of such technology is a prerequisite just to participate in national business activities [56]. But, as a general statement, the extended use of IT by one society or another does have a
direct effect on TFP and, hence, on GDP. Public officials understand that the use of IT is critical to the evolution of their societies
and economies [57].

IBM's own research on public administration has identified six
patterns of behavior which, while broader than public policy toward IT or economic behavior, are so tied to the style of administration that is spreading around the world that they are worth list-
ing because officials can turn to these and ask to what extent are
their own IT-centered policies and practices taking into account
such broad patterns of behavior [58]. As Table 3.3 documents,
these also reflect similar patterns of behavior evident in the private sector [59]. In short, the appetite of public officials to inject IT
into their economic strategies has not slackened. Current tactics
are indicative of their intent. As recently as 2008, the EIU reported
the continued growing activity of governments around the world

Table 3.3. Six trends transforming governments

Trend	Description
Changing the rules	Changing laws, administrative requirements, and organizations to shape behavior of officials and citizens
Using performance management	Using results-oriented methods to achieve intended outcome goals
Providing competition, choice, and incentives	Can include outsourcing, public–private partnerships, and vouchers
Performing on demand	Improving speed and quality of responsiveness to citizen demands for services, 7 days/week
Engaging citizens	More active participation by citizens in consuming government services and information, and participating in public decision and policy making
Using networks and partnerships	Increased use of networks of groups and people to carry out the work of government

Source: Adapted from Mark A. Abramson, Jonathan D. Breul, and John M. Kamensky, *Six
Trends Transforming Government* (Washington, DC: IBM Center for The Business of Government, 2006).

to facilitate the narrowing of digital divides, further extension of the availability and use of broadband Internet connections, and now, increasingly, wireless communications and links to the Internet, all with a growing surge of activity now as well in developing countries in Africa and in parts of Asia and Latin America [60]. So, what are these current trends?

First, public officials are continuing to support expanded, faster, and more intense connectivity among people and organizations via the Internet and telecommunications. In the poorest nations, telephony has long been a primary area of focus and investment and continues to be so at the present; in more advanced economies it is further expansion of broadband, and, in the most advanced, use of Internet-based wireless communications. In all areas of the world, policy makers are also implementing economic incentives to drive down the cost of communications, hence increasing the affordability of these for citizens and organizations. These incentives vary, such as capital investments in telecommunications infrastructures, tax incentives, and privatization of telephony. These also are in evidence when combined to encourage and facilitate competition within IT and communications industries that, in turn, create economic environments that facilitate innovation in the use of technology. Normally evident is the exercise of the power of laws and regulatory authority. By the early 2000s, WiFi had become the one specific technology drawing the greatest attention, building nicely on wired broadband that either already existed in a society (such as in South Korea) or that represented a convenient leapfrogging tool in Central European and North American coffee shops, airports, and other public spaces in large urban centers. No area of the world is immune from this cumulative trend.

A second major long-standing area of focus for governments concerns the preservation of a business environment that is both stable and open. It is imperative that these non-IT considerations be foremost in the minds of officials as they deal specifically with fostering competition, because that drives down costs of goods and services and leads to innovations in offerings and uses. Such practices often lead to predictable and equitable taxation practices that avoid unfair burdens on firms that limit their competitiveness in national and global markets. Additionally, expanded borderless competition and movement of goods, services, and people facilitate the ability of a national economy to export, import, and attract workers, products, and other offerings. Nurturing business environments continues to gain momentum. The EU, for example, is the source of many incentives for the most recent 10 new members in Central and Eastern Europe aspiring to full integration in the greater European economy. The WTO has rapidly become a force to reckon with around the world as nations aspire to become integrated into the global economy, while at the same time creating unique internal competitive advantages for themselves. The environments keep changing and there are no guarantees. For instance, the EIU's rankings of the quality of U.S. business environments have been dropping slightly over the past several years when compared to that of Canada, for example. To be sure, the U.S. economy is still massive, powerful, and not to be discounted, particularly when compared to that of the much smaller Canadian one, or for that matter, to the very large European or Chinese economies. Nonetheless, its relative competitiveness is not assured; public officials will have to continue to nurture it as we witnessed with the events of the banking crisis of 2008–2009.

Emerging economies offer many examples of how officials are raising the bar for economic performance around the world. Over the past several years, for example, Chile has emerged as a useful case study. It has implemented policies encouraging economic liberalization and structural reforms since the 1970s. These efforts include patent and copyright protections, additional securities for land and property, investments in IT and communications infrastructures, and facilitating business transactions. By-products of these have included the creation of investment and taxation environments that, when compared to those in other Latin American countries (e.g., the large economies of Brazil and Mexico), are attractive.

It seems that media in most countries discuss consumer use of IT more than the role of IT infrastructures in telecommunications or use within businesses or government agencies. However, the role of individuals remains crucial to economic development. That is why all major surveys of the social and economic well-being of nations invariably include discussions and rankings on education levels, healthcare, personal security (the issue of crime), and access to the Internet and other forms of IT and information. The most "advanced" economies (i.e., those that rank the highest in various studies) continue to be those in which public officials ensure there exist what some economists call "entrepreneurial cultures" [61] and a highly IT-literate workforce and student population. As with other facets of economic development, public officials find these elements slower to develop than business environments, but they are nonetheless essential to overall economic development. Ultimately, and to be more precise, governments use their considerable powers to influence the evolution of environments toward some intended outcome, and avoid creating or developing them directly. North America, Western Europe, and three nations in Asia (Australia, South Korea, and New Zealand) are the current benchmarks of success. However, central and eastern Europe (specifically Slovenia, Czech Republic, and Hungary), growing numbers of nations in Latin America (Brazil, Argentina, and Chile), and parts of the Middle East (most notably Israel, United Arab Emirates, and, arguably, Turkey) are also rapidly improving when compared to their neighbors or to their economic and political competitors.

However, there are obstacles to overcome. One recent report on the role of the Internet and society pointed out for these rapidly evolving nations that "as governments and enterprises increasingly migrate services online, those without reliable Internet access are in danger of being disenfranchised," requiring enormous and rapid efforts on the part of both public and private sectors collaborating to expand affordable access to the Internet [62]. This issue is not just about citizens with low personal GDP gaining access, it is also about senior citizens in wealthy nations too. Governments are turning to the needs of this latter population, one that is growing in number in many advanced economies. For example, the Spanish government is investing billions of Euros to educate the elderly and women on how to use the Internet. The same is occurring in Austria [63].

In many of these tech-savvy advanced economies, public officials can take credit for having done a credible job in creating legal environments that facilitate two key activities: business transactions in an open yet secure manner and the free flow of information. Laws, regulations, and public policies have allowed contracts to be enforceable, property to be protected, and information to move about openly enough to inform the work and actions of citizens. Today, the major work effort for officials is to take these conditions and facilitate their extension to the world of the Internet and to virtual economic activities. Officials in the United States and in other countries are dealing with copyright issues for software and recorded music, both of which can be downloaded off the Internet easily with broadband connections, which can result in the loss of royalties to their producers. In parts of Europe and Asia, officials are dealing with the cross-border movement of information that historically they could censor. From an IT perspective, and based on prior positive experiences, officials will probably continue to protect intellectual property rights of things gone digital, and promote and protect technical and legal ways to ensure the secure and accurate flow of transactions and information. Authentication of online transactions is crucial and remains an area requiring considerable attention. Censorship of information remains an equally problematic issue in all societies, including those that consider themselves quite open (for example, the United States or the Netherlands). The ability of new businesses to register and do business over the Internet is also imperative at the moment. Much of what global organizations do in these areas is to articulate requirements and recommendations, such as those of the EU, UN, and WTO.

An ugly side of all these issues is the growing problem of cybercrime. This is not just an issue of the notorious and well-understood constant flood of banking scams over the Internet coming out of Nigeria. Criminal activity has moved into the networked economy. In the United States, for example, the U.S. Federal Bureau of Investigation (FBI) and many local police departments have investigative units devoted to detecting cybercrime of all kinds, not just the pursuit of those exposing children to pornography [64]. Hacker activities and denial-of-service (DoS) attacks are increasing around the world and threaten economic and social activities, for example in Australia, where DoS has become the fastest growing form of crime in the nation. Japan's cybercrime grew by nearly 12% in the first six months of 2006, especially online fraud [65]. South Korea has an even worse problem because of some 200,000 criminal sites online [66]. In both countries, special police units had to be created to concentrate on cybercrime, much as the Americans did more than a decade earlier.

Censorship has also moved to the Internet. Bloggers are arrested in Egypt for criticizing government policies, while censorship is alive and well in China, where many Internet sites are blocked from being seen by citizens. Online censorship is not limited just to these two countries, or even to African nations. Others include Burma, Iran, Tunisia, and even republics that were once part of the Soviet Union, such as Uzbekistan. In addition to the serious implications for free speech and the functioning of republics and democracies are the effects on business. Business leaders normally prefer conducting business in nation states where there is open flow of information and protection of privacy and patents and copyrights. Thus, censorship can constrain the flow of data and insights needed to optimize business transactions; that circumstance makes it more difficult for firms to be competitive within their internal economies and in a global economy. It also causes management in corporations not operating in a particular society that has a reputation for censorship to think twice before either investing in doing business there or in expanding their markets. Above all else, business leaders value social stability and flexibility in conducting transactions. Underpinning the latter is the combination of the free flow of information and respect for rights and signed contracts.

There also remains the political problem that as governments foster economic and technological innovation, they must perforce encourage winners and create losers as the leaders of the future are cheered on and often political supporters from the past have to be displaced. This problem of the political and financial influence of vested interests is not limited to democracies; it exists in all manner of regimes from the most open and egalitarian to the most corrupt and authoritarian. Yet each has a history of being able to stimulate innovations, both desired and undesired.

IMPLICATIONS FOR BUSINESS LEADERS

As the number of firms becoming involved in commercial transactions around the world increases, both big and small companies face a number of issues. They deal with two types of activities: (1) products or services that are made or done for them and (2) what they sell and do for customers in other countries. Large companies and innovative firms may establish globalized value chains or supply chains to acquire goods and services and to deliver products and perform work internationally, and, thus, they must worry about the physical space in which these occur. The landmass upon which humans conduct business is still controlled by governments. Thus, eBay still has to worry about French laws, Google about the wishes of the Chinese government, and manufacturing firms about the environmental laws of the United States and the regulations of the European Union. Managers also need to rely on governments to create attractive market environments that include protection of property and rights, enforcement of contracts, availability of capital, promotion and sustainability of local standards of living and economic development that makes one's products and services attractive and affordable, provides political and physical security, and reduces corruption (because it increases the cost of doing business, often in unpredictable ways). In short, the private sector needs to participate in the economic development of a nation while collaborating with public officials to facilitate the growth and possibility of doing business.

There are some economies in which conducting business is attractive because all the necessary requirements are there: Western Europe, all of North America, and large swaths of East Asia. But there is the opposite as well: nations with poverty, political instability or war, poorly managed economies, and substantial corruption. Depending on what industry a company is part of, these can outnumber the ideal economies. The problem with this scenario is that the growth potential for many firms lies in those countries that in general can be characterized as having, in addition to their problems, substantial natural resources (e.g., oil in Nigeria) and rapidly growing local populations (e.g., Sub-Saharan Africa). International corporations and many smaller enterprises seek to enter those markets as local conditions improve. That is largely why most managers knowledgeable about international affairs cheer on the work of public officials in stabilizing and improving market conditions in their countries.

Besides the obvious act of managers assessing when and where to expand business, often working with local public officials to gain incremental economic advantages, such as reduced taxation or construction of infrastructures (e.g., roads, electrical supplies, or training of workers), they look at risk. Risk is not necessarily a bad thing; good prudent risk taking is how large new businesses have been grown in market-driven economies for centuries. In the second half of the twentieth century, however, a variety of scientific, statistical, mathematical, and managerial practices emerged that help managers determine the extent of risk they face in taking new actions and these are being applied to the question of which economy to participate in. Public officials and business managers cannot ignore these, but must engage in dialogue about them where they exist, and often that conversation should be initiated by a business manager. The kinds of risks that could negatively affect a business are considerable in number, from emergencies (e.g., natural disasters and strikes) to unreliable infrastructures (e.g., irregular supply of water or electricity), to geo-political crises (e.g., civil unrest), and extend even to the availability of a sufficient source of suppliers, customers, properly trained and productive workers, considerations about culture (e.g., legislation dictating how much vacation time must be given to workers or flexible labor laws), and economic conditions (e.g., the banking and credit crises of 2007–2009).

Risks can appear in surprising places. For example, many West European countries have labor laws that, to put it bluntly, make their pools of workers far less competitive to employ than those in China, India, and even in parts of Africa. A government in Europe might find it politically impossible to change that situation, but a corporation can simply move work to another country. The other dimension of risk is the likelihood of a risk actually occurring. Financial risk can be very high, happen all the time, and can be reflected in many ways: inflation in salaries, imposition of tariffs for goods coming into a nation, and, more frequently it seems, changing monetary exchange rates. On the other hand, some risks are low in probability of happening, such as natural disasters, disease, collapse of an existing telecommunications network, or the disappearance of customers.

This discussion of risk is not intended to discourage international trade or noncommercial forms of globalization. Rather, it is a dose of reality that gets injected into the discussion about economic growth. So, what is a manager to do? I would argue that there are six major activities that can be listed briefly because they are obvious and already proven.

First, understand the local economy, the political stability of a country, and how business is conducted. Take the time to appreciate a nation's recent history and each of the risk and opportunity factors already discussed in this chapter and elsewhere in this book. Having local partners is not a bad thing either, as is investing in local business partners who are familiar with regional business practices and speak the language.

Second, when negotiating with governments and local businesses, take the time to craft agreements that really are a win–win for both so that each has economic and other advantages to be won by carrying out the agreement, even in countries where contract compliance is still an evolving concept. This is one of the lessons learned by the International Monetary Fund and the World Bank over the years as they came to realize how to distribute funds in developing economies; it is a best practice that managers going global should learn as well.

Third, make sure you understand what role your firm should play in a particular economy and then work with local public officials to make that happen. In one country, it may be that a company outsources software development to a local firm if that is not core to its own mission; or it outsources core work because it can be done less expensively or quicker than in-house. How these activities may be done through partnerships with local firms, with other international companies already there, using local distribution channels for goods and services, or by establishing local branches of one's own company.

Fourth, determine how the financials will work out. What are the local banking regulations and laws? Do they need to be modified? If so, negotiate with local governments. Stable supplies of local capital is often a crucial factor weighing on the decision to enter a local economy, particularly in developing nations or in those with a history of monetary instability, such as has often been the case in Africa and in Latin America. Foreign direct investments (FDIs) play one of the most essential roles for any public official attempting to develop their economy, so managers must pay careful attention to this issue.

Fifth, each opportunity has its own advantages and disadvantages that must be optimized or mitigated with the help of both local companies and governments. Each region has its inherent attractions that one should leverage. In North America, the transportation infrastructure, access to markets, and cost of living are very appealing to foreign companies. Western Europe is attractive because it provides easy access to markets and its work force is highly educated and trained. Both regions have excellent political stability and low corruption, and, most important of all, for over a half century economic and financial stability, despite the banking and recessionary pressures that existed at the time this book was published. Similar attributes can be found even in areas of the world that have a reputation of being the opposite. But not all African countries are fighting wars and suffering poor economic conditions, not all Latin American countries are plagued with inflation and weak monetary systems, and not all Asian countries have workforces that can only do First Industrial Revolution work.

Finally, the movement of work, customers, markets, and attractiveness of one location versus another is dynamic, a point made in the first chapter and facilitated by the diffusion of modern IT, transportation, and high-tech-supported banking systems. If the world's standard of living rises, and I believe it is doing that, then the volatility described in the pages above should diminish. Workers making payments on car loans are not interested in fostering revolutions. Governments eager to participate in the European Union and its large market are highly motivated to stabilize their monetary systems, control public spending, and implement wide-ranging laws that protect property, contracts, patents, and copyrights. Nations with young populations are seeking ways to educate children and young adults and then to find them jobs. Even Communist Cuban officials made sure that, for all intents and purposes, the entire population became literate and had a growing amount of education. African governments worry about health, education, and employment as well. There is a global rise in standards of living underway; one does not need to rush to large compendiums of UN statistics to verify this trend. Barring some unforeseen circumstance, corporate management can expect this to continue, making it even more important to implement these six recommendations.

THE WAY FORWARD WITH POLICIES AND PRACTICES

We must, however, return to the role of public officials because they still have the primary responsibility and wherewithal to ensure that this trend continues. Prior historical experiences and current practices can be mined for future actions that can be taken by public officials to stimulate further economic development. Ultimately, they ask: What can governments do in terms of their daily operations that in turn facilitate effective use of IT in the nation's economic development? As often the largest consumer of goods and services in a national economy, there are actions officials take that go beyond simply legislating and regulating. A combination of strategies and tactics are currently being implemented by public administrators that warrant replicating in ways tailored to the realities of individual countries. These are presented, admittedly like much of the rest of this chapter, in a trenchant style because the evidence exists to support their value. They are also approachable, however, and, as previously described, are already in evidence around the world.

First, one can begin by looking inside one's own departments and agencies for ways to stimulate more IT-dependent behavior in the marketplace. For example, require providers of services to a government agency to submit proposals and invoices using e-procurement methods. Concurrently, governments should create payment systems to pay their suppliers electronically, by transferring funds directly into the bank accounts of these vendors. The entire two-way process should be transparent, that is to say, subject to valid accounting audits. One effective way to begin is with a tech-savvy agency. Then spread the practices across other agencies and departments through waves of deployment. An early and effective role model of this behavior is the government of the United States, to which it is nearly impossible today to submit a paper bill, a point made earlier in this book. Vendors are paid electronically, although individual citizens can still be paid by check.

Second, because of the unique one-time circumstance that governments in many countries face today of their public workforces about to retire in great numbers, agencies should automate and reengineer as many processes as they can in order to capture the experience and knowledge of these retiring workers, while simultaneously reducing the amount of labor content required to perform the work of government. This action means reducing paperwork and perhaps bureaucracy, but many governments know how to do this. What is unique to government is that often the political will to do so has not been present or sufficient. But with increasing numbers of IT literate workforces available, the ability to move work around within a national economy and across agencies in a government, and even within a region (e.g., within the EU), unique opportunities present themselves for innovative practices that will not require layoffs of public employees. To date, however, this kind of work intended to reduce labor content due to impending retirements has really not begun, although political leaders in Western Europe and in North America have started to raise the issue, most notably in the United States and in Great Britain.

Third, extend governmental services to the public via the Internet. Recall that Finland gave its citizens e-mail addresses, the U.S. government now prefers initial e-mail contacts by the public to its various agencies for information and forms, and the British government is quietly building e-commerce capabilities so as to lower the cost to the private and public sectors for doing business with government agencies. Even in economies in which one would not expect to see e-commerce, opportunities exist for innovation. For example, the Asian Development Bank (ADB) is executing online banking services in Afghanistan, where there had previously not been any online financial services. ADB is implementing a classic technological leapfrogging strategy by bypassing prior ways of conducting paper-based business [67]. That kind of creative thinking can be especially effective in the least teledense societies, providing that the public can be educated on the rudiments of their use.

Fourth, since public officials have paid insufficient attention to several technological trends involving IT that go far beyond access to the Internet—affordable broadband or even personal computers and other portable consumer electronics—they need to pay attention to these. Specifically, actions and policies should involve establishing ways to have trusted identification of people and information about goods and property on the one hand, and open systems on the other. In fact, on the latter point, there is now another round of innovations underway around the world involving technical standards. Each has its issues; none should be ignored. Several warrant additional discussion.

Security issues are clearly an obvious collection, specifically those related to "trusted" identification of people and goods. The term "trusted identity" is a term used within IT circles, and increasingly in government agencies responsible for security and border management [68]. The challenge for all is to determine how to make sure that an individual is who he or she says they are. And more than just simply creating a technologically foolproof passport or national identity card that has tamperproof digital images, even biometric proofs (such as fingerprints, and images of one's iris), there are a series of back office operations to consider. Additionally, there are the socially charged issues concerning privacy and law. At the moment, there are rapidly emerging technologies that make it possible to create identity cards that are almost tamperproof and that would largely assure that who someone is matches who they say they are. 9/11 helped along the continued innovation of the technology, but it is a process that has been underway since the first digitized fingerprinting systems became available to law enforcement in the 1960s. There is hardly a national government in the Americas, East Asia, and across all of Europe today that is not revisiting the whole issue of national identity cards in light of the variety of technological innovations that have emerged in just the past two to three years [69]. That is the easy part.

A more difficult issue concerns what to do with the information, how to create and manage the cards and the data they contain. What data needs to be on a card? What should be in some national or regional database? Who should control or use the information? How should it be used? [70] What needs to be done with it? For example, it is now customary for many governments to share with each other names of individuals flying to another nation while these passengers are on a flight so that the receiving country can quietly determine what kind of individuals are about to enter their territory. It is a practice that has long been used to determine what ships, for example, to inspect before arriving at a port.

Additionally, there is the highly charged issue of privacy. In many countries in Europe and North America, for instance, the issue of "big brother" watching over us is so volatile that policy makers are reluctant to confront it. In most instances, they are addressing it in an incremental manner. For example, in the United States the issuance of a national identity card is politically out of the question. However, the number of citizens who now are required to have one increased substantially beginning in 2007 because of a new requirement that citizens moving in and out of Canada and Mexico must have one; a requirement that did not exist before, when a state drivers license or a birth certificate were adequate proofs of identity. In the past, such documents could easily be forged; less so a modern American (or European) passport. In a concurrent initiative, the American government established mandatory national standards for the issuance of driver licenses by the 50 U.S. states as a way of reducing forgeries. More incremental and just emerging as an issue is that of U.S. state governments beginning to entertain the notion of requiring citizens to have a state issued identity card (a drivers license being one possible form) in order to vote, as a way of blocking access to voting by immigrants living illegally in the United States. Each of these three initiatives has been fraught with controversy and difficult to implement even though the technology exists to provide high degrees of tamper-free trusted documents for identification of individuals. The challenge to officials is a reflection of the social and political values of their citizens that cannot be ignored.

There is also the issue of open systems and the related one concerning technical standards, mentioned earlier but worth further comment. The theory behind open systems is that governments, industries, and firms would want to have software and networks that anyone with new software and IT tools could plug into and interact with. The idea is that oligopolistic or monopolistic constraints on an economy, industry, or product could be reduced. The EU, for example, has had ongoing issues with Microsoft to expand the ability of other suppliers of software that do the same things as the former to be made available in Europe, thereby enhancing competition among software firms, encouraging local companies to innovate in creating new products and services, and all the while encouraging vendors to lower the price of software for consumers and organizations alike. Companies like IBM and Oracle have intensified the discussion with arguments expounding the virtues of open systems as ways of increasing the volume of uses to which IT can be put. In the case of IBM, it has gone further than any other major IT company to put into the public domain various software tools and patents as a way to facilitate what has now become known in many circles as the "open-software movement" [71]. The whole subject has reached critical mass such that public officials can no longer ignore it; indeed, there is much to suggest that they can use it to facilitate the further extension of IT and networking in their economies.

A related issue, indeed, one could argue that it is the flipside of open systems, is that of technical standards. For over sixty years, computer scientists have known that when technical standards are agreed to by those inventing machines and writing software, the more widely used a technology becomes. With the adoption of IBM's large-mainframe standards in the 1960s, for example, the IT industry grew at a compound rate in the United States by on average 20% a year all through that decade [72]. With the arrival of browsers in the mid-1990s, such as Netscape, Internet usage went from several million users to nearly a third of the world's population in just over a decade. Microsoft's operating system, and some of its applications subsystems (such as Word), dominate, used by nearly 95% of all PC users. Although one might quibble over the technical quality of its products, one can easily see how convenient it is to have a widely used set of standards for creating products that work with Microsoft and the convenience to PC users of being able to work with various PCs and software products that are compatible with Microsoft's or with some other widely accessible sets of technical standards.

Most industries have established various forms of technical and operating standards such as the ISO series. Firms insist that their suppliers adhere to them as well. Government agencies do the same; for example, the U.S. Department of Defense is beginning to require its suppliers to use RFID tags on goods, based on preset technical specifications [73]. European governments represent the famous case of standardization with the technical conformity to one form of wireless telephony, which resulted in the earliest and most extensive deployment of cell phones in the world, and for most of the past decade, the best quality wireless telephony. Increasingly, world organizations are also establishing standards for what data is collected, organized, stored, and presented. Border management agencies have been imposing standards for what information accompanies cargo around the world as a security measure. This initiative represents one of the most visible forms of imposed standards in evidence today, and is one that has not yet fully played out. In fact, one can expect that trusted supply chains will continue to be enhanced this way for years to come.

But standards also raise important questions for officials. What standards should these be? How will they advance or retard economic well-being and comparative competitive advantages of one economy or industry over another? What role do standards play in fostering open systems? Indeed, are they the basis of how open systems can function, since the concept of open systems is itself a de facto standard? What effect do they have on the debate regarding the security of information, especially about people and the facts of their lives (e.g., financial transactions and medical records)? These are fundamental issues that public officials face as they play their IT cards in the economic development game. Although they may seem familiar to those who have been in government for more than twenty years, these have intensified as IT-centered economic development and recent innovations in technology have simultaneously become high-priority issues.

Thus, part of the way forward is for officials to pay close attention to the emerging issues related to identity management, open systems, and open technical standards. It is difficult to imagine that any national economic strategy dependent on IT would ignore these. It is equally hard to conceive of any major governmental initiative intended to leverage IT for its own internal operational efficiencies not taking these into consideration. In short, they are already becoming the next turn in the road for public officials working in our highly digitized societies.

We now can move from broad questions of national economies, global effects of IT, and public policies to a more micro view of how managers make decisions to acquire and use technologies, with the understanding that they operate in the larger context described in the first three chapters of this book.

NOTES AND REFERENCES

1. Quoted in Jeannine Klein Menzies, "Island Among the Elite in Economist Intelligence Unit-ebusiness Survey," *The Royal Gazette,* April 5, 2006.

2. There is hardly any government in any advanced economy that today avoids tracking the volume of IT activity in their nation or that does not have important IT policy initiatives underway. Although the United Nations, OECD, and the European Union are the most obvious sources for such tracking, an examination of the activities of individual governments yields similar material. In the case of the United States, for example, policy emanates from the White House and the Departments of Commerce and Labor, whereas the Office of Management and Budget and the General Accountability Office track internal governmental activities concerning IT. Similar comments can be made about such other large economies and their governments as Japan, United Kingdom, Australia, and Germany.

3. Manuel Castells, *The Internet Galaxy: Reflections on the Internet, Business, and Society*, Oxford: Oxford University Press, 2001.

4. Literature on this topic is now vast. Each year, however, public officials around the world do comment publicly on the annual Economist Intelligence Unit's report on their role, for example, *The 2007 E-readiness Rankings: Raising the Bar*, London: Economist Intelligence Unit, 2007, published since 2000. For one example of further awareness, see Kimball P. Marshall, William S. Piper, and Walter W. Wymer, Jr. (Eds.), *Government Policy and Program Impacts on Technology Development, Transfer and Commercialization: International Perspectives*, New York: Haworth Press, 2005.

5. In addition to the EIU survey cited above, see also the United Nations, *UN Global E-government Readiness Report*, New York, United Nations, annual.

6. Reported in James W. Cortada, Ashish M. Gupta, and Marc Le Noir, *How the Most Advanced Nations Can Remain Competitive in the Information Age*, Somers, NY: IBM Corporation, 2007.

7. See, for example, Dan Breznitz, *Innovation and the State: Political Choice and Strategies for Growth in Israel, Taiwan, and Ireland*, New Haven, CT: Yale University Press, 2007; William J. Baumol, Robert E. Litan, and Carl J.

Schramm, *Good Capitalism Bad Capitalism and the Economics of Growth and Prosperity*, New Haven, CT: Yale University Press, 2007.

8. Richard R. Nelson, *Technology, Institution and Economic Growth*, Cambridge, MA: Harvard University Press, 2005, pp. 162–164.

9. Described in more detail in James W. Cortada, Ashish M. Gupta, and Marc Le Noir, *How Nations Thrive in the Information Age*, Somers, NY: IBM Corporation, 2007.

10. Mark A. Abramson and Roland S. Harris III (Eds.), *The Procurement Revolution*, Lanham, MD: Rowland and Littlefield, 2003. E-business means the use of online systems, such as the Internet, with which to conduct business (e.g., purchases) or to communicate and share information (e.g., e-mail or collaborative Internet-based tools whereby multiple organizations can look at the same data).

11. Yoon Je Cho, "Government Intervention, Rent Distribution, and Economic Development in Korea," in Masahiko Aoki, Hyung-Ki Kim, and Masahiro Okuno-Fujiwara (Eds.), *The Role of Government in East Asian Economic Development: Comparative Institutional Analysis*, Oxford: Clarendon Press, 1996, pp. 208–232.

12. "OECD Internet Access Price Comparison" (undated), http://www.oecd.org/document/23/0,3343,en_2649_34225_1884055_1_1_1_1,00.html (last accessed 7/21/2007).

13. Economist Intelligence Unit, *The Means to Compete: Benchmarking IT Industry Competitiveness*, London: Economist Intelligence Unit, 2007.

14. Susanne Berger, *How We Compete: What Companies Around the World Are Doing to Make It in Today's Global Economy*, New York: Currency/Doubleday, 2006, p. 282.

15. Ibid.

16. Rishab A. Ghosh, *An Economic Basis for Open Standards*, Maastricht: University of Maastricht, 2005; Committee for Economic Development, *Open Standards, Open Source, and Open Innovation: Harnessing the Benefits of Oppenness*, Washington, DC: Committee for Economic Development, 2006; James W. Cortada, *Using IT Standards as a Competitive Tool in a Global Economy*, Toronto and New York: Paradigm Learning, 2005.

17. Richard Coopey (Ed.), *Information Technology Policy: An International History*, Oxford: Oxford University Press, 2004, pp. 12–21.

18. For multiple case studies on measurements, see John M. Kamensky and Albert Morales (Eds.), *Managing for Results 2005*, Lanham, MD: Rowman & Littlefield, 2005.

19. EIU, *The Means to Compete,* pp. 8–9.

20. Remarks made in response to the subprime banking crisis that took place in the summer of 2007, precipitated in part by the actions of French and American banks, Emma Vandore, "French Finance Minisster Says Globalization Is "Here to Stay," Associated Press, *Wisconsin State Journal,* August 29, 2007, p. C7.

21. Barry Eichengreen, *The European Economy Since 1945: Coordinated Capitalism and Beyond*, Princeton: Princeton University Press, 2007, pp. 18–419.

See European Union reports and programs, http://europa.eu/scadplus/leg/en/lvb/l25056.htm.

22. Carl Shapiro and Hal R. Varian, *Information Rules: A Strategic Guide to the Network Economy*, Boston, MA: Harvard Business School Press, 1999, pp. 3–9; Michael D. Smith, Joseph Bailey, and Erik Brynjolfsson, "Understanding Digital Markets: Review and Assessment," in Erik Brynjolfsson and Brian Kahin (Eds.), *Understanding the Digital Economy: Data, Tools, and Research*, Cambridge, MA: MIT Press, 2000, pp. 125–126.

23. Access has been the subject of many studies. However, for an introduction to recent trends on a global basis see Naazneen Barma, "The Emerging Economies in the Digital Era: Marketplaces, Market Players, and Market Makers," in John Zysman and Abraham Newman (Eds.), *How Revolutionary Was the Digital Revolution?* Stanford, CA: Stanford Business Books, 2006, pp. 148–170, and especially Table 7.1, p. 153.

24. Richard Florida, *The Rise of the Creative Class: And How It's Transforming Work, Leisure, Community and Everyday Life*, New York: Basic Books, 2002; and *The Flight of the Creative Class: The New Global Competition for Talent*, New York: HarperBusiness, 2005. Recently, Manuel Castells has started to comment about these themes in the context of the emerging experiences societies are having with the Internet; see *The Internet Galaxy: Reflections on the Internet, Business, and Society*, Oxford: Oxford University Press, 2001.

25. Friedman, *The World is Flat.*

26. Eichengreen, *The European Economy Since 1945,* pp. 26–27, 392.

27. James M. Popkin and Partha Iyengar, *IT and the East: How China and India Are Altering the Future of Technology and Innovation*, Boston, MA: Harvard Business School Press, 2007, pp. 101–125.

28. Espen Moe, *Governance, Growth and Global Leadership: The Role of the State in Technological Progress, 1750–2000*, Burlington, VT: Ashgate, 2007, p. 3.

29. *Economic Development in a Rubic's Cube World: How to Turn Global Trends Into Local Prosperity*, Somers, NY: IBM Corporation, 2008.

30. See, for example, EIU, *The 2007 e-Readiness Ranking,* p. 24.

31. For a more detailed description of these dimensions, see James W. Cortada, Ashish M. Gupta, and Marc Le Noir, *How Nations Thrive in the Information Age*, Somers, NY: IBM Corporation, 2007.

32. Highly influential in this regard are Carlota Perez, *Technological Revolutions and Financial Capital: The Dynamics of Bubbles and Golden Ages*, Cheltenham, UK: Edward Elgar, 2002; Angus Maddison, *Growth and Interaction in the World Economy: The Roots of Modernity*, Washington, DC: American Enterprise Institute, 2005; and Manuel Castells, *The Information Age: Economy, Society and Culture,* 3 vols, Oxford: Blackwell, 1996–1998.

33. Recently described by Richard H. K. Vietor, *How Countries Compete: Strategy, Structure, and Government in the Global Economy*, Boston, MA: Harvard Business School Press, 2007.

34. Vietor, *How Countries Compete;* but see also Dale W. Jorgenson, *Productivity,* vol. 2, *International Comparisons of Economic Growth,* Cambridge, MA: MIT Press, 1995.

35. One of the key points made by Thomas L. Friedman, *The World is Flat: A Brief History of the Twenty-First Century*, New York: Farrar, Straus and Giroux, 2nd ed., 2006, pp. 457–504.

36. Which is why the annual e-rankings on which we collaborated with the EIU always show disparities in the performance of nations and even regions.

37. Clair Brown and Greg Linden, "Offshoring in the Semiconductor Industry: A Historical Perspective," in Susan M. Collins and Lael Brainard (Eds.), *Brookings Trade Forum 2005: Offshoring White-Collar Work*, Washington, DC: Brookings Institution Press, 2006, pp. 279–322; Jan Mazurek, *Making Microchips: Policy, Globalization, and Economic Restructuring in the Semiconductor Industry*, Cambridge, MA: MIT Press, 1999.

38. To be sure, economists play a central role in informing officials about options in which they draw upon their training and on economic theories to which they subscribe.

39. Nelson, *Technology, Institutions and Economic Growth,* p. 108.

40. Ibid., p. 111.

41. Baumol, Litan, and Schramm, *Good Capitalism, Bad Capitalism,* pp. 35–59.

42. It continues. For example, the development of the software industry in India in recent years was made possible in part by the policies implemented by the Indian government. For an account of its role, see Kaushik Basu (Ed.), *India's Emerging Economy*, Cambridge, MA: MIT Press, 2004, pp. 215–262.

43. World Bank, "Country Brief: Russian Federation, Economy," http://web.worldbank.org/WEBSITE/EXTERNAL/COUNTRIES/ECAEXT/RUSSIAN-FEDERATIO (last accessed 5/2/2007).

44. This issue is not to be confused with an equally critical one that public officials face, namely, how to keep salaries from increasing so quickly that corporations have to divert funds to this budget item rather than invest in expanding their businesses, hence increasing the number of new jobs, which in turn support national economic growth. For a clear description of this balance of needs for use of funds as applied to Europe since World War II, see Eichengreen, *The European Economy Since 1945.*

45. Described by Tapan Munroe, *Dot-Com to Dot-Bomb: Understanding the Dot-Com Boom, Bust and Resurgence*, Moraga, CA: Moraga Press, 2004.

46. As evident during the adoption of IT over the past sixty years; see James W. Cortada, *The Digital Hand: How Computers Changed the Work of American Public Sector Industries*, New York: Oxford University Press, 2008. The problem was first identified in modern times by economist William J. Baumol, when he noted that labor intensive work did not always lend itself to the rates of productivity increases evident in industries that relied more heavily on machinery, technology, and automation. His insight was named "Baumol's Disease," which he and W. G. Bowen first described in "On the Performing Arts: The Anatomy of Their Economic Problem," *American Economic Review* 55, 12 (March 1965), 495–502. They demonstrated that musicians playing classic music took as much time in the 1960s to do that as in the previous century. Government work, because it is so highly labor intensive, has been suggested as subject to similar conditions and circumstances.

47. "Palmisaro to Obama: Smart Infrastructure is Best Path," January 28, 2009, http://www.crn.com/government/21290 3237 (last accessed 6/28/2009).

48. Chad Berndtson, "Palmisano to Obama: Smart Infrastructure Is Best Path," *ChannelWeb,* January 28, 2009, http://www.crn.com/government/212903237 (last accessed 3/3/2009).

49. *2009 US Technology Policy Agenda,* www.bsa.org/technology (last accessed 3/3/2009).

50. Robert D. Atkinson and Daniel D. Castro, "A National Technology Agenda for the New Administration," *Yale Journal of Law and Technology* 11, 190 (2009), p. 10.

51. Daniel Castro and Rob Atkinson, "Ten Ideas for Policymakers to Drive Digital Progress," *IEEE Internet Computing* 13, 2 (March/April 2009), pp. 69–73.

52. See, for example, Eichengreen, *The European Economy Since 1945,* pp. 400–402.

53. Ibid., pp. 403–404; but also Daniel E. Sichel, *The Computer Revolution: An Economic Perspective*, Washington, DC: Brookings Institution Press, 1997.

54. TFP is discussed usefully by Dale W. Jorgenson, *Productivity, vol. 1,* Postwar U.S. Economic Growth, Cambridge, MA: MIT Press, 1995, pp. 138–140.

55. A conclusion reached by Eichengreen, *The European Economy Since 1945,* p. 403.

56. James W. Cortada, "The Digital Hand: How Information Technology Changed the Way Industries Worked in the United States," *Business History Review* 80 (Winter 2006), pp. 755–766.

57. Based on unpublished papers cited in Ibid., pp. 404–405. However, OECD's own research over the past two decades on similar issues arrived at similar conclusions. Because this is an ongoing issue of interest, one should routinely visit OECD's website, particularly http://www.oecd.org/publications (last accessed 5/1/2007).

58. Mark A. Abramson, Jonathan D. Breul, and John M. Kamensky, *Six Trends Transforming Government,* Washington, DC: IBM Center for The Business of Government, 2006.

59. Graham Tanaka, *Digital Deflation: The Productivity Revolution and How It Will Ignite The Economy,* New York: McGraw-Hill, 2004.

60. EIU, *The 2008 e-Readiness Rankings,* p. 4.

61. Ibid., 12.

62. Ibid., 13.

63. "ES: Spain Takes Steps to Ensure Internet Use Is Inclusive," November 27, 2006, http://ec.europa.eu/idabc/en/document/6292/194 (last accessed 5/1/2007); V. Risak, "ICT In Austria: Institutions, Regulations, Challenges and Applications In Academia, Industry and The Public Sector," www.ifip.org/it_star/report_austria.pdf (last accessed 5/1/2007).

64. James W. Cortada, "The Digital Hand: How Information Technology Changed the Way Industries Worked in the United States," *Business History Review* 80 (Winter 2006), pp. 136–137, 349.

65. For details, see http://www. news.softpedia.com/news/A-New-Apex-of-Cybercrime-in-Japan-33318.shtml (last accessed 5/1/2007).

66. Ludmila Goroshko, "South Korea to Create Unit Fighting Cybercrime," July 10, 2004, *Computer Crime Research Center,* http://www.crime-research.org/news/10.07.2004/477/ (last accessed 5/1/2007).

67. For details as they evolve, see http://www.adb.org/Afghanistan/default.asp (last accessed 5/1/2007).

68. Bryan Barton, Dennis Carlton, and Olivier Ziehm, *Identity Management in the 21st Century,* Somers, NY: IBM Corporation, 2007.

69. *Card Technology* is an online journal that publishes on this topic, available at http://www.cardtechnology.com/article.html?id=20061219IX4CKCL5.

70. This is not a question about the management of technology or digital databases, but rather often about constitutional practices. For example, following World War II, the Allies forced the West German government to adopt a constitutional clause that forbade the national government from collecting identification information on the nation's total population. Rather, each of the German states would do that. Later, laws mandated that even the states expunge certain classes of information on people every six months.

71. For a broad perspective on the concept as applied to both software and administration of an organization, see Chris DiBona, Danese Cooper, and Mark Stone, *Open Sources 2.0: The Continuing Evolution*, Sebastopol, CA: O'Reilly Media, 2006; and Don Tapscott and Anthony D. Williams, *Wikinomics: How Mass Collaboration Changes Everything*, New York: Portfolio, 2006.

72. Emerson W. Pugh, *Building IBM: Shaping An Industry and Its Technology*, Cambridge, MA: MIT Press, 1995, pp. 296–300.

73. Mark Roberti, "DOD Releases Final RFID Policy," *RFID Journal,* August 9, 2004, http://www.rfidjournal.com/article/articleview/1080/1/1/ (last accessed 5/1/2007).

4

HOW MANAGERS AND OFFICIALS DECIDE WHAT TECHNOLOGY TO USE

> The first rule of any technology used in a business is that automation applied to an efficient operation will magnify the efficiency. The second is that automation applied to an inefficient operation will magnify the inefficiency.
>
> —BILL GATES

Depending on whose definition of the information technology (IT) market one uses, each year business managers and public officials spend globally between $1 and $2 trillion on new acquisitions of software, hardware, and services [1]. These expenditures do not include other outlays for using and maintaining these IT products or services, nor do they take into account the economic effects on a firm, let alone on an economy. In the case of the latter, using the United States as one large example, over two-thirds of all capital expenditures made in the 1990s went into IT. Economists were later able to establish that technology improved the nation's productivity by as much as 2–3% in some industries [2]. Additionally, with the increasing convergence of IT and telecommunications, one can reasonably assume that these figures are probably understated, yet there is no consensus about by how much. But clearly, management spends an enormous amount on IT and, therefore, is called upon to make many decisions about how to acquire and later dispose of IT products, services, and applications. Who makes the decision to acquire IT has been shifting over the past fifteen years too; today, it is not unusual for roughly two-thirds of all IT acquisitions to be made outside of the traditional CIO's organization and the "glass house" [3]. Very little research has been done on how nontechnical managers do, or should, make such decisions [4].

In prior chapters our discussion has centered on macro issues—the spread of computing around the world and how national governments encourage the use of IT across nations and economies—but in this chapter we turn our attention to the millions of decisions that translate the macro trends already discussed into tangible actions. This will not be an account of how computers and other IT and telecommunications were used, rather why they were selected and the considerations involved. Historical perspective helps today's business and government leaders make prudent decisions. For if there is anything we can draw from the $2 trillion dollars in institutional investments in IT, it is that managers must understand how best to make such acquisitions because there is too much money and too many potential consequences at stake to afford fundamental errors. That is why this chapter's subject is so crucial to the bigger story told in this book.

Nothing remains static, of course, and technology is emblematic of that reality. The subject of IT acquisitions has become more complicated over time as the variety of possible decisions has increased. In the period from the 1950s through the 1980s, most decisions centered on what hardware and software to acquire or make, and what uses of computing to embark upon. Timing correctly the adoption of some new technology became part of the decision process. In manufacturing industries, for example, moving from batch to online systems, replete with either hierarchical or, later, distributed database management software, drew considerable attention of data processing managers in the 1960s and 1970s [5]. For retail firms in the 1990s, the issue often centered on when and how to leverage the Internet [6]. Beginning in the 1970s, but becoming a major decision-making gale force in the 1990s, was the whole issue of whether or not to outsource management of a data center (or network) and, later, whole functions of a firm, such as customer and employee support for IT and myriad human resource and financial matters, a subject that actually grew in importance to management in the early years of the new century. In the past several years, we have seen yet a new aspect of IT acquisition decisions involving the emerging software as a service option. In short, the whole topic of acquisition/deacquisition remains murky and continues to evolve.

Historical evidence is increasingly demonstrating, however, that there are commonly exercised practices that IT experts and historians characterize as "best" and "bad," which today's managers and public officials can learn from as they make their decisions. By drawing upon examples, surveys, and anecdotal evidence gathered from over 35 industries' experiences over the past six decades in the United States, we can begin to identify these patterns of behavior. What is remarkable is that current practices related to how acquisitions of information technology and services have been made remain relatively consistent from one decade to another. The evidence is drawn from industry trade magazines, surveys conducted by industry associations and government agencies, and projects by consultants [7].

THE KINDS OF DECISIONS MADE BY MANAGERS

The historical record demonstrates that there is a set of decisions that are routinely made by managers but that vary in importance and emphasis over time. Table 4.1 illustrates the key types of decisions. The first involves acquisition of one of three categories of IT use: hardware, software, or services. These decisions can be com-

Table 4.1. Decisions made by managers

Type of decision	Spectrum of IT	Examples
Acquisition	Purchase of hardware or software; contracting for work	Purchase of PCs or servers; consultants to write software; funding a new application; buying an ERP tool
Outsourcing	IT decisions on vendor selection; IT work sent to another firm	Outsourcing decisions often made with help of consultants; moving processing to India
Deacquisition	Replacing old hardware and software; terminating a badly managed IT project; replacing an old use with a new one	Frequently done with machines over 3 years old; move to new software; canceling IT contracts due to new business models

bined into one decision or broken out into components. For example, it is not uncommon for companies to leave the acquisition of individual items to their IT organization, such as the purchase of a particular brand of PC, computer memory, or communications equipment. But over time, the services one might acquire from an outsourcer or specialized consultancy has been made by line management, with or without the collaboration of a CIO. The key example of this behavior from the 1990s was the wide adoption of ERP applications by manufacturing firms. On the other hand, the acquisition of infrastructure technologies and services were, and continue largely to be, the preserve of the CIO, such as what e-mail services to provide. This has particularly been the case for communications and Internet-based services, and, most recently, software to enhance the security of an organization's digital applications and records [8].

A second set of decisions involves whether or not to do work within the firm or agency. As technology improved in the 1980s and 1990s, IT innovations facilitated movement of data from one organization to another, making outsourcing of work increasingly more practical and cost-effective than in earlier years, particularly for companies. By the end of the 1990s, many large firms had had over a decade of considerable experience in sending work around the world [9]. Semiconductor firms designed chips in California but sent production plans to factories in East Asia. Insurance companies sent data entry activities to India or elsewhere, while telephone call centers scattered to Ireland, India, and to other countries where labor costs were lower than in the United States. Most industries participated in this movement in the 1990s and beyond, and largely in a successful manner [10].

Three circumstances facilitated this trend. First, the technology made it possible to run data centers in many countries, using the best practices for data centers developed over the period from the 1970s through the 1980s, when today's call center technologies and practices were essentially honed in the United States. Second, so long as there was a pool of English-speaking labor, one could set up quickly (within months) in another country. Over time, local firms could provide industry-specific services to American companies. Third, as the volume of work involving data management increased, so too could such work be outsourced to firms in other countries that were either less expensive or specialized. The most obvious historic and current example is the writing and maintenance of software. Microsoft's recently introduced new operating system, Vista, was written largely in India. A great deal of IBM's software often is too. Yet in both cases, decisions to do work in another nation were made by managers in the United States and Europe, and the end products were used in nearly 200 countries [11].

A third set of decisions, just now attracting the attention of managers and academics alike, involves the confederated enterprise that is, in effect, made up of a variety of legal entities scattered around an economy, various industries, and in different countries. Charles B. Handy and others had talked about the coming of these types of organizations made possible by IT as early as the 1970s, and they were certainly the topic of much conversation and limited experimentation in the 1980s and 1990s [12]. But with the rapidly evolving and robust capabilities made possible by the Internet and other forms of communications emerging in the late 1990s and beyond, senior managers could realistically begin considering how to build whole companies made up of parts of other firms [13]. Thus, the acquisition of IT once again became a "top-of-the-house" activity [14]. Early examples became legendary: Amazon.com taking orders for books and then letting publishers fulfill these, Charles Schwab & Company selling stock online, and eBay becoming the world's largest auction house or "garage sale." The examples are so numerous that one can reasonably conclude that no large or midsized firm today has ignored participation in this kind of IT-dependent activity in some fashion or another. These new business models represent a "hot" topic in corporate strategy and have been the subject of many recent studies and discussions, a process well underway [15].

Conversely, there have always been decisions about when to relinquish use of a particular class of IT, device, software, or service. Often, these decisions remained in the hands of the technologists working for the CIO, particularly those regarding when to replace an old computer or piece of software, or when to change IT vendors. But as these decisions became linked to corporate strategic imperatives, decision making shifted to line management and up the organizational ladder. For example, decisions by auto makers to integrate suppliers into their parts fulfillment processes and, later, design activities were not made by CIOs at any major firm. These were collaborative efforts involving senior design and manufacturing executives, whether at Toyota or at General Motors, and, to be sure, with the participation of senior IT executives and managers. Technologists described the possible, while line management drove the transformations [16]. Old uses of computing were changed in an evolutionary manner over time. For instance, providing production schedules for a factory was a batch job run overnight in the 1960s and 1970s with delivery of the next day's schedule of activities to a factory manager. These practices were evident in automotive firms, at manufacturers of home appliances and industrial equipment, and with their suppliers [17]. In the 1980s, this process went online and became a continuous-flow operation in most manufacturing industries, particularly in the automotive industry, for example [18]. In the 1990s, suppliers of components helped design new products and were able to provide considerable just-in-time and mass-customized short and long production runs [19]. By the early 2000s, extensive use of Internet-based ordering by customers of products drove the production schedules of increasingly numbers of manufacturers and their suppliers through much more complex IT-intensive supply chains that were cross-industry and global (see Figure 4.1).

In other words, decision making regarding acquisition and deacquisition of hardware, software, and applications moved from simply buying and disposing of old IT to increasingly complex, strategic decisions by line management. To be sure, IBM sales personnel still show up at IT glass houses to sell computers and software, Cisco worries about what telecommunications devices to introduce into the marketplace, and Microsoft battles advocates of open-source operating systems and Apple Computer's software too. But many firms have reached the point where hardly any of their executives or officials in a medium or large enterprise or public agency in the industrialized world can avoid for long par-

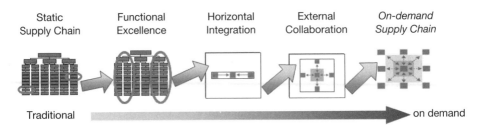

Figure 4.1. Supply chains.

ticipating in one of these four types of decisions regarding the use of IT.

The challenges faced by management in arriving at these decisions can be enormous. For example, when a firm has to replace an existing critical use of computing with a new one, should management attempt to shut down the old one on a Friday and go live the following Monday with a new one? This was the challenge many thought they might face when replacing old banking applications in the 1990s in response to the potential threat of Y2K. Bankers and brokers spent billions of dollars replacing most of their core software applications; they had no choice, government regulators demanded that their economies not stop functioning and that required financial sectors to get ready. They succeeded and there were hardly any problems, but many senior executives wondered if they were not betting on the success or failure of their firms in those critical years of 1997–1999 [21]. Often, CIOs and other technologists will liken transforming a major system to the act of changing a flat tire on a moving car. As a firm or agency became increasingly dependent on a use of computing for its core activities and, hence, its survival and economic success, transforming or improving IT-based applications and infrastructures in the face of available new IT tools became a major issue in the decision-making process. Today, this reality of not being able to stop the car to change a tire is nearly ubiquitous. The problem is often even more massive for a government agency that may have a larger number of transactions to conduct, such as tax collection or air traffic control, than a private firm. For them, the analogy is more realistically about changing tires on a large truck driven at a high speed.

TYPES OF JUSTIFICATION

Historically, there have been three types of justification for the use of IT. Although they may appear obvious, nonetheless they were never easy to make. Perhaps the most evident and the hardest-to-document results involved cost justification. For over a half-century, the most attractive form of justification was the use of IT to do work less expensively than before. In countries, industries, and firms with high labor costs or extensive use of manual procedures, this was normally the case. High labor costs in the United States, for example, led to mass automation of manufacturing in the automotive industry and to automated systems in the telephone industry to reduce the labor content of work. The more successful unions became in winning increased wage contracts, the more attractive automation became to management. The same applied to hardware; one machine was compared to another. It was not uncommon for every new generation of IT hardware to be anywhere from 5 to 20% less expensive to buy and use than the predecessor generation of equipment [22]. In addition, the newer devices usually had the added advantage of being more reliable, normally had more capacity to do more work, and operated faster [23]. This form of cost justification is always driven by the imperative of a department that "owns" the budget and responsibility for a particular IT machine, software, application, or support to contain costs while providing more capacity, such as an IT organization.

What management rarely did, however, was to go back after a decision had been implemented to determine if the benefits touted at decision time were realized. There is no empirical research on why that is the case. Yet, long experience in these matters would suggest several possibilities. First, a year or more would have gone by since the original decision had been made and budgets allocated and spent, so it becomes "water under the bridge." A second possibility is that often managerial turnover occurs during the postdecision period, leaving either the original decision maker or his or her successor unaccountable for delivering on promised results. Yet a third consideration is that such an analysis might be superfluous, either because circumstances had so changed that the original premise of a decision had become moot, or because one could not reverse the action if one wanted to do so. Many large U.S. and Western European government applications of technology fell into this category: the hundreds of procurement systems in the U.S. Department of Defense, tax filing systems at the U.S. Internal Revenue Service, the various criminal and crime tracking systems at the Federal Bureau of Investigation, and across Western Europe [24].

A second form of justification for the acquisition of IT involved the ability to do new things not possible before. The historical record indicates clearly that the majority of this class of decisions was an extension of the cost containment practices just discussed above. The vast majority of decisions to use IT over the past half-century were made in response to the desire of a firm, government agency, and many individual managers to control costs that were within their purview to manage. Entering new markets and offering new services and products were often of secondary consideration for companies, despite the fact that the vast and overwhelming volume of literature and attention to IT centered on new uses of IT to acquire additional customers, enter new markets, or to offer additional services. To be sure, these latter activities occurred often enough in spectacular fashion, but they were often initially a secondary by-product of the original decision process. Most decisions centered first on cost containment. In many instances, it was only after that had occurred that new capabilities became incrementally possible to implement, which in turn led to new products and offerings. We can class this phenomenon under the heading of positive unintended consequences or as an extension of classic path dependency [25].

But before discussing that latter circumstance in more detail, it is important to understand the cost-containment issue further. When a new technology appeared, it became possible to do things less expensively while simultaneously begin adjusting one's business model. In the late 1960s, online order taking became possible, thanks to new systems and improved communications, allowing firms to take orders 24 × 7 days. Another round of improvement in that capability surfaced in the late 1990s and early 2000s using the Internet, making available even richer offerings, often with less labor than the original order processing applications. In the 1970s, to order clothing from the retailer Land's End, for instance, one still had to talk to an employee; two decades later, that was not necessary. A customer could simply go to the firm's website, see graphical representations of its products as good as what it had presented for years in its catalogs, and order quickly online without necessarily talking with an employee. Airlines became some of the most extensive users of this application, essentially decimating within a decade a great deal of the travel agency business in the United States and in large parts of Europe [26].

Third, there is the strategic decision whereby someone concludes that a novel use of IT makes possible a new offering or business model, building on existing functions. It is an incremental approach that essentially answers the question, "Now that I have this installed and paid for, what else can I do with it?" This question is more than simply renting out excess capacity or becoming an outsourcer for someone else's work. This is about what new things could be done since they had an installed technology and understood deeply its strengths and weaknesses. For example, many companies created websites with information about their products in the late 1990s [27]. When software next became available by the end of the decade that could ensure secure transactions, these programs began making it possible for customers to order products online, while directing employees to conduct internal transactions, using intranet channels, such as for processing expense reimbursement requests. In both instances, additional applications and functions were added over time [28]. The same occurred with the use of technologies at a personal level: first, the big PC on one's desk with some distributed processing, laptops next, blackberries third, and now even smaller devices such as the current generation of high-function cell phones. At the same time, the labor of expensive professional classes of workers (fashionably called knowledge workers) was replaced by ever-lower-paid clerks with inexpensive technologies, such as cell phones and hand-held wands for inventory control [29].

MANAGERIAL PRACTICES

What seems to work well most of the time for most managers and their firms and government agencies? Do sixty years of decision making about what to acquire and why to acquire it reflect some best practices? Although the concept of "best practices" is subject to many definitions, for our purposes these are practices generally preferred by managers, not necessarily those validated later by business professors, historians, or economists as necessarily the most effective. The reason for relying on this definition is because most managers would not have significant insight from those other students of business and public administration practices when making decisions, only their own personal experiences and those of others around them with whom they interacted on a daily basis, such as colleagues within their firms, industries, agencies, and associations, or among the vendors who were persuading them to take one action or another. With that definition in mind, the answer in general to the two questions is yes, that several practices satisfied the largest number of managers over time across all industries, at least in the United States and in Western Europe.

First, managers preferred to invest in IT and to implement new applications in an incremental fashion. This practice often flew in the face of the vast literature of the past half-century that tended to tout such things as "blown to bits," or urged managers to create a "revolution." Consultants, professors, reporters, and vendors all talked about the need for radical change either to be implemented or underway [30]. But managers normally did, and do, the exact opposite. They incrementally changed existing IT and work processes for two reasons [31]. First, they often had to fund these changes within the confines of their budgets; to ask for more funding either was out of scope with their responsibilities or just required too much work going through the bureaucracy of their firm or government department (or even legislature). Start-up firms often talked about how simple it was to make decisions, to take actions without the bureaucracy that made larger firms move too slowly.

To be sure, there is a substantial managerial literature that documented the general appetite of managers to make incremental decisions, of not wishing to take large risks, and to focus on internal operations, particularly in times of uncertainty. The historical record for IT confirms that this preference of management applied as well to decisions involving technology [32]. But because of the constant turnover of decision makers in IT, what the academic literature assures us is normal and well understood does not necessarily reflect the reality of the daily work of managers. There is little evidence to suggest that managers, for example, understand what the managerial literature would advise them to do.

Second, there were personal and market risks that could result from a failed project. It was one thing to make a mistake in selecting the wrong $700 laptop to buy; it was quite another to take on a complex ERP application that could cost the corporation millions of dollars in overruns and disgruntled employees or customers [33]. Similar personal risks exist for public officials. Furthermore, it was not always obvious what the next big thing might be that one should embrace.

As a result, managers made continuous incremental changes to their uses of IT. The results they achieved proved cumulative, because as one moved from a decision to a second one, the later was based on the circumstances prevailing after the first one had been implemented. Every new release of an operating system or software of an existing application, for example, reflected that process. Most of the process improvement work of the 1990s and early 2000s also reflected that cumulative consequence [34]. Mundane decision making and implementation were almost always forgotten but, when looking back, it seemed that a manager could conclude that over the previous decade, "we made a revolution." Figure 4.2 graphically presents the process of incremental improvements affecting cumulatively the results of management's decision making, suggesting the existence and nature of a continuous progression of changes and the role of effects.

Third, managers overwhelmingly prefer to make decisions in support of improving internal operations. Once again, I want to stress that this practice stands in sharp contrast to the publicly accepted wisdom that IT can be used most effectively to create new markets and opportunities or to better serve citizens. Although that is in fact often possible, management finds that their more controllable actions and needs revolve around the issue of improving existing internal operations to improve productivity and lower operating costs. As economic historians are beginning to point out, the world went awash with excess capacity of goods and services after about 1975, which drove down costs and prices, putting pressure on profits not seen before in modern times, indeed not since the eighteenth century. Yet the need for profits had not withered. These circumstances forced management to hunt for profit more than for revenue, a process still un-

Figure 4.2. Process of incremental improvements versus cumulative change.

folding because the circumstances that created the overcapacity (something one can blame many technologies for facilitating) has not yet played out [35].

There were two by-products of this process. The first and most obvious was that productivity increased. While economists were debating the "productivity paradox" in the 1990s, managers were busily investing record amounts in IT. By the early 2000s, it had become quite clear that many American, Western Europe, South Korean, and Japanese firms had become some of the most productive in the world, enjoying the cumulative impact of prior decades' investments in IT and the effects of newer forms of technology, such as the Internet and more portable devices [36].

The second effect was that as internal operations improved (i.e., modernized and automated) they became increasingly similar from firm to firm, what management called best practices. It is not completely clear if the same occurred in public administration; however, officials all over the world expressed a keen interest in the managerial practices of the private sector. Figure 4.3 illustrates the historic trend. In those industries where common operational and business models were important, such a trend proved positive, as occurred in banking, for example, where banks had to share information about transactions (e.g., check cashing), or where suppliers and their customers had to collaborate (e.g., sharing common product databases in the automotive industry). It is no accident, for example, that such large firms as Wal-Mart and

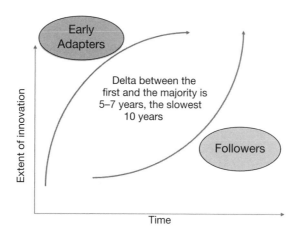

Figure 4.3. Adoption patterns of common practices.

General Motors imposed common practices, standards, and even software tools and databases on their suppliers.

How should one respond to the counterargument that management is also able to make bold IT decisions that are not incremental or focused on cost containment? Are those bad practices? The examples of Wal-Mart making use of IT central to its growth strategies for over a quarter of a century, from deployment of massive and effective inventory management systems to the most recent requirement of its suppliers to start using radio-frequency identification technologies (RFID), is currently an exception, a case (RFID) of a way of operating that is possibly an example of what might become common at some time in the future, but is not today. History is replete with examples of firms taking bold steps in IT that are successful and, thus, these kinds of decisions are not bad practices. They are simply options and exceptions to what is more properly the norm. It is why so many writers like to discuss them, following the reporter's time-honored notion that "man bites dog" is more newsworthy than "dog bites man." Yet even in the example of Wal-Mart, these applications of IT were created, expanded, and modified in an incremental fashion over the course of three decades, thus aligning with the pattern of adoption described in this chapter.

Extant evidence suggests that so far the best results from making inward looking operational improvements returned more positive economic consequences to a greater number of firms in aggregate than using technology to go out and acquire new customers. This does not mean that using technology to expand markets was a bad move; it normally could be a good one, but results often generated incremental expansion. When a new technology finally comes on stream that is effective, then the proverbial "everyone" seemed to adopt it quickly as a market multiplier, with the result that such a move became the minimum price of admission to the new market. ATMs illustrated this effect. In the late 1960s, one bank in New York installed ATMs and it proved quite popular with customers. Within a very few years all banks in the United States were busy at work installing ATMs, soon afterwards incrementally linking whole networks of ATMs across multiple banking corporations, and by the dawn of the new century, these morphed into international networks. By the early 1990s, if a retail bank did not have ATM offerings, it could not compete in many of the OECD nations [37]. Bar coding in the grocery and later other retail industries in the United States is also an instructive example of the process at work after ATMs [38]. We are seeing the process at work again with how the recorded music industry has to provide music through downloads and how television companies have to make their programming available on portable devices that pull in content from the Internet [39].

Looking inward to determine what technologies and applications to embrace makes sense to many managers, because tangible results expected from such decisions can best be understood by looking at internal operations. This is a function of the fact that managers know their own departments and processes better than the vagaries and generalities of the marketplace. They also have more control over what their employees do than over their customers' activities. Managers can meet internal expectations a great deal easier than they can predict the actions of customers. Additionally, most employees in a company do not have direct responsibility for dealing with customers, and so are held accountable for only improving the functions of their department or set of tasks.

SOME POSSIBLE LESS EFFECTIVE PRACTICES

Do managers make IT decisions that one can characterize as bad practices? Indeed, the historical record is replete with examples. Five of the most common are cataloged in Table 4.2.

The first is to acquire IT because it is fashionable. It is first because it was the initial one in evidence in various industries across the American economy and has remained in practice. In the 1950s, the notorious cases consisted of firms that acquired computers with tape drives whirling away behind glass windows and made sure that everyone walking into their building could see how "modern" the firm was. As security problems mounted in the 1960s and 1970s, these "glass houses" went underground or behind concrete walls. But the rationale for acquiring IT because "everyone else is doing it" remains with us. Today, "everyone," it seems, has to have a website. But if there are not specific, rational business reasons for having one, then not having a website might make sense too. If a manager understands why he or she needs a particular technology or use, then the chances are much better that the results will be positive. During the Clinton Administra-

Table 4.2. Bad IT practices

Type of bad decision	Spectrum in IT	Examples
Buying because of fashion	Applications; outsourcing just to save labor costs	ERP systems; sending IT call centers to India
Adopting a best practice "as is"	Type of hardware, software, process with software	A software programming method; a manufacturing technique used by a rival as well
Avoiding total cost of computing considerations	Multiple incremental decisions by device or department	Capital purchases without consideration of maintenance of hardware; applies also to software
Failing to link IT to business objectives	Networking, standards, hardware and software; operational practices	Multiple incompatible networks, software, and hardware
Keeping IT too long	Hardware and software	PCs that cannot support wireless use; old releases of software no longer supported by the vendor

tion, all U.S. federal agencies were told to get on the Internet and they dutifully did so. The result was that some were relatively useless sites with minimal or outdated information and were not improved to the extent of others which had been created for the express purpose of delivering information and services to specific audiences relevant to the agency. Successful examples of having good reasons and good results are the websites created by the U.S. Internal Revenue Service (IRS) [40].

A second possible bad practice is a variant of the first: adopting a use because it has become a best practice in one's industry. It has been well understood now for well over a decade that a "best practice" does not mean one should simply implement exactly what some other firm has done [41]. No two enterprises are quite the same. A bad practice in most circumstances is simply lifting a practice "as is" from another firm and putting it into one's own, regardless of technology or industry. Every good idea that emerges first in another firm is worthy of attention but must be implemented in a form that is suited to the particular circumstances of the second enterprise. That is a good practice [42]. An example of a bad practice is described in the next paragraph.

For many years, implementing Japanese-style employee-suggestion processes in American companies proved quite popular, but most of them failed. Japanese firms had for decades received over a dozen suggestions per year per employee, so their IT-supported suggestion processes reflected that reality. Americans, on the other hand, submitted suggestions at the rate of less than 10 per 100 employees, in other words, hardly at all. So, elegant suggestion systems were dropped into these American companies in the 1990s at great cost but with no significant improvements in the rate of suggestions submitted by employees. Proper preparation of employees and attention to changing the culture of American firms with respect to submitting suggestions for how to improve operations were rarely implemented in an effective manner [43].

A third practice seen as less than optimal, and that seems never to go away, is to avoid recognizing that a decision will have long-term operational and budgetary implications that should be thought thoroughly about and at least recognized at the time it is made. Often, the cost of operating a new piece of equipment or software is left out of the decision-making equation for myriad reasons: ignorance, budgetary constraints, because support comes from another department or division, and so forth. The notion touted by IT experts of calculating the "total cost of computing" is rarely implemented. There are very few documented examples of comprehensive analysis being done either in the private or public sectors. What exists are considerable numbers of examples of what does not occur. For instance, one of the largest collections of negative IT "war stories" can be found in the hundreds of case studies prepared by the U.S. General Accountability Office, an audit arm of the U.S. Congress, which goes into government agencies to study troubled operations, including IT decisions [44]. Invariably, they note the due respect agencies give to examining private-sector best practices, use of private-sector consultants, relying on the wisdom and experience of public subject area experts, and so forth, but then invariably made narrowly focused decisions that did not take into account the complexity of a project, how long it would take, its cost, and, of course, the lack of sufficient long-term managerial oversight to make sure expectations were achieved. Other examples can be found in the private sector and in public agencies in other countries, so the problem is not limited to American agency heads and their IT staffs.

A fourth decision-making bad practice involves not linking effectively an IT decision to the overall business objectives of the enterprise or agency. This can take many forms. In a state or provincial government, it could be favoring a vendor who politically supports the party in power, bypassing the local formal procurement practice, thus leading to possible decisions not in the best interest of the organization. It could be that decisions are made to acquire equipment and software that are incompatible with the overall objective of the institution to be able to communicate across multiple systems to share information; an incompatible e-mail system within a firm or public institution is a notorious and wide-spread example [45]. It can be implementing a technology whose life is about to come to an end, to be replaced by the next generation of cheaper, faster, and better devices or software. This error, which happens often although there are no formal studies about how often, is often carried out in response to a near fire sale of an older technology. Nothing will bring terror into the heart of an IT manager faster than being the last person to install a piece of equipment coming off a production line because, in very short order, the manufacturer will stop supporting that product, new software will probably not run on it, performance will degrade, and residual values of the hardware will drop faster than the depreciation schedule they were put on in agreement with the accounting department.

One final bad practice involves organizations relying on an IT product or software for too long. Often, the problem a manager faces is that an installed application is working in some reasonable fashion and its replacement cost is either not in the budget or the effort to replace it would distract staff away from other urgent business at hand. From a financial perspective, it is very much the story of someone whispering into the decision maker's ear, "Let's squeeze one more year of profits out of this one." The problem is normally well understood in business circles regarding what platforms to be on or not, such as when to move from vinyl records to tape, to CD, to DVD, or from one video format to another. Taking action is another matter. Stay too long on the old technical platform, product, or format and one is leapfrogged by a competitor who cannot subsequently be overtaken. The same rules of behavior apply to IT used by a firm. Stay too long with an application or technology and the hurdle to the most current one may be insurmountable [46]. This happened to many small regional telephone companies in the United States, for example. They were overwhelmed by the regional Bell companies or more aggressive local firms, such as TDS in the Midwest and now operating also in New England and in the South [47].

The problem of staying with a technology or its use too long is a chronic problem across many, if not most, government agencies, particularly those that were early adopters of a technology or use. They face several major challenges. First, the use may be so massive, involving literally millions of users and transactions, that just the act of moving from one use to another is daunting, if not nearly impossible. Automated tax processing systems and university-wide grade management applicsations are examples. A second problem is that the necessary decision making, budgeting, and project planning may take so long that in the process agency heads change, political administrations transform, and the financial wherewithal of a legislature shifts too. This is not about incompetent public administrators at work, but rather about structural attributes of government that make it difficult to make changes in a timely fashion with adequate resources applied to the effort.

Implicit in each of these situations of less than optimal behaviors is the notion that a detachment exists between well-grounded business objectives and IT acquisitions. It is a canon of managerial practice that decisions should always be made in support of an organization's strategy and objectives. It is also universally recognized that personal and departmental agendas and self-interests conflict with the larger objectives of the enterprise. So, can we ask why some IT decisions appear irrational within the context of the mantra that all decisions should be made in direct support of an enterprise's objectives? Although there are so few formal studies of the question, one can postulate several possibilities. The most pervasive is the fact that enterprises and government departments and agencies are ecological systems, made up of various communities within an organization, much like neighborhoods in a city. Observers of corporate cultures and enterprises and of public administration have embraced this view for over a quarter of a century [48]. The emergence of the "extended enterprise" in the past decade or more as both a notion and a reality simply reinforces the view that corporations are not highly disciplined, organized entities as one has been led to believe [49]. In such an eclectic environment, the reader could reasonably expect that decision makers will be motivated economically, socially, and from a career development perspective to make short-term decisions that are personally of immediate advantage to them and to their part of the enterprise in the short term. This is exactly what happens more often than not. Furthermore, this occurs at every level of management. The manager deciding what PCs to acquire for his department would make one decision, for example, to buy Apple computers for a graphics department, while the rest of the firm doing standard business computing chose Dell PCs and Microsoft products. A division-level CIO might make decisions in support of her own division's best interests, while a senior vice president would take into consideration the needs of a yet larger proportion of the enterprise.

To combat this parochialism, for at least three decades senior management has implemented two fundamental strategies, most frequently in the private sector in large enterprises. The first, which became evident initially in the late 1960s, involved promoting data processing management to higher positions in the organization, leading to the latter's evolution into management information systems (MIS) executives, and later into chief information officers (CIOs). In the 1980s, it was fashionable to have the lead MIS executive report to the CEO of the firm. In many organizations, that proved to be overkill, because the lead IT executive was involved in too many operational details to warrant diverting attention of the CEO and so, by the 1990s, one saw CIOs relegated down one notch in the organizational reporting structure. Today, CIOs exist at multiple levels in an enterprise and government departments, and rarely report directly to the most senior executive in a firm or cabinet-level unit of government [50]. A second strategy has been to create a council of CIOs to share ideas, define standards, and make collective decisions. This practice is today widespread in the largest enterprises and government agencies. For example, the U.S. Department of Defense and the U.S. Department of Homeland Security each has such a council. They make decisions affecting the work of the two largest departments of the American government, each of which has as many people working for them as the number of residents in some U.S. states and manage budgets that are bigger than some national GDPs [51].

The point is that perceived "bad" practices are not usually irrational when considered from the perspective of an individual manager or organization operating within the confines of one's own ecology that rewards optimization of an individual's role within the ecosystem of one's company or government. That system of rewarding individual performance is such a hallmark of corporate culture in so many countries that it need not detain us here [52]. These practices, however, can be seen as sometimes not as effective as others. For example, simply porting over into one's organization a practice from another organization without any alteration to fit the specific cultural and operational dynamics of one's firm, is not irrational, it is simply not effective [53].

SPECIAL ROLE OF INDUSTRIES

Industry associations, publications, and colleagues doing similar work often influence decision makers to such an extent that their role in affecting the behavior of management has to be acknowledged. Traditionally, one thinks of the vendor as being the major source of influence on how decisions are made [54]. However, the role of industries increasingly needs to be taken into account because the historical record points to a large body of activities carried on within an industry that does three things: stimulates demand for specific uses of IT, sets expectations as to what results one should receive for using a specific technology, and describes how to arrive at such decisions to acquire IT. For example, through its various publications and conferences, the American Banking Association (ABA) discusses emerging uses of IT, and has for over a half century. It routinely publishes case studies of how various companies have successfully implemented some new use, particularly through its flagship publication, *ABA Banking Journal,* for over a half-century [55]. In the life insurance industry, LOMA has done the same thing in essentially the same way.

My examination of over 50 trade journals in some 45 American industries found no exceptions to this practice of presenting IT as a positive, innovative initiative from one decade to the next. These publications constantly celebrated such decisions to acquire IT by publishing articles naming firms and specific managers who did this. Firms lent themselves to this kind of publicity as a way of promoting the image of their management and company as progressive and modern. Annual conferences of the key industry associations routinely have sessions on emerging applications and technologies. These are normally well attended and do provide frameworks, guidelines, examples, and information in support of IT decision making. One cannot help but conclude that these activities, so pervasive in American business and increasingly in East Asian and European economies, are effective and indeed welcome sources of help to managers. This has particularly been the case in more recent years as the percent of IT acquisition decisions have shifted from IT organizations to management in the lines of business.

In a related manner, as the number of managers who have personal experience in adopting or using IT increases, their experience within an industry or firm influences more explicitly their decision making. In the 1970s and 1980s, there were few senior American or European executives outside the computer industry who had ever made a decision to acquire computing. By the end of the century it was difficult to imagine anyone becoming a senior executive without having run a line of business and, thus, having made such decisions as to acquire an ERP system, for instance, and, equally so, having had to be the line executive responsible for its successful implementation. Today, it is not uncommon for executives to make IT decisions that tactically make sense to them in support of widely accepted industry practices or the strategy of their firm. That trend is consistent with the growing body of evidence that management is behaving in observable ways similar to colleagues throughout their industry [56].

As Figure 4.4 illustrates, one can now begin to track behavior by industry. The composite evidence drawn from the experiences of over three dozen American industries suggests common patterns of behavior that have worked in general for most companies and agencies over the past six decades. In this instance, Figure 4.4 illustrates that as the extent of collaboration of firms within an industry increases, such as sharing data or serving as partners or suppliers to one another, the greater the dialogue and cooperation that occurs, which, from an IT perspective, requires greater adherence to industry technical standards for data formats, telecommunications, reporting, and so forth. The greater the demand for such collaboration, the more necessary it becomes for some third-party organization to serve as the intermediary facilitating such coordinated activities. Often, these are established industry organizations and their publications, such as APICS, ABA, and LOMA, to mention a few. Each quadrant of the figure reflects patterns of be-

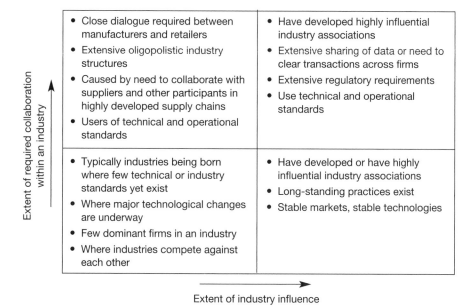

Figure 4.4. Patterns of behavior as industry influence increases.

havior evident as collaboration and industry influence increase in intensity. When one takes the behavior reflected in these quadrants and overlays them on any particular firm's IT decisions, one begins to see those behaviors affecting decisions. This observation should be of no surprise because as the dependence on IT increases over time, and as IT becomes more embedded in the processes and strategies of a firm, one should expect that these broad, nontechnical business considerations would affect decisions regarding the acquisition, change, and disposal of IT artifacts and applications.

PATH FORWARD

What are the lessons for management going forward? As Figure 4.5 illustrates, taking the same quadrants as in Figure 4.4, we can document specific considerations management can take into account as they make decisions within the broader context of the industry and, hence, markets in which they function. Although these recommendations are largely aimed at the private sector, public insti-

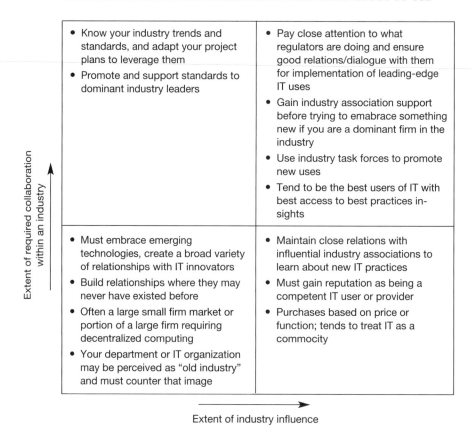

Figure 4.5. Industry influenced managerial actions.

tutions have much to learn from these as well. These suggestions reflect many practices deployed positively across many firms today, as documented anecdotally in the numerous case studies and examples reported on within the industry press or in the thousands of pages of marketing case studies produced by such firms as IBM, Accenture, Hewlett-Packard, and others.

To be sure, there are exceptions, such as innovative startups, but they are not the norm. The historical truth remains that the constellation of dominant and midlevel firms in any industry tend to behave roughly the same across many dimensions, or have been the key players for a long time [57]. Besides, many of the innovators are eventually absorbed into the more established players. This is particularly the case, for example, in the pharmaceutical industry, which is experiencing fundamental changes caused by the new science of genomics [58], continuously in software, of course, and increasingly in telecommunications, management consulting, and across the entire financial sector. Note, however, that everything described in this chapter is based on the American experience. Extant evidence does not allow us to extrapolate with confidence about what is happening in Europe or East Asia, for example.

Elsewhere, I have argued that almost all industries are moving to a post-Second or Third Industrial Revolution style of operation on the way to an emerging protodigitally dependent style of doing work [59]. Space does not permit a detailed discussion of that fundamental transformation. However, briefly put, the idea is that IT has made new business models a reality, along with novel ways of doing work. The move from mass production to mass customization was merely one early and small manifestation of this transformation; the myriad uses of the Internet are collectively another more profound example of the type of changes underway. We are in what appears to be in the early stages of this transformation. However, the key point to make is that decision making about the acquisition of IT is routine and integrated into the activities of most managers and of all firms, because no major work function today operates without some IT content. Increasingly as well, decisions and points of emphasis for management are also becoming global. One can see this in the decisions made by multinational firms attempting to become global enterprises [60], and by industry associations and NGOs setting globalized standards for operations.

There are several recommendations for management that suggest ways forward in how they make decisions regarding IT.

First, a decision maker should understand how firms in one's industry acquire IT and why. They should understand the historical perspective and also observe and understand why something is an effective practice.

Second, leverage industry associations to acquire insights about some of the better uses of IT within one's own industry. This approach is particularly effective in determining current and anticipated trends and up-to-date sources of economic benefit of using technologies of all kinds, not just computing or telecommunications.

Third, while accepting the realities of currently installed technologies and applications, what is normally called path dependence, make decisions within a context of some forward-looking plan that anticipates the strategic and operational realities of the firm over the next five to ten years.

Fourth, understand what is going on in other industries. One's industry magazines often report on trends as if they had not arrived earlier in other industries. The historical record demonstrates overwhelmingly that the future arrives at different times in different industries. For example, bar coding as a concept arrived first in railroading to track cars but failed (1960s). The grocery industry had a task force that found and liked it, and asked companies such as IBM and NCR to improve on the concept (1980s). That is why we have the bar codes today in all industries.

Fifth, remember that hype always comes before reality. Over the past half-century, it has not been uncommon for industry proponents and vendors to promote use of a new technology or application four to seven years before an industry adopted it. The evidence from historical experience does not suggest that being "first" is bad, just risky, and unless there is a compelling business case for doing that, and a plan to mitigate risks, one should understand where they are in the adoption cycle before engaging. In some cases, it makes sense to be a laggard and in others, a rapid adopter, and in yet other instances the leader. Because those three conditions are so strategic, they would require separate treatment apart from this chapter.

As Figure 4.6 catalogs, there are some historical lessons and advice for decision makers. There are those who want to be first with an application, such as the financial institution that installed the first ATM in America or Great Britain, and those who want to follow closely behind, such as most banks. On one extreme end of the decision spectrum are the "heat seekers," the decision makers who have the most novel ways of using IT, or more frequently tend to be the first in their industry with a new device, software, or application. Historically, about 10% of all customers of IT products and services fall into this category and they work in all industries and at all levels of management. The vast majority of decision makers are followers behind the heat seekers, who have for various reasons come to the conclusion that being first does not make sense. One should not assume, however, that this strategy is bad; many reasons can account for this behavior, ranging from regulatory constraints, as the U.S. brokerage industry experienced in the 1980s when it sought to provide banking services, to the relative expense of new versus older technologies or costs of transformation. However, there is also a small minority that does not change IT so much and thus make the fewest IT decisions. Being the last nearly always conveys no economic advantage and is not an effective business strategy [61]. So timing, while not "everything," is nonetheless an important factor one should take into account when making any decision to embrace a technology or new application.

Figure 4.6 is not a list of recommendations proven to be effective for either group; rather, it catalogs actions by each that one normally sees. Extant evidence does not necessarily demonstrate that one action or another is more or less effective. Rather, we see all these behaviors. These behaviors are subsets of actions taken within the broader contexts of those described throughout this chapter and are mentioned because they are sufficiently evident so that they cannot be ignored as part of the managerial landscape. There have been many studies on the strategic value and costs of being first-entrant or follower enterprises, but Figure 4.6 is about the style of performance of individuals, not firms. If either of these styles characterize the behavior of a senior official, then that style might or might not characterize firm-wide activity. For example, one can reasonably conclude that Steve Jobs at Apple Computer

Heat Seekers:
- Buy in increments, frequently
- Minimize risks of decisions
- Buy features and functions of IT
- Reinforce progressive nature of decision
- Leverage industry trends
- Stay current on technology and trends
- Think biggest firms can afford to be "out there"
- Personal relationships mean everything, such as trust in the unknown and the untried
- Leverage industry and application knowledge
- Checking references is not so critical, although still useful, especially if from another industry
- First on their block to acquire a new IT

Followers:
- Buy in increments, frequently
- Minimize risks of decisions
- Buy productivity; cost justifies everything
- Value practicality of an option
- Rely less on industry trends, but do not ignore them
- Feel less need to stay current on technology
- Think smaller firms can't risk bleeding-edge IT
- Personal relations not as important as a sound business case
- Leverage industry and application knowledge
- Rely on references from their own and other industries
- Lag in acquiring new IT

Figure 4.6. Patterns of behavior of early adapters versus followers.

has more often than not behaved like an effective "heat seeker," with outstanding results accruing to his company [62], but that behavior is an exception. The key observation is that within all firms one can find both kinds of individual managers who are simultaneously making decisions about the role of IT. They are part of the mix that reinforces the observation of so many management experts that an enterprise or government agency is a community, an ecological system controlled by individuals with various styles of management.

The final recommendation to management that appears in almost every book that has ever been written on the effective use of IT calls for measuring results. Given all the complexity of decision making and various styles of management, what is to be done about the nagging bad habit of managers of not auditing the results expected from some new use of IT? This is not the place to analyze the reasons for that failure, but there is an action one can take so that an audit of benefits received does not have to be conducted. In some companies, IBM being one of them, an action can be taken when a decision maker is presented with a business case for doing something new with IT and is given to believe that an operating cost will decline as a result of using the technology, and that the benefits would flow over the course of some period of time in which action can be taken. The manager making a decision can agree with the statement of benefits and then simply reduce the requester's budget by the amount of savings promised to take affect in those time periods that the business case said they would. Conversely, if the benefits involved are increased quantities of new revenue, financial targets can be adjusted upward beyond what they might otherwise have been to reflect what should be the new cash inflows. Either action places the onus on the requester of additional IT to achieve the targets described in their business case. This tactic is simple, works, and is also very unpopular with requesters.

IT has become part and parcel of what managers deal with on a regular basis. Learning how to acquire, use, and discard IT is as much a central part of how they learn their trade as understanding accounting, human resource management, and business law. It is part of the emerging postindustrial style of management. If we can predict anything with confidence, it is that managers not only will make IT acquisition decisions in the years to come, but probably more of them will be increasingly critical to their personal and their enterprise's success. That is why it is so essential for managers to understand deeply how to acquire, modify, and dispose of IT and services based on these technologies. Appreciating some patterns from historical experience is a first step.

When we combine the work of private sector management and public officials, we can begin to see social change accumulating, much as one can see the process at work within organizations. The next chapter is intended to discuss whether or not we are entering an information age and begins to suggest milestones and markers to help both executives and public officials judge the progress they are making in optimizing their markets, economies, and societies through the use of IT.

NOTES AND REFERENCES

1. IBM market intelligence; but similar data is routinely reported by IDG and Forrester, among others.
2. First reported in Daniel E. Sichel, *The Computer Revolution: An Economic Perspective*, Washington, DC: Brookings Institution Press, 1997.
3. Based on internal IBM market data, 1995 to present.
4. For an early pioneering work, see Peter Weill and Jeanne W. Ross, *IT Governance: How Top Performers Manage IT Decision Rights for Superior Results*, Boston, MA: Harvard Business School Press, 2004, pp. 25–56.
5. For a sense of the issues faced, see David F. Noble, *Forces of Production: A Social History of Industrial Automation*, New York: Oxford University Press, 1986; Gideon Halevi, *The Role of Computers in Manufacturing Processes*, New York: Wiley, 1980.
6. U.S. Department of Commerce, *The Economic and Social Impact of Electronic Commerce*, Washington, DC: U.S. GPO, 1998; and *The Emerging Digital Economy II*, Washington, DC: US. GPO, 1999.
7. Reported in considerable detail in three volumes, James W. Cortada, *The Digital Hand*, New York: Oxford University Press, 2004–2008.
8. *Computerworld* has routinely been reporting on the interest in security software since the turn of the century, as have all U.S. industry IT magazines and newspapers.
9. The most mature example at an industry level is the experience of semiconductor manufacturing firms. See Cortada, *Digital Hand,* vol. 1, pp. 197–207.
10. Described in considerable detail on an industry-by-industry basis in the first two volumes of Cortada, *The Digital Hand.* There is no history as yet of the role of industry associations affecting the role of IT, but it has been mentioned briefly. See, for example, JoAnne Yates, *Structuring the Information Age: Life Insurance and Technology in the Twentieth Century*, Baltimore, MD: Johns Hopkins University Press, 2005, pp. 82, 87, 128–129, 217–218.

11. For an introduction to the subject, see Anthony P. D'Costa and E. Sridharan, *India in the Global Software Industry: Innovation, Financial Strategies and Development*, New York: Palgrave Macmillan, 2006.

12. See, for example, see an early work by Charles B. Handy, *Understand Organizations*, Baltimore, MD: Pengiun Books, 1976; and then his most influential study, *The Age of Unreason*, Boston, MA: Harvard Business School Press, 1989.

13. Many observers were commenting, such as Don Tapscott in a series of books, but see *The Digital Economy: Promie and Peril In the Age of Networked Intelligence*, New York: McGraw-Hill, 1996; and more recently Tapscott with Anthony D. Williams, *Wikinomics*, New York: Portfolio, 2007.

14. Once again, because when computers first appeared, they were so expensive that often the president, chairman or board of directors had to make the "acquire, don't acquire" decision, a circumstance that prevailed into the 1980s. In federal agencies, such projects often even required U.S. Congressional action, such as the acquisition of computing by the Internal Revenue Service in every decade since the early 1960s.

15. The *California Management Review, Harvard Business Review,* and other journals have published on this theme over the past five years, while the Harvard Business School press publishes books annually on the topic.

16. Kurt Hoffman and Raphael Kplinsky, *Driving Force: The Global Restructuring of Technology, Labour, and Investment in the Automobile and Components Industries*, Boulder, CO: Westview Press, 1988.

17. Gideon Halevi, *The Role of Computers in Manufacturing Processes*, New York: Wiley, 1980.

18. Well described by Steven L. Goldaman, Roger N. Nagel, and Kenneth Preiss, *Agile Competitors and Virtual Organizations*, New York: VNR, 1995; and by Rebecca Morales, *Flexible Production: Restructuring the International Automobile Industry*, Cambridge, UK: Polity Press, 1994.

19. B. Joseph Pine II, *Mass Customization: The New Frontier in Business Competition*, Boston, MA: Harvard Business School Press, 1999, paperback ed..

20. Karen Butner and Derek Moore, *Building Value in Logistics Outsourcing*, Somers, NY: IBM Corporation, 2006.

21. Lauren Bielski, "Did Y2K Deep Freeze Data Processing?" *ABA Banking Journal* 91 (May 1999), pp. 38–41.

22. Gerald W. Brock, *The Second Information Revolution,* Cambridge, MA: Harvard University Press, 2003, pp. 92–95.

23. Discussed in a series of contributed papers in William H. Dutton, et al., *Transforming Enterprises: The Economic and Social Implications of Information Technology*, Cambridge, MA: MIT Press, 2005.

24. Described in considerable detail in Cortada, *The Digital Hand*, vol. 3.

25. Articulated recently for two IT industries by Alfred D. Chandler, Jr., *Inventing The Electronic Century: The Epic Story of the Consumer Electronics and the Computer Science Industries,* New York: Free Press, 2001.

26. Jeffrey R. Yost, "Internet Challenges for Nonmedia Idustries, Firms, and Workers: Travel Agencies, Mortgage Brokers, Personal Computer Manufac-

turers, and Information Technology Services," in William Aspray and Paul Ceruzzi (Eds.), *Internet and American Business*, Cambridge, MA: MIT Press, 2008, pp. 317–326.

27. Described in considerable detail in William Aspray and Paul Ceruzzi (Eds.), *Internet and American Business*, Cambridge, MA: MIT Press, 2008.

28. Ibid.

29. Mizuko Ito, Daisuke Okabe, and Misa Matsuda (Eds.), *Personal, Portable, Pedestrian: Mobile Phones in Japanese Life*, Cambridge, MA: MIT Press, 2005, offers an excellent example of these kinds of studies, with bibliography.

30. Titles from the period suggested the strident hype: *Blown to Bits* by Philip Evans and Thomas S. Wurster, Boston, MA: Harvard Business School Press, 1999; or Frances Cairncross, *The Death of Distance*, Boston, MA: Harvard Business School Press, 1997.

31. A growing body of research can be found in *Quality Management Journal,* which has published on this theme for nearly a decade.

32. A key finding of Cortada, *The Digital Hand,* 3 vols.

33. ERP applications are worth studying empirically but this has not been done. However, SAP, a leader in providing such software, has been the subject of some initial study, with insights on how various firms fared with ERP. See, for example, Gerd Meissner, *SAP: Inside the Secret Software Power*, New York: McGraw-Hill, 2000.

34. Although there are few empirical studies of the enormous effort American industry went through in the 1990s to redesign their processes, there is one large collection of hundreds of contemporary testimonials: James W. Cortada and John A. Woods (Eds.), *Quality Yearbook*, New York: McGraw-Hill, 1994–2002, with some 8000 pages of material that documents the experience of many firms.

35. Discussed thoroughly by Graham Tanaka, *Digital Deflation: The Productivity Revolution and How It Will Ignite the Economy*, New York: McGraw-Hill, 2004; Robert Brenner, *The Economics of Global Turbulence*, London: Verso, 2006.

36. Robert E. Litan and Alice M. Rivlin (Eds.), *The Economic Payoff from the Internet Revolution*, Washington, DC: Brookings Institution Press, 2001, p. 2; Dale W. Jorgenson, Mun S. Ho, and Kevin J. Stiroh, *Productivity,* vol. 3: *Information Technology and the American Growth Resurgence*, Cambridge, MA: MIT Press, 2005; the first two volumes of *Productivity* review activities in other countries, Cambridge, MA: MIT Press, 1995–1996.

37. Mark Arend, "Are Your Bank's ATMs Earning Their keep?" *Banking* 83 (November 1991), pp. 37–38, 42.

38. For an excellent history of this application, see Stephen A. Brown, *Revolution at the Checkout Counter*, Cambridge, MA: Harvard University Press, 1997.

39. William W. Fisher III, *Promises to Keep: Technology, Law, and the Future of Entertainment*, Stanford, CA: Stanford University Press, 2004.

40. Described by President's Clinton's head of the IRS, Charles O. Rossotti, *Many*

Unhappy Returns: One Man's Quest to Turn Around the Most Unpopular Organization in America, Boston, MA: Harvard Business School Press, 2005.

41. I have commented more thoroughly on this issue in James W. Cortada, *Best Practices in Information Technology*, Upper Saddle River, NJ: Prentice Hall PTR, 1997, pp. 1–16.

42. Described early during the Quality Management movement by J. Edward Russo and Paul J. H. Shoemaker, *Decision Traps*, New York: Simon and Schuster, 1989.

43. John Savageau, "World Class Suggestion Systems Still Work Well," *Journal for Quality and Participation* 19, 2 (March 1996), pp. 86–90.

44. GAO maintains a searchable database of its papers published since the early 1960s, representing a goldmine of managerial studies hardly consulted by the private sector for operational insights, http://www.gao.gov.

45. As this chapter was being written in 2007, the State of Wisconsin had some $200 million in troubled IT projects that were being investigated by the legislature's audit department involving bypassed procurement practices, faulty procurement criteria, and bad project management.

46. An early description of the issue, which itself is a demonstration that the problem has been around for some time, can be found in Kenneth Primozic, Edward Primozic, and Joe Leven, *Strategic Choices: Supremacy, Survival, or Sayonara*, New York: McGraw-Hill, 1991, pp. 41–60; and part of an older discussion about the role of "experience curves," Pankaj Ghemawat, "Building Strategy on the Experience Curve," *Harvard Business Review* (March– April 1985): 143–149.

47. K. C. August, *TDS: The First Twenty Years*, Chicago, IL: Telephone and Data Systems, Inc., 1989; rev. ed., 1993.

48. For examples, see Russell L. Ackoff, *Re-Creating the Corporation: A Design of Organizations for the 21st Century*, New York: Oxford University Press, 1999, which summarizes his work of many years; Anthony Sampson, *Company Man: The Rise and Fall of Corporate Life*, New York: Times Business, 1995; Carl Kaysen (Ed.), *The American Corporation Today: Examining the Questions of Power and Efficiency At the Century's End*, New York: Oxford University Press, 1996; James Brian Quinn, *Intelligent Enterprise*, New York: Free Press, 1992.

49. The literature on this theme has become nearly vast. For a very recent example of the discussion, which includes a heavy dose of IT influence as is normal for this literature, see Don Tapscott and Anthony D. Williams, *Wikinomics: How Mass Collaboration Changes Everything*, New York: Portfolio, 2006, and the earlier, highly influential study, William H. Davidow and Michael S. Malone, *The Virtual Corporation: Structuring and Revitalizing the Corporation for the 21st Century*, New York: Harper Business, 1992.

50. In every decade since the 1950s, books and articles have appeared on the role of IT management. Two recent studies have influenced my current views: Peter Weill and Jeanne W. Ross, *IT Governance: How Top performers Manage IT Decision Rights for Superior Results*, Boston, MA: Harvard Business

School Press, 2004; Marianne Broadbent and Ellen Kitzis, *The New CIO Leader: Setting the Agenda and Delivering Results*, Boston, MA: Harvard Business School Press, 2004.

51. U.S. Department of Commerce, *Statistical Abstract of the United States: 2006*, Washington, DC: United States GPO, 2005, pp. 317–320.

52. This becomes most apparent when comparing American practices to those in other countries, such as Japan. For an example of Japanese practices, see Hideshi Itoh, "Japanese Human Resource Management From the Viewpoint of Incentive Theory," in Masahiko Aoki and Ronald Dore (Eds.), *The Japanese Firm: Sources of Competitive Strength*, New York: Oxford University Press, 1996, pp. 233–264.

53. In an earlier research initiative, I documented how this problem played out in IT: James W. Cortada, *Best Practices in Information Technology*, Upper Saddle River, NJ: PTR/Prentice-Hall, 1998.

54. Neil Rackham, *SPIN Selling*, New York: McGraw-Hill, 1988, describes the relationship process and the relative importance of risk in decision-making in IT; pp. 10–11, 53–66.

55. See Cortada, *Digital Hand*, vol. 2, pp. 508–510 for examples of articles.

56. Recently described in some detail by Anita M. McGahan, *How Industries Evolve: Principles for Achieving and Sustaining Superior Performance*, Boston, MA: Harvard Business School Press, 2004.

57. Famously described by Alfred D. Chandler, Jr., *The Visible Hand*, Cambridge, MA: Harvard University Press, 1977.

58. Alfred D. Chandler, Jr., *Shaping the Industrial Century: The Remarkable Story of the Evolution of the Modern Chemical and Pharmaceutical Industries*, Cambridge, MA: Harvard University Press, 2005.

59. James W. Cortada, "The Digital Hand: How Information Technology Changed the Way Industries Worked in the United States," *Business History Review* 80 (Winter 2006), pp. 755–766.

60. Thomas W. Malone, Robert Laubacher, and Michael S. Scott Morton (Eds.) present papers on early examples of this unfolding process, in *Inventing The Organizations of The 21st Century*, Cambridge, MA: MIT Press, 2003. For a CEO's perspective on intentions and directions, see IBM's CEO, Samuel J. Palmisano, "The Globally Integrated Enterprise," *Foreign Affairs* 85, no. 3 (May–June 2006): 127–136.

61. Richard Foster, *Innovation: The Attacker's Advantage*, New York: Summit Books, 1986, pp. 161–164.

62. Jobs and Apple have been the subject of considerable attention by journalists and academics. For a useful introduction to his managerial practices, see Jeffrey S. Young, *Steve Jobs: The Journey Is The Reward*, Glenview, IL: Scott, Foresman, 1988, which covers his early and middle career, and for the period involving iPod, consult Steven Levy, *The Perfect Thing: How the iPod Shuffles Commerce, Culture, and Coolness*, New York: Simon & Schuster, 2006, which is replete with comments on Jobs' managerial style.

5

ADDING UP THE RESULTS SO FAR: DO WE NOW LIVE IN THE INFORMATION AGE?

> Now the real IT revolution is about to begin. . . .
> —*Thomas L. Friedman* [1]

Have we entered the Information Age? Did we recently depart some other one, such as the Cold War era? Or, do we live in the New Economy? Why should we care about such questions? It seems that everyone plays the naming game—historians, journalists, scientists, sociologists, and political scientists—leading one to wonder if defining an age is suspended somewhere between a marketing ploy and a method of analysis, or even if the topic is useful in support of one's work. With so many people involved in naming an age, we should at least suspect that the method for doing so is not clearly defined or agreed upon. The subject has been made more urgent because of the widespread use of the label Information Age (or New Economy) by the press and by many academics either studying the period or attempting to make their presentations and publications "relevant," "modern," or "hip." But why care who names a period? What do they have to teach business managers and public officials, let alone serious academics, such as computer scientists and engineers? Historians, in particular, have long used the process of naming a period as a useful mechanism for organizing their research, viewing specific years, and in framing issues to address. By turning to them, one can learn some useful lessons. As one historian put it, naming periods "is essential because the past in its entirety is so extensive and complex" [2]. As managers, what can we do with that insight?

If we look at the issue, we can, first, sharpen our focus regarding the processes of naming a period. Then we can begin to determine if, in fact, the late twentieth–early twenty-first century should be called the Information Age. Finally, and this is our key point, we can apply those insights to business management's daily work and to the development of their strategies. It is important also to understand what that age would look like in a very broad sense because an increasing number of governments aspire to have their societies and economies participate as part of that new period and there are many corporations that can profit from that initiative. Therefore, how can leaders in the public and private sectors know what it takes to participate in the Information Age and measure what progress they are making to that end?

To discuss these issues, it is convenient to begin by summarizing why historians find naming a period useful, then move to a brief analysis of why it is so difficult to do so, and review what historians and others have said about the process and its scope. We should, additionally, look at the notion of the Information Age in light of methodological issues so as to begin drawing conclusions about whether it is appropriate and useful to name our current era the Information Age, identify its implications and, subsequently, define what management should do as a result of reaching such a conclusion, a step normally not discussed by commentators about how the world has become global, digital, flat, or curved [3]. It is also an idea closely linked to one facet of modern society—the use of computing. However, the issues would be the same if one were to take an economic-centric example, such as the equally popular New Economy. Finally, those managers who believe we work in such an age, need to implement elements of the Information Age and track progress toward it, to swim, so to speak, with the current. In short, this chapter blends a great deal of history with orthodox thinking about managerial practices. On purpose, it is the most intellectual and abstract of all the chapters in this book—context provided through historical perspective.

WHY NAMING AN AGE IS A USEFUL EXERCISE AND SO HARD TO DO

Naming a period helps provide definition to a subject, much the way a name does for a nation, person, or thing. A name helps one to focus, helping students of the past to determine what should be included in their studies or not, and, equally important, situates narrower research in some larger context. Terms such as "ages" or "eras" serve as shorthand, facilitating communications between students of the past or observers of the present and their constituents. For example, a historian can signal that his or her particular topic is political in scope, religious, or about some other thematic emphasis, such as the increased use of information, computers, or other technologies in recent times. For some decades, historians and others spoke of the Cold War era as the central set of political events of the second half of the twentieth century. With the collapse of the Soviet Union, it seemed that era was over, and so the hunt was on for a new name for the period that followed. The naming of an era should be a familiar exercise to managers and consultants because think tanks and lobbyists frequently make their publications and points of view appear relevant by positioning them as dealing with some newly emerging or contemporary era, such as "The Information Age" or the "Digital Economy," or about "Digital Democracy," for instance.

As is true for good nicknames, that for an age can take on a permanence that subsequently affects how we view a period. The Age of Jackson (U.S. history of the 1820s–1830s) is an obvious example drawn from American history, or the Bronze Age for an earlier time. And who can forget the "Cold War?" There are many ways to name a period. Historian George Basalla argues that studying artifacts (e.g., stone tools for ancient times, digital computers for our age) is crucial to any understanding of the important role of technology in human history, so that could be the basis of the naming process [4]. Art historians organize their thinking about periods in the history of art based on shared styles of painting (e.g., Impressionism or Modernism). Political historians focus on patterns of political behavior to arrive at a name.

Whereas it is easy to recognize that naming a period is useful, it is also fraught with difficulties that are better described as limitations. The most immediate issue is that whatever features are used

to define an age can lead to minimizing other important characteristics of the same period. For example, when historians refer to a
specific period in human history, such as the Bronze Age, they
could possibly minimize too much the fact that during a great part
of that long age, humans also used stone tools and continued to
rely on bronze weapons for thousands of years after the arrival of
the subsequent Iron Age. A second problem involves the actual
chronology of an age. When should we say a period has begun or
ended? Related to this second question is the fact that the names
of periods change as historians and others place emphasis on
varying issues over different times, as happened when historians
began rethinking whether to view World War I and World War II,
the two world wars of the twentieth century, as two independent
sets of events or as some continuum, such as one long war with a
pause in between hostilities [5].

A third consideration is more serious. Without careful attention
to the analysis of any historical issue, it is easy to impose today's
views or values on prior events, causing some issues to be overem-
phasized at the expense of others, because some became more important today than they were in the past, a problem lawyers and
managers face in reconstructing scenarios and case studies. On the
other hand, a topic of interest to a later generation can cause historians to revisit old issues, such as the role of women and children,
which was not the subject of as much research in the first half of
the twentieth century as it was in the second half [6]. In a recent
exercise designed to look at historical precedents of what one
might call the Information Age in America, a team of scholars
looked at the role of information in American history back to the
1700s. They concluded that information had played a significant,
increasingly growing, if not fully understood, role in North American life over hundreds of years. But they struggled with the real
danger that they might extend the notion of some idea of an Information Age back too far, to a time when the concept could not be
justified [7]. On the other hand, at least one student of the Information Age (not a professional historian) squarely fell into the
trap when he entitled his history of the telegraph as *The Victorian
Internet: The Remarkable Story of the Telegraph and the Nineteenth Century's On-Line Pioneers* [8]. In no way can one realistically call this technology the direct predecessor of the Internet, or
even use the concept of the Internet (and the notion of on-line) in
the same sentence. The two were profoundly different and came

more than a century apart [8]. As the *Victorian Internet*'s title suggests, naming problems are developing for our own era [9].

WHAT HISTORIANS CAN TEACH US ABOUT THE PROCESS

In recent decades, historians have looked at the role of technologies and worked through how best to situate them in periods of time, an exercise still underway that has also caused them to deal with the issue of naming eras. Some emphasized the role of artifacts [10]. Others thought in broad terms of economic transformations [11], and yet others formed their views within the context of information [12]. Their deliberations ranged from events in the eighteenth through the twentieth centuries. But there is no consensus when it comes to naming our time the Information Age. Closely tied to this lack of consensus are some basic questions: When did it begin? What made it worthy of that name? The indisputable consensus that computers and telecommunications have profoundly influenced societies and national economies during the second half of the twentieth century may not necessarily be enough justification. The variable concerning timing and degree of effects intensifies our concern over the issue as well.

If we look at the specific problem of the Information Age, one sees that computer-like technologies emerged in various laboratories in the United States and Europe in the 1920s and 1930s. These became digital computers as we know them today in the mid-1940s, whereas commercial use of this technology did not start in earnest until the mid-1950s. By 1960, there still were still only about 6000 computers in the entire world. In the 1960s and 1970s, large computers and telecommunications began converging into integrated systems, which later made the Internet and PCs of such enormous value. But telephony had been around since the 1870s. The PC, which made computing available to the "common man," emerged initially in the 1970s, became widespread by the late 1980s, and relatively ubiquitous in advanced economies by the late 1990s. So when might we date the start of the Computer Revolution? What about the Information Age? Answers to such questions remain unclear without some useful set of criteria.

Historians compound the problem by changing their focus many times, a normal activity as they gain additional insight about a subject. They moved from just looking at the machines themselves to adding software, telecommunications, uses of computing, and management of technology. They next started examining the book in America, the telegraph, telephone, television, underwater telephone cabling, satellites, newspapers, magazines, and so forth as part of a larger story about information, media, and telecommunications [13]. So, now what should be the starting date for the Information Age?

The question assumes that one has resolved the methodological problems of defining its features in the first place, because the Information Age is not solely about computing, reading, or shuffling data. Boundaries separating information technologies from what might otherwise be perceived as low-tech activities, such as entertainment, became fuzzy at best, especially so, for example, with video games [14]. Using entertainment as only one of many examples, various information technologies make up entertainment, such as radio and television. So, are they also part of the Information Age?

Historians looking at the Information Age through the venue of the computer have used such early dates as 1930, 1945, or the mid-1950s to signal the start of the computer period [15]. But this neat typology has been altered by others arguing the case that telecommunications was an important part of the story [16], whereas still others added television, radio, books, magazines, and newspapers to the mix [17]. To be sure, it has become a messy process, compounded by the fact that for many observers of computing and other technologies these various uses and artifacts were rapidly converging [18].

Convergence means that more than one technology was used within a device, which led to new uses and to novel definitions. A laptop computer that can automatically dial a telephone to access the Internet is a good example; it combines chips, computers, and telecommunications all in one device. Television sets that have the capability of personal computers represent another case of converging technologies. With CD-ROMs, one could use a laptop as a portable movie theater running simultaneously as it downloaded music off the Internet, which one could listen to later on the same machine [19]. These cases are made possible by use of shared technologies, the highly flexible computer chip and software. A most dramatic transformation is underway, coming out of this convergence and holding out the promise of changing how computing and information are used in the next decade or so [20].

If results are as profound as experts on the technology and its social implications think possible, will the chronology of the Information Age, and even its name, change? Developments in the study and use of DNA, driven by use of computers as a cook uses a pot and spoon, conjure up additional complications facing anyone who attempts to date or characterize the Information Age as a unique period. With present-day knowledge suggesting that an age is more than its artifacts, what is left to date a period?

We may have a way of dealing with the issue of how to date the Information Age that also helps the nonhistorian to think with a historical perspective, by looking at the work of the late historian Arthur Marwick, who studied the years 1950s through the 1970s, lived in the period as well, and wrote extensively about that time. Marwick was also a master craftsman and the author of several books on how to ply this craft. In a massive history of the 1960s [21], he suggested a path for anyone wanting to frame a period, not just a method for use by historians. To reach his conclusion that the times that came before and after the 1960s were sufficiently different, such that Marwick could call the 1960s a period with its own characteristics, he grouped together many kinds of events. He ranged across ideas, artifacts, politics, racial and gender issues, multiple countries, entertainment, music, and technology. In each category, he saw both emerging discontinuities and various continuities with the past [22]. Concluding that a wide variety of considerations had to go into the naming of a period, in the process he gave us a useful list of possible types of defining attributes as a resource.

When writing about the information (or other nearly contemporary) age, historians of technology face the same problems Marwick did because they, too, lived through most, or all, of the modern computer-centric era.

It is almost obligatory in one's preface to any history of computing, or to the era in which the computer came into prominence, to acknowledge problem of the immediacy of events clouding one's judgment [23]. It is quite possible that not enough has changed—after all, computers represent only one facet of modern society—or maybe a great deal has changed. In the former case, for instance, how programmers wrote software programs in the 1950s is so different from how it is done today that one is easily tempted to say everything about programming is now different [24]. There is a growing body of evidence in support of this finding in the form of memoirs, interviews, studies about programmers from the earlier period, and an expanding collection of biographies of William Gates and other software developers, yet their working culture remained remarkably the same [25].

Some things are obviously different today. No company used a computer in 1945 to create invoices but today one cannot imagine receiving a hand-written bill. A computer of 1980 could do many times the work of a machine from 1950, and today's handheld calculators are more powerful tools than those mechanical "brains" used by the American and Soviet governments at the dawn of the Cold War [26]. But in the 1940s, as at the end of the twentieth century, there existed the requirement to create invoices, pay bills, and fight wars, using all available technologies.

In a study I did on the office appliance industry of the late 1800s and early 1900s, I kept finding business requirements similar to those I experienced as a business manager in the 1980s and 1990s. Yet management also evolved in how they did their work and how they reacted to the arrival of the computer in the 1950s. The next generation of managers had grown up with that technology and could thus approach the subject with knowledge, experience, and confidence not available to their predecessors, even when dealing with the same business issues as had earlier generations of managers [27]. The closer one moves toward the present, the more complicated it is to detach personal views and experiences from the subject at hand. In the instance of the computer's influence, one could argue that even what occurred in the 1950s and 1960s was so similar to what happened in the 1980s and 1990s that it really was too early even to call it history. To argue that this perspective is faulty might seem a safe strategy. However, too many events occurred that make it possible for scores of books to have been published on the history of computing and the Information Age, with many documenting and analyzing events that took place just within the past two decades [28].

Marwick established a list of factors with which to screen events useful to today's management seeking either to understand current conditions or to develop a future strategy. Historians analyzing what happened in the 1960s and beyond are perhaps well equipped to perform these duties, because they can accept the fact that things have not changed so much, which can make their work easier (as happens, for instance, to those examining the history of the PC) [29]. Or they can view events through some other lens (for

example, the motivating influence of the Cold War on the expanded use of computing). They can put some historical distance between them and the events of the past by examining these in a
structured way. They can create criteria against which they compare their evidence to determine if indeed we are living in an Information Age [30]. When Marwick laid out his case for why 1958
to 1974 represented an integrated time, he pointed to 16 characteristics that bound together events in those years. The number he selected is more important to our discussion than what they were,
because he reminded us that for any period to be seen as distinctive from others, a large set of unique shared features should be
present and be identified. For management, the lesson is clear:
identifying the forces at work on our activities and lives today requires probing a long list of interconnected activities evolving
over some period of time. It is complexity and ambiguity writ
large.

Therein lies a fundamental problem with notions of our immediate case, the Information Age: It seems to have so few identifi-
able features *thus far.* The most important one already identified
relates to the extensive use of computers, the continuing evolution
of this technology, and, just now emerging, an understanding of
how things were done as a result of melding computing into a nation's work practices and entertainment. Of course, before the invention of computers there were none, and if many computers are
in use, more information is woven into the work and play of society, hence changing it. That logic rests, unfortunately, on only one
dimension of post-1950 life: the computer or, for some, the Internet.

One can argue that various information technologies, and use of
data in modern societies, predate the arrival and use of computers
and, later, the Internet. For the United States and Europe, one
could argue that more fundamental information-handling technologies appeared in the period 1875–1935 than in the years
1940–2000 [31]. In the first epoch, workers and consumers around
the world were introduced to adding machines, various types of
calculators, punched-card tabulating equipment, telephones, radio, film, typewriters, and television, and witnessed expanded use
of the telegraph, inexpensive magazines, newspapers, and books.
In the second period, computers appeared in various forms, along
with satellites, the Internet, and advanced versions of every technology introduced in the first era [32]. Both periods could be

called the Information Age if one used the criteria of use of an existing information technology [33]. Yet, historians did not name the earlier period the Information Age. The reason is straightforward: there was a great deal more going on in the earlier period than simply typing, telephoning, and adding. Wouldn't the same logic extend to discussions about the late 1900s and early 2000s?

Although the answer is yes, the notion that information or some specific technology plays a greater role in modern society should not be ignored either. In business and work, for example, recent studies demonstrate how computing profoundly changed the way things were done. Tasks were automated and computers made an increasing number of minor decisions previously made by people. Management routinely accumulated and analyzed more data before when making decisions. New activities can be done today that were not possible a half-century ago [34]. Robots do a better and faster job of painting cars than people; computers can transfer money around the world thousands of times faster than banks did in the early 1900s, spaceships function because of navigational software, and almost all research done on DNA and genomics is made possible by using computers; the list is endless. It gets worse: More information per capita exists today than ever before [35]. In the United States, over 50% of all homes have a PC, 98% a TV, and there is a phone in nearly 99% of all households. Over 25% of the U.S. population uses a cell phone (over 60% in Europe), and over 60% of Americans interact with a computer in order to perform their jobs. Every single automobile manufactured in the United States, Japan, and Western Europe since the late 1970s has one or more computer chips (hence, computers) to manage and improve performance [36]. Today, it is not uncommon in any given year for over 5% of the U.S. gross domestic product to be spent on computing, closer to 20% if we add telecommunications, and two-thirds of all capital expenditures go toward the purchase of computing products by businesses and government agencies [37]. So, one could begin to make a case that we may be living in the Information Age.

But if one thinks about what Marwick had to go through, it becomes evident that before one labels the current time the Information Age or the New Economy (or use some other technology as a label for any period) we should take into consideration a variety of issues not yet discussed here. On the basis of information earlier historians have used to help define a period, these can include political trends, economic sectors, cultural values, the arts, religion, and use of groups of technologies.

Following Marwick's lead, before anyone labels our time the Information Age, a number of features of modern life would have to change sufficiently. Historians and economists know that change comes at different speeds and in various forms and forces, so whatever list one imposes on the present as the filter will contain elements that have undergone more considerable transformation compared with previous ones. For example, it is true that no major work process today is really performed without at least some use of computers, an illustration of one major change that has led to a new style of management, a new style of work in almost all OECD countries; but that fact does not hold as true for the other some 100 nations absent from the list [38]. Computing and telecommunications have changed how we interact with each other in many countries (even in addition to those tracked by the OECD), but not all that communication is information, unless we include conversations. Research done at the University of California at Berkeley would suggest that today over 90% of all information moving about the world is already in digital form, clearly a marker of perhaps something new afoot, but not everywhere, a fact that executives running a global enterprise must not forget [39]. The U.S. military community, which spends 50% of the world's budgets that are devoted to defense and war, and which dominates the warfighting practices of NATO and all modern military forces, is an extensive user of information technology. That use has fundamentally altered its (and the Allies') views on military strategy and warfare. But how many other institutions have changed so much, thanks to information technology? How many have to in order for all of us to alter our views? [40]

THE CASE AGAINST THE INFORMATION AGE

One would have to question how extensively digital technology has changed our taste in music and art, people's views about religion and social values, and the intents and events in our political and public lives. Have governments changed a great deal as a result of living in some sort of digital world? Has our worldview become different because of computing? Has information technology altered our sexual practices? Have we become more tolerant of other life styles due to some digital influence? I think we can safely say, not yet. Furthermore, is it necessary for the entire world to have moved to some new form for a new period to be declared? Historians have overwhelmingly voted no through their practice of often defining a period just within a nation, region, or otherwise constrained view of a subject. Perhaps experts of world history might want to apply a more global label, but none have yet used the title Information Age. Nonetheless, the physical artifacts of computing and telecommunications continue to spread rapidly and in vast quantities around the world, affecting dramatically how work and play are done. Those trends, however, are perhaps initial steps toward some new form of society, in much the same way as the extensive deployment of steam in the early 1700s in Europe served as an initial step toward what eventually became known as the Industrial Revolution, when the amount and nature of work done by humankind not only changed, but also shifted fundamentally away from predominantly agricultural to industrial over the course of some 200 years.

There are other compelling worldviews that compete for our attention as well and, thus, are rivals for the naming of our time as the Information Age. One case illustrates how different these can be. Samuel P. Huntington, a distinguished political scientist and author of important studies on modern political systems, argued in the 1990s and early 2000s that the world was increasingly clustering around mega-civilizations characterized by, among other things, shared religious heritage. Islamic states were clustering together, Christian states were doing the same, and a similar process was at work in Asia. He argued that international and even national economic and political behaviors were rapidly becoming culture-centric, that is to say, Muslims were aligning together, Christians doing the same, and so forth [41]. We do not need to debate the merits of his ideas; however, what we should recognize is that Huntington paid minimal attention to information and its technologies. He argued that the Western dominance in most technologies (including computers) was a "blip," and was waning as the rest of the world was catching up in its deployment of technologies of all types, thereby returning people of all nations to a technological balance-of-power closer to what the world had in 1800 or before [42]. Huntington's view—that for the same years as the Information Age it is possible to characterize compelling alternative ages—became increasingly fashionable, indeed relevant, to many observers of the modern scene following 9/11 and as warfare and tensions between the Islamic Middle East and the United States and many other non-Islamic nations increased. Huntington was prescient and shrewd to be sure, but historians fifty years from now may consider his worldview obvious and relevant, or possibly not.

The alternative view provided by Huntington has a direct effect on managers and public officials. It turns out that senior public officials around the world embraced his view of changing circumstances as they set policies—indeed went to war in the early 2000s—than they did notions of an Information Age. Business managers, on the other hand, paid more attention to Information Age models of the world than they did to notions of religious mindsets. Not until at least a few years into the new century did managers begin taking into consideration the possibility that their technocentric worldviews needed adjustment, the point made in the last chapter when discussing the role of risk in business operations. In short, a word of warning: just because someone puts a label on an age, and publishes books and articles promoting it, does not necessarily make it so. Strategies and tactics have to rely on a base of assumptions and facts that are not always aligned with popular aphorisms about contemporary life.

CAN WE COEXIST ON THE FRONTIERS OF A NEW AGE?

Is Huntington right? Or are those who view us now as being in an Information or Networked Age correct? Put more usefully, what name should we give to the second half of the twentieth century and beyond to help managers, computer scientists, other members of the IT tribe, policy makers, and historians understand the events of this period in their full richness of diversity and complexity? Is it premature to position our period as the Information Age? Do we need to wait decades to gain that all elusive "perspective" and "context" historians so cherish? Answers do not have to suppose a "winner-take-all" approach in which a historian or journalist with the most novel name or the most widely supported approach wins for the most contemporary periods. As we get closer in time to our age, names of periods change more frequently. It is less important whether someone gets a name right, which somewhat resembles a person picking a winning horse at a racetrack, than to have someone explain the rationale for his or her choice, defending it with solid evidence and clear thinking, thereby enriching our understanding of a period and especially our time. As Marwick reminded us, "different historians will identify different chunks, depending on their interests and the countries they are dealing with" [43], which reads very much like the work habit of a business strategist, but without Powerpoint slides.

Historians of technology have taken turns dealing with issues raised in this chapter. Carroll Pursell, for example, has argued the case for placing the history of technologies (and not just one) within conventional political categories. These include such well-accepted ages as Progressivism and the New Deal. Thomas P. Hughes demonstrated a second strategy, by writing an alternative national American history that focused heavily on the role of various technologies, such as electricity. A third approach holds that one could see as an extensive combination of the approaches offered by Pursell and Hughes. Social historians see the subject of technology in yet a different way, looking at such issues as tools and practices used in the home and the effects of such popular topics as the railroad and computers [44]. The fact that historians of technology have not settled on one perspective is not as important as what they have done by providing various strategies for dealing with the issue of how to categorize technologies and the times in which they were important in the lives of people and societies.

This discussion about the Information Age and effects of technologies on views of our times suggests basic lessons regarding historical methods, periodization, and the naming of ages. First, for historians and other students of a modern time, it is helpful to attempt naming a period in order to stimulate a deeper understanding about certain facets of a time, to give scholars and other commentators a way of placing the topic within the broader context of national or global history, even at the risk that the name will have to be changed later. In our case, we must solve a problem that is less about naming this period and more about examining how IT makes a difference in modern life. Second, it is advantageous to have multiple candidates for period names in order to sharpen our understanding of the relative importance of one set of characteristics and events over another. Contrasting views about the nature of modern life presented by individuals such as sociologists Daniel Bell or Manuel Castells, when compared to those of someone with a profoundly different perspective, for example, Huntington, provides enriched perspectives. This is the same logic that makes alternative scenarios and gaming exercises so useful to business and government leaders.

Using the analogy of scaffolding is a convenient way to structure periods and organize issues and can be applied to the case of the Information Age. Scaffolding supports painters, window washers, and the like. It is temporary; at the end of the task it will be taken down. To carry the analogy forward, the ideas of historians or political scientists who name a period can be likened to scaffolding. The analogy can be applied neatly to a modern age, but students of the past and managers attempting to understand the present and glimpse at the future need to embrace several notions about its use.

One ought to accept the idea that whatever name or view is first devised for a period is probably not going to survive the test of time. It is a temporary construct to facilitate organization of research and data and to provide structure and scope for perspectives and text. Thus, World War I or World War II might be in the early stages of retiring as scaffolds for organizing vast quantities of historical research, to be replaced with a more permanent one— the Twentieth Century Global Wars, for example. The point is, however, that the names World War I and World War II were of extraordinary value to historians, students, and readers. In the case of the Information Age, that name facilitates the transformation currently under way in the study of modern technological conditions that veers away from focused discussions on machines and moves increasingly toward information itself and to its uses in business and government, and by individuals.

That the label Computer Age was useful in the 1970s and 1980s for purposes of calling attention to the need to study the history of machines and to understand their effects on engineering, technology, science, business, and society, cannot be overestimated. The focus was appropriate and relevant. Now it is anachronistic.

Whereas a history of a specific machine, as appeared frequently in the 1970s and 1980s [45], is still useful, such an approach marginalizes our view of what really happened and could continue to do so. Students of history are moving to broader, more complex themes reflecting and recognizing effects of technologies (both computers and telecommunications), the information systems, societies, and economies, and are being joined in this more expansive view by sociologists and economists [46]. Use of the title Information Age helps point many in a direction for new perspectives and urgently needed research [47].

For the academic community and business consultants in particular, one can ask: How does historical perspective on the modern period—the act of giving it a name and the label itself—influence our thinking about what happens in the period still unfolding? The age-old question asks, if one could go back in time, would that influence the course of events, and how? This issue was raised so entertainingly in the American movie *Back to the Future* (1985). Historians have known for centuries that the past affects the present and notions of the future; it is a fundamental working assumption of every generation of scholars. Does the present continue to unfold as new chapters in the history of the Information Age? Since most historians are not asked to comment on the present and future, it may be a moot issue. However, if they are, and there seems to be a growing appetite for historical perspective to influence management's decisions, then it could be a new issue for them concerning how they work, but not so for managers, who want "lessons of history" and have accepted the economists' notion of *path dependency* without having to do a lot of reading about the past. Already, individuals who are not historians apply loosely "lessons of history" to current events. If they believe they live in a period that is the Information Age, or view modern international events the way Huntington has, does the historian (or nonhistorian) encounter the problems of *Back to the Future*? Yes, but we also know that all decisions are made with the influence of some bias (for example, prior experience, national heritage, etc.), so historical bias is an option that is brought to bear in some cases [48].

Most of the examples of this going on inside government and more so in business are shrouded in secrecy because the activity is part of the development of business and operational strategies. I have seen many of these strategies across a dozen industries and, more frequently than not, they begin with a description of the emerging world, era, and, of course, markets and opportunities. Over the past decade, many began by describing some sort of "networked age" or a "flat world," citing academics such as Manuel Castells, Carlota Perez, and such journalists and social commentators as Thomas L. Friedman and Chris Anderson. I have recently come across a new crop of labels, such as a "Rubik's cube world" and "connected world" as descriptors of our time, both of which at least attempt to broaden the definition of contemporary times to include nontechnical facets. In short, labeling is a popular sport among managers, academics, writers, engineers, and strategists.

LESSONS FOR MANAGEMENT AND A STRATEGY FOR CHANGE

It should be clear that labeling a period can influence one's view of a time; it certainly affects the experts that managers and public officials often rely on for advice. What lessons can be drawn from this discussion that would be helpful to those affecting the role of IT in any business, industry, or society? When a government announces that it wants its society to become an "information age" one, as have the Japanese, or a "knowledge economy," as has the European Union, what does this mean? How is one to judge how far down the path a particular society has gone? How can businesses use that insight to determine when and where to invest in growing their revenues? For executives, it becomes an issue of alignment and momentum, of having the wind to one's back so to speak. Getting that right may be one of the two or three key success factors for any firm that survives longer than a couple of decades in our increasingly globalized economy.

These are serious questions because management is also paying attention to those describing ages. For example, historian Carlotta Perez has written a book about phases in technological revolutions. While her list is fine, it is too neat and tidy for many historians. By her schema, we now live in a period in which IT is essentially being deployed across all economies, implying that it will, thus, not be as transformative as prior experiences. Her chart showing phases of technological evolution over the centuries appears in PowerPoint presentations made by corporate strategies in many industries. Most, if not all the historians mentioned in my chapter, would probably shake their heads at the naïve attachment those presenters display toward such a view of history [49]. My fear is that an executive would conclude that innovations in IT in the years to come might not be profoundly transformative, yet we know there are things going on in laboratories that, when they finally emerge as products over the next decade or so, will be dramatic in their impact, such as the effects of a whole new class of small, lightweight batteries. In short, we have to be careful not to be lulled into viewing the world too simplistically.

That said, what elements are needed to comprise an information age society, economy, or market? Given what the historians, sociologists, political scientists, and others have suggested are components of such a culture, some obvious features should be present. These include high levels of literacy and education among the general public, a workforce skilled in the use of IT and who are dependent upon those technologies to do their work, and an economy that uses IT extensively in manufacturing and that has a high percentage of GDP derived from services that also use IT and require advanced levels of education. In manufacturing, the role of services fits the mold. For example, in a plant that manufactures computers, a minority of the workforce actually makes things, bends metal so to speak; the rest operate high-tech devices, work in management and supply chain management, labor in a clean-room laboratory or in human resources (HR), even serve as guards on the property or as cooks in the cafeteria. Economies that rely heavily on IT also tend to have higher per-capita GDP and more advanced infrastructures, such as telecommunications, transportation, media, and schools and universities. Crime tends to be lower, while laws protect property rights, patents, copyrights, and enforce contracts. Capital and other forms of credit and finance are available and cost-effective. Note that in this list there is no emphasis on the requirement to invent or manufacture IT hardware or software; integrating these into the daily work and private lives of citizens is enough. A manager in search of an information age economy can use the attributes listed above as a short list of things to look for in a society. For a public official aspiring to transform an economy into such a society, the list is essentially the same.

Next, we must ask: How do we know what progress is being made toward becoming an information age society? At the risk of answering this question too glibly, there are many surveys and ranking reports published today that can provide good indications of the characteristics of an economy or society relative to others. There is no need to reinvent these. They are a good place to start. The United Nations and the OECD routinely look at such issues, and the Economist Intelligence Unit has long published various rankings based on some one hundred variables and thousands of data points that are both numerical and qualitative. To reinforce this recommendation to begin by relying on existing frameworks and road maps, start by thinking in terms of the three categories of nations presented in Chapter 2, which describes the most advanced, advancing, and least developed economies in their use of IT, and lists non-IT features of each type of society, which are often more important considerations than any individual technology. For a manager, annual reports of this type describe the progress (or lack thereof) in the evolution of an economy and its salient features, such as levels of education. For a public official, it is a score card of progress and relative status. Such reports describe trends by country and region over time. It is against these rankings and frameworks that public officials can then do the next level of work required to create a strategy for improving their information age status and features, and to understand the desired economic and social benefits required of any strategy for national development.

It is in the context of such an approach that historians, economists, management and public policy consultants and experts, and political scientists can be consulted to gain their perspective on what is possible and which issues to consider as one advances with plans. Thus, if investing in Africa, understanding tribal politics is essential for a business executive, so consulting a historian of the region or a banker from the World Bank can be an extremely useful exercise, just as management does before entering a European economy by understanding the role of the local political parties, even the availability of broadband and software programmers. There is the famous story of when Margaret Thatcher was asked by the West Germans to endorse the merger of East and West Germany into one nation in the 1980s. Fearing the possibility of the return of another Nazi Era or, more immediately, the resurgence of the historic economic dominance of Germany in Central Europe at the expense of Britain, France, and other neighboring countries, she corralled a group of historians who were experts on twentieth century German history, asking them for their opinions on the matter. She was not enthralled at the prospect of a united Germany under the command of a chancellor (Adolph Hitler had once held that title), nor where the British people who remembered World War II. But, the historians told her that the problems of the past would not be repeated, that the German public and polities were different than they had been in the 1930s and 1940s, and that Germany would not dominate European politics

and economics the way it had in the past. She reluctantly con-
doned the merger of the two Germanies. No doubt those experts
helped reassure her that the decision would not be really dangerous to her nation, merely unpopular with the British electorate!
Historical and political perspectives have their uses and are important. In this instance, the historians had concluded long before
the British prime minister approached them that Europeans were
now living in a different age than had their parents' generation.

At this juncture, a senior public official, or a business executive,
might ask about what milestones or phases one should establish
and then set targets for forcing progress toward some measurable
end point. The problem, of course, is that no two companies or
countries start the process at the same time or with the same circumstances. No two nations have the same GDP, let alone similar
mix of industries and firms contributing to their national income.
Even something as simple to measure as the number of years on
average of formal education of a population does not speak to the
issue of the quality and content of that schooling. However, what
economists have been advocating for decades still makes sense
here, specifically, formulating a point of view of what a nation's
aspirations should be, understanding the constraints officials,
managers, and citizens face, and all the while appreciating deeply
what are the core competences of an economy, society, or industry. These are the same steps taken by any manager or executive
who is creating an enterprise-wide business strategy. But there are
several additional considerations one will want to take into account that are unique to the challenge of evolving into an economy that has high-tech features to it.

First, the business/government side of using IT is quite different
than the consumer's experience. It takes an industry's firms normally 3–10 years to implement a major new application of technology, such as ERP systems in manufacturing or finance, but it
only takes a nation's consumers between 2–3 years to embrace
widely a new product, such as iPods or novel cell phones. So the
cadence varies between the two largest groups of users of IT and
that has to be taken into account in developing a national economic plan. Furthermore, they affect each other. In the case of South
Korea, until the manufacturing side of the economy became high-
tech, local consumers could not afford to buy consumer electronics, let alone appreciate for what they should be used. Yet in the
United States, the standard of living was so high when digital con-

sumer goods appeared that consumers were able to reach out to many of these as early adopters; the Europeans, for similar reasons, did the same with cell phones. So, speed of adoption varies by economic sector and player, not to mention by country.

Second, implications of the role of technology also vary by nation. In an African country, where the costs of land lines is so high and cell phones relatively low, one ought to expect that wireless communication would take precedence over other forms of digital products. That embrace of one form of digital technology over another affects how a society uses IT and its related attitudes, policies, and practices. Emerging economies in general use technology differently than the most advanced economies; they even finance them differently. In those nations that have reliable, well-operating banking industries and reliable supplies of electricity and broadband, capital goods tend to be acquired by firms earlier rather than later; the converse occurs where capital and secure banking services are rarer.

Third, the role of government in an economy is as varied as the countries themselves. We have dictatorships, democracies, and republics. Some are run by fiscally conservative regimes, others recoil from raw capitalist practices and instead embrace more socialized approaches to public administration. Yet other governments are more or less protective of patents, copyrights, and contracts. Some have extensive corruption while many others are relatively clean and honest. Therefore, one cannot generalize about the role of government; it will vary from one nation to another, despite a megatrend of many administrations attempting to create common rules of economic and social behavior, as we are seeing today with the regulatory practices of the EU across two dozen European countries, and with the WTO with respect to trade around the world.

Fourth, an increasing variable to factor into setting targets and defining aspirations involves environmental issues. In some instances, the interest concerns safety (as in Europe), in other cases the availability of clean water (India) and air (China), in still others the issue centers on driving down the cost of energy used in transportation, manufacturing, and even in heating buildings (United States and Germany); the list is long. Increasingly, environmental factors of some sort are being taken into greater consideration than in the past as companies and governments develop strategies for the evolution of their societies. Some sort of tipping point has been reached in recent years and, true to our discussion, at different speeds and in varying forms.

Fifth, there is uncertainty, which disrupts business and often has to be responded to directly by governments. These are events that interrupt the predictable march toward some sort of information age. Wars are the most obvious, but also climatic change and natural disasters, and, recently, the banking and credit crisis, all of which are rarely predictable as to when they will strike or their magnitude. The ubiquitous spread of media seems to bring the story of a problem to everyone at the same time, and thus creates a crisis of mindset for many people, globalization can help to dampen conditions that would otherwise disrupt economic and social evolution even further. For example, when a natural disaster strikes, it is the use of IT and digital communications that normally speeds up the response of public officials to the crisis, from cell phones and radio communications to faster transportation of needed supplies to an affected area. More quietly behind the scenes, economic globalization can help. There is the little publicized case of when India and Pakistan were headed toward military confrontation in the early 2000s. Officials in India were quietly told by third parties not to descend into war because that would disrupt its rapidly growing software industry and use of Indian call centers by American and European companies would quickly decline [50], thereby setting back India's aspiration to become a knowledge-based country with a growing standard of living for millions of its citizens. This discussion goes back to the topic of risk described in the previous chapter.

Although there are many other elements one could mention that should go into any modeling of what a nation might do to become an information age society, these five are some of the most obvious. If Huntington is right, that the world is headed for some sort of technological balance of power, then most economies will eventually arrive at some set of circumstances that will cause historians and others to declare that they are now information age economies, regardless of any overt actions taken to speed up the arrival of this new era. Given the appetite evident all over the world for increasing one's reliance on IT, regardless of age, education, ethnic background, or financial circumstances, he is probably right. How those uses will affect one's values, behavior, careers, and standard of living are only just now becoming the subject of speculation and, realistically, have been minimally documented.

CONCLUDING THOUGHTS

This chapter began with the premise that historians had something to teach business managers, public officials, and others about the Information Age. It also argued the case that how one defines an age is not merely an interesting intellectual exercise but could also inform the strategic intentions of large organizations within a society and, especially, their leaders. If we are really entering an age in which digitized information is prized as essential to the daily work and play of people, then it makes perfect sense that various communities of experts would have to collaborate and learn from each other, which in preinformation age times would not have been necessary. Historians debating national and corporate development with executives and public officials would certainly be an example of what would likely not have taken place. But the idea is an old one whose time, perhaps, has come. As far back as the mid-1980s, two scholars had proposed such a thing: Richard E. Neustadt, professor of public administration at the John F. Kennedy School of Government at Harvard University, and Ernest R. May of the same institution's history department. They wrote a book on how public administrators could use history to inform their work, entitled *Thinking in Time: The Use of History for Decision Makers.* The book has long been out of print but not out of style, and is worth the effort to find and read. Through a series of case studies, they explored how the craft of the historian could meld with that of the leader. Although they offered many ideas, such as thinking of the present as "it may be when it becomes the past" [51], a great deal of their value lay in exploring what leaders should look for in understanding current situations and patterns of behavior (i.e., trends), and how to address these. Although they also encouraged people to read history (many senior public officials do this routinely, such as U.S. presidents and European prime ministers), it is interesting to note that some of the biggest fans of history have also been important leaders: Abraham Lincoln, Franklin D. Roosevelt, Winston Churchill (also a historian), and John F. Kennedy. Others were practicing historians, such as Antonio Canovas del Castillo, who dominated Spanish politics in Spain from the mid-1880s until his assassination in 1897 and was known as a Spain's Otto von Bismarck, and Woodrow Wilson, president of the United States during World War I. A similar list could be created cataloging history fans among business leaders and commentators; my favorite is Peter Drucker, who rarely published an article or a book without reference to some historical precedent or insight.

Our discussion about a possible future that so many managers and public officials aspire for their nations leads us back to some of the questions these two Harvard professors suggested national leaders ask before making momentous decisions. These are questions that historians can help answer: "Will it work?" "Will it stick?" "Will it help more than it hurts?" "If not, what?" [52] These questions are applicable to the operation of a company or country and represent a productive way to end our discussion about the Information Age and the more specific roles of IT. With such questions, what might otherwise be an intellectual question of interest only to historians now becomes one of the most important that a leader of an organization can ask. One additional question also then needs answering as well: "What are the implications for us?"

Much of what has been discussed in this and the previous chapters addresses today's reality. Given the enormous dependence on the evolution of society upon what is happening with information technology itself, and the mega forces of globalization, we need to turn our attention to navigating into a time beyond the immediate. Much of what managers and public officials do today will be with us in the next several decades, a period in time that will also witness significant changes in technologies. Thus we also need to explore the role of computer scientists and engineers.

NOTES AND REFERENCES

1. Thomas L. Friedman, *The World Is Flat: A Brief History of the Twenty-First Century*, New York: Farrar, Straus and Giroux, 2nd ed., 2006, p. 233.

2. Arthur Marwick, *The Sixties: Cultural Revolution in Britain, France, Italy, and the United States, c. 1958–c.1974*, Oxford: Oxford University Press, 1998, p. 5.

3. For a sober view of globalization, see Harm de Blij, *The Power of Place: Geography, Destiny, and Globalization's Rough Landscape*, New York: Oxford University Press, 2009.

4. George Basalla, *The Evolution of Technology*, Cambridge, UK: Cambridge University Press, 1988.

4. Eric Hobsbawm, *The Age of Extremes: The Short Twentieth Century 1914–1991*, London: Michael Joseph, 1994.

6. Snuggle up one night with a wonderful book written by a historian of women's history who also experienced the holocaust: Gerda Lerner, *Why History Matters: Life and Thought*, New York: Oxford University Press, 1997.

7. Alfred D. Chandler, Jr. and James W. Cortada (Eds.), *A Nation Transformed by Information: How Information Has Shaped the United States from Colonial Times to the Present*, New York: Oxford University Press, 2000.

8. Tom Standage, *The Victorian Internet: The Remarkable Story of the Telegraph and the Nineteenth Century's On-Line Pioneers*, New York: Berkley Books, 1998.

9. As any experienced book author will attest to, editors are often eager to spice up a book's title to help sell more copies, which may have happened here. However, although it is a great marketing tool, the author still owns the responsibility for what messages the title of his or her book communicate.

10. Richard R, John, *Spreading the News: The American Postal System from Franklin to Morse*, Cambridge, MA: Harvard University Press, 1995; Basalla, *The Evolution of Technology*.

11. Most notably, David Landes, *The Unbound Prometheus: Technological Change and Industrial Development in Western Europe from 1750 to the Present*, Cambridge, UK: Cambridge University Press, 2003, 2nd ed.

12. Peter J. Hugill, *Global Communications Since 1844: Geopolitics and Technology*, Baltimore, MD: Johns Hopkins University Press, 1999; and Daniel R. Headrick, *When Information Came of Age: Technologies of Knowledge in the Age of Reason and Revolution, 1700–1850*, New York: Oxford University Press, 2000 are two examples.

13. Richard D. Brown, *Knowledge Is Power: The Diffusion of Information in Early America, 1700–1865*, New York: Oxford University Press, 1989.

14. Boundaries are melting between movies and video games, for instance, which I discuss at length in James W. Cortada, *The Digital Hand: How Computers Changed the Work of American Financial, Telecommunications, Media, and Entertainment Industries*, New York: Oxford University Pres, 2006, pp. 412–430.

15. A typical example is by historian Paul E. Ceruzzi, *Reckoners: The Prehistory of the Digital Computer, From Relays to the Stored Program Concept, 1939–1945*, Westport, CT: Greenwood Press, 1983; I also did so early in my own work, *The Computer in the United States: From Laboratory to Market, 1930 to 1960*, Armonk, NY: M.E. Sharpe, 1993.

16. For example, see John Bray, *The Communications Miracle: The Telecommunication Pioneers from Morse to the Information Superhighway*, New York: Plenum Press, 1995; George P. Oslin, *The Story of Telecommunications*, Macon, GA: Mercer University Press, 1992; David C. Moschella, *Waves of Power: The Dynamics of Global Technology Leadership, 1964–2010*, New York: AMACOM, 1997; Manuel Castells, *The Informational City*, Oxford: Blackwell, 1989.

17. James C. Carey, *Communication as Culture: Essays on Media and Society*, Boston, MA: Unwin Hyman, 1989; Joshua Meyrowitz, *No Sense of Place: The Impact of Mass Media on Social Behavior*, New York: Oxford

University Press, 1990; Sara Kiesler, *Culture of the Internet*, Mahway, NJ: Lawrence Erlbaum, 1996; William Mitchell, *City of Bits*, Cambridge, MA: MIT Press, 1995.

18. Jorge Reina Schement and Terry Curtis, *Tendencies and Tensions of the Information Age: The Production and Distribution of Information in the United States*, New Brunswick, N.J.: Transaction Publishers, 1995, pp. 47–70.

19. For an excellent introduction to the issue of converging technologies, including historical case studies, see David B. Yoffie (Ed.), *Competing in the Age of Digital Convergence*, Boston, MA: Harvard Business School Press, 1997.

20. See two important anthologies: Peter J. Denning and Robert M. Metcalfe (Eds.), *Beyond Calculation: The Next Fifty Years of Computing*, New York: Copernicus/Springer-Verlag, 1997; Peter J. Denning (Ed.), *The Invisible Future: The Seamless Integration of Technology into Everyday Life*, New York: McGraw-Hill, 2002.

21. I do not differentiate between era and age, although there are subtle differences; discussing those here would take us astray from our purpose.

22. Marwick, *The Sixties*, pp. 3–22.

23. See, for example, Ceruzzi, *A History of Modern Computing*, pp. ix–x, 2–5, and Paul N. Edwards, *The Closed World: Computers and the Politics of Discourse in Cold War America*, Cambridge, MA: MIT Press, 1996, for how one uses sources for history and yet critiques them, pp. xvii–xx; Janet Abbate, *Inventing the Internet*, Cambridge, MA: MIT Press, 1999, pp. 2, 6; Martin Campbell-Kelly and William Aspray, *Computer: A History of The Information Machine*, New York: Basic Books, 1996, p. 6.

24. For programming practices over time, see Susan Lammers (Ed.), *Programmers at Work: Interviews*, Redmond, WA: Microsoft Press, 1986.

25. On Gates, for example, see Ibid., pp. 70–90; on the earlier period, see John Backus, "Programming in America in the 1950s. Some Personal Impressions," in N. Metropolis, J. Howlett, and G.-C. Rota, *History of Computing in the Twentieth Century*, New York: Academic Press, 1980, pp. 126–127.

26. On computing at the start of the Cold War, see Ceruzzi, *A History of Modern Computing*, pp. 13–46.

27. Richard L. Nolan, "Information Technology Management Since 1960," in Chandler and Cortada, *A Nation Transformed by Information*, pp. 217–256; Cortada, *The Computer in the United States*, pp. 102–124.

28. The case of the PC is illustrative for it did not exist until the mid-1970s and now there are both millions of these devices and nearly a dozen histories of them. For examples, see James Chposky and Ted Leonsis, *Blue Magic: The People, Power and Politics Behind the IBM Personal Computer*, New York: Facts on File Publications, 1988; and Michael S. Malone, *Infinite Loop: How Apple, The World's Most Insanely Great Computer Company Went Insane*, New York: Currency/Doubleday, 1999.

29. See Ceruzzi, for example on the PC, *A History of Modern Computing*, pp. 207–242, and Campbell-Kelly and Aspray, *Computer*, pp. 233–258. The same held true for the Internet.

30. Edwards, *The Closed World*; Abbate, *Inventing the Internet*.

31. James W. Cortada, *Before the Computer*, Princeton, N.J.: Princeton University Press, 1993, pp. 281–287.

32. Jeffrey R. Yost, *The Computer Industry*, Westport, CT: Greenwood Press, 2005.

33. See conclusions by contributors to Chandler and Cortada, *A Nation Transformed by Information;* also my observation when I looked at various aspects of American life over three centuries (e.g., work, leisure, religious practices, etc.), *Making the Information Society; but see also James Beniger,* The Control Revolution: Technological and Economic Origins of the Information Age, Cambridge, MA: Harvard University Press, 1989; and Alfred D. Chandler, Jr., *Inventing the Electronic Century: The Epic Story of the Consumer Electronics and Computer Industries*, Cambridge, MA: Harvard University Press, 2005. Robert Gordon has made a similar point in "Does the 'New Economy' Measure Up to the Great Inventions of the Past?" *NBER Working Paper Series* (August 2000).

34. There are hundreds of books and thousands of articles. For example, see Michael L. Dertouzos, *What Will Be: How the New World of Information Will Change Our Lives*, New York: HarperEdge, 1997; James Martin, *Cybercorp: The New Business Revolution*, New York: AMACOM, 1998; and Stephen A. Brown, *Revolution at the Checkout Counter: The Explosion of the Bar Code*, Cambridge, MA: Harvard University Press, 1997.

35. Peter Lyman and Hal R. Varian have done research on the question about how much data exists. Their ongoing study is the most important ever conducted on the subject, "How Much Information?" (undated), available at how-much-info@sims.berkeley.edu.

36. Chandler and Cortada, *A Nation Transformed by Information,* passim.

37. Daniel E. Sichel, *The Computer Revolution: An Economc Perspective*, Washington, D.C.: Brookings Institution Press, 1997, pp. 39–74.

38. The central finding of my, *The Digital Hand,* 3 vols, New York: Oxford University Press, 2004–2008.

39. Lyman and Varian, "How Much Information?"

40. Many commentators argue that little has changed yet, particularly in government. For a recent example, see "The Electronic Bureaucrat. Special Report: Technology and Government," *The Economist,* February 16, 2008: 1–18, 56.

41. Samuel P. Huntington, "The Clash of Civilizations?" *Foreign Affairs* 73, 3 (Summer 1993): 22–49, and *The Clash of Civilizations and the Remaking of World Order*, New York: Simon & Schuster, 1996.

42. Huntington, *The Clash of Civilizations,* pp. 86–88.

43. Marwick, *The Sixties,* p. 5.

44. Caroll Pursell, *The Machine in America: A Social History of Technology*, Baltimore, MD: Johns Hopkins University Press, 1995; Thomas Hughes, *American Genesis: A Century of Invention and Technological Enthusiasm, 1870–1970*, New York: Viking, 1989; Roe Smith et al., Inventing America. New York: W.W. Norton, 2000; Ruth Schwartz Cowan, *A Social History of Technology*, New York: Oxford University Press, 1996; Cortada, *Making the Information Society.*

45. See for example, Nancy Stern, "The ENIAC: A Case Study in the History of Technology," *Annals of the History of Computing* 1, 1 (July 1979): 9–20; Ceruzzi, *Reckoners;* William Aspray, "The Mathematical Reception of the Modern Computer: John von Neumann and the Institute for Advanced Study Computer," *MAA Studies in Mathematics* 26 (1987): 166–194.

46. Each issue of *IEEE Annals of the History of Computing* reviews such material; see also newsletters: *Charles Babbage Institute Newsletter* and the *IEEE History Center Newsletter.*

47. Chandler and Cortada, *A Nation Transformed by Information,* which includes chapters by historians Alfred D. Chandler, James W. Cortada, Richard D. Brown, Richard R. John, JoAnne Yates, and Margaret Graham.

48. Using history to influence events has been explored by historian Ernest R. May and political scientist coauthor Richard E. Neustadt, *Thinking in Time: The Uses of History for Decision Makers*, New York: Free Press, 1986. For recent trends about applications, see my "Learning from History: Leveraging Experience and Context to Improve Organizational Excellence," *Journal of Organizational Excellence* (Spring 2002): 23–29; and "The Case for Applied History in the World of Business: A Call for Action to Historians" *The Historian* 62, 4 (Summer 2000): 835–847.

49. Carlotta Perez, *Technological Revolutions and Financial Capital*, Cheltenham, UK: Edward Elgar Publishing, 2002, p. 11, but see also table on p. 18.

50. It is not uncommon for large corporations to have call centers in more than one country, prepared to take over the work of another call center. This can be done in a matter of hours, whereas setting up a new center in another country can be accomplished in less than 60 days, or faster if need be. In the early 1990s, while in a prior role at IBM, I designed two call centers; best practices and flexible technologies have been around for a long time.

51. Richard E. Neustadt and Ernest R. May, *Thinking in Time: The Uses of History for Decision Makers*, New York: Free Press, 1986, p. 254.

52. Ibid., p. 270.

6

AN EXPANDING ROLE FOR SCIENTISTS AND ENGINEERS

> Being the best provider of technical information and services should be the society's most important mission.
> —IEEE Computer Society

Computers and communications have become such a part of our lives across some 200 countries that we have almost forgotten the millions of computer scientists and engineers around the world who invented and continue to refine these technologies. They are a relatively silent, often nearly invisible community, and yet, without their continuing role, even the existing technologies would atrophy in time and, of course, not be improved. They are part of the high-tech infrastructure of our modern age. Along with all the programmers, manufacturers, systems analysts, computer operators, repair personnel, and call center experts who we most often think about as the IT community, the technologists who create and sustain IT are rarely discussed outside the closed circles of their working worlds. Yet, they have long played an influential role in shaping our world, a mission that perhaps needs to be further appreciated.

Why are they nearly invisible to the public? For one thing, many work as professors scattered in small groups across thousands of universities and institutes all over the world. For another, many others spend their lives in corporate or government research centers, often working on projects that either are too technical for the public to appreciate (or be interested in), or that are shrouded by corporate policies designed to protect competitive positions. Their opportunities for exposure are few. Although many awards are granted to these individuals, such as the Turing Prize, they are given by technologists to other technologists. There are no Nobel prizes for computing; the closest is for physics, which itself receives less media exposure than the other Nobel prizes for economics, literature, medicine, and peace. Their articles and books are highly technical; one has merely to look at the fine books published by the IEEE Computer Society to see that, though useful to technologists, they will probably never make the *New York Times* Best Seller list. So another avenue of exposure to the greater world is blocked. But this near invisibility does not mean they are without influence. We have the basic fact that the world is filling up with computer technology as the ultimate testimony to their influence. Despite their near anonymity, we know some things about their role, enough that we can conclude that their influence may actually expand over time and, indeed, should.

This chapter describes briefly their role, but I also advocate that this community step outside its traditional comfort zone and promote and help deploy public policies and practices, and lead by example and wisdom, among the wider society to further optimize the great good that IT and its professions can do for people and nations. Because IT is now so prevalent in societies around the world—hopefully a point prior chapters have made evident—the IT community has to play a central role in saying grace over how the technology is leveraged and protects us from potentially negative consequences, such as the mounting pile of e-trash, including my old PCs and laptops. For that reason, this chapter on purpose takes on a more strident tone than earlier ones.

THE RISE OF THE COMPUTER SCIENTIST

In the beginning, there were no computer scientists. Electrical engineers, experts on radio technologies, mathematicians, and a few physicists banded together around computer-like projects in the 1930s, 1940s, and 1950s. Not until the late 1950s did this community come to realize that its members had evolved into a new field and that it had acquired the name "computer science." It was a slow process and this is not the chapter in which to tell their story. However, several historical trends are important to highlight, because they continue to influence the personality of this field and other emerging areas of study, such as biotechnology and services science [1].

They came together on specific projects, such as in the development of early American, British, and Russian computers in the 1940s and 1950s, collaborating in some instances in groups of several hundred, as happened, for example, at Bletchley Park in Great Britain and at MIT in the United States. As corporations began building computers on behalf of government agencies and, later, as their own commercial products, they too began to hire electrical engineers, mathematicians, and others, as IBM did in the early 1950s, in this case situating them in Poughkeepsie, New York, and Burroughs in Detroit, Michigan. Another clustering of experts occurred around the development of transistors and memory systems in California. British, American, French, and Canadian universities created some of the earliest communities of what came to be known as computer scientists and the first computer science departments. Other centers emerged in Boston, Grenoble, Amsterdam, and Moscow. In time, the academics gave definition to their new field through the formation of defined lines of research and instruction (e.g., software, programming languages, and systems architectures), granting advanced degrees in this new field, forming associations (about which we have more to say below), and publishing journals in which their voices could be heard and their research shared. These were worldwide trends. Ten years ago, we only knew that the Americans, British, and Russians did this; now we know that these activities took place in scores of countries that historians have yet to describe [2].

Economic and government demographers eventually came along to tabulate statistics on how many of these people functioned in a nation's economy. There is little aggregation of data on a global basis, however. This does not matter for our purposes as it is enough to know that it is a large number. A few data points suggest the extent. The IEEE Computer Society, the single largest group of experts on computers, for over a decade has had a global membership of between 75,000 and 100,000 members and, if asked, its leaders would argue that there are more computer scientists and engineers running around who were not members. One company, IBM, has a combined population of computer scientists, computer architects, software programmers, and other technologists that easily exceeds 300,000. Add in the technologists at Microsoft and Hewlett Packard, those of Tata in India, and SAP and other firms in Europe, and one begins to realize that the population runs into the millions.

One way that people track computer scientists is by defining that portion of a nation's workforce with academic degrees in the field. Since the United States continues to be one of the largest producers of graduates in the field of computer science, it is informative to look at its numbers. In 1980, American universities and colleges awarded just over 11,000 undergraduate degrees in computer science. In 1990, that cohort of graduates had grown to over 27,300 and then to 37,400 in 2000. Today, that community routinely increases its membership by about 60,000 per year [3]. However, the more important numbers concern the advanced degrees—Masters in Science and Ph.D.s—since it is this community of recipients who normally spend their entire careers in the field and often in roles in which they shape the nature of the technology. In 1980, the total number of advanced degrees awarded in the field in the United States just exceeded 3600, in 1990 it reached nearly 9700, and in 2000 it was ten graduates shy of 15,000. In subsequent years, the number of degrees awarded kept rising by roughly an additional 1000 per annum [4]. If we use U.S. Government census data and add the total number of people in the workforce who are programmers, systems engineers, scientists and so forth working in the field, the number climbs to 28.3 million individuals, of which 700,000 alone are characterized as computer scientists and systems analysts [5]. If we include Europe and East Asia into the mix, doubling the numbers suggests a reasonable, if quite conservative, estimate of the size of the global community.

Computer scientists are as tribal as other professionals, particularly in the United States. One can see that just by looking at the number of associations that exist to serve their needs. Table 6.1 lists the most obvious. A few that existed and no longer do, but the others are very active today. Some are user organizations, but they too have members who are computer scientists, analysts, and engineers. This list is not a definitive one either. The observation to draw from this inventory of associations is that the community of computer experts has social and institutional vehicles that facili-

Table 6.1. Information technology professional associations, 1950s–2000s

American Federation of Information Processing Societies (AFIPS)
American Society for Information Science (ASIS)
Association for Computing Machinery (ACM)
Association for Educational Data Systems (AEDS)
Association for Systems Management (ASM)
IEEE Computer Society (CS)
Data Processing Management Association (DPMA)
Institute of Electrical and Electronics Engineers, Inc. (IEEE)
Instrument Society of America (ISA)
International Federation for Information Processing (IFIP)
Joint Users Group (JUG)
National Computer Conference (NCC)
SHARE
Society for Computer Simulation (SCS)
Society of Information Display (SID)

tate their learning and networking, and offer a forum to raise issues relevant to them and to society.

The IEEE Computer Society (CS) is a good example to look at as it is the largest of these associations. It has consciously encouraged use of various technologies and discussed their related operational issues. In recent years, much effort went into promoting the evolution, training, and deployment of web/net graphics and software engineering, for example. It provides a forum for scientists to publish their research findings and to train people in various subfields of computer science, as has the Association for Computer Machinery (ACM) for many decades.

CS developed and evolved along with its industry and members. In the mid-1940s, a committee was formed within the Institute of Electrical Engineers (IRE) of interested parties, and during the 1950s interest grew around technical computing issues, leading to the establishment of a more formal committee within the IRE and then to publications. Training and sharing of information within the emerging computer community led to rapid growth and in the mid-1960s the group became known as the Computer Group, ending the decade with some 10,000 members. The name was changed to the Computer Society in 1971, and the base broadened with more members, meetings, training, and publications in the 1970s, reflecting the growing community of computer technologists, with special emphasis on those working in software. CS, in turn, established committees focused on the interests on specific technologies as well and ended the decade with 44,000 members. The history of the 1980s and 1990s saw CS grow in size, expand its number of publications and training programs, and become increasingly involved in setting and influencing technical standards in computer and IT products and technologies.

But it was not all about technologies per se. In the 1980s, CS as an institution and its members through personal activities concerned itself with new issues, most notably professional ethics and, more important for the themes of this chapter, governmental activities and public policies. By doing that, CS set the precedent of accepting a role as a major organization in modern society having a responsibility to engage in the great technical issues of the age. Managerially, it established a Committee on Public Policy to channel its thinking and actions in a coordinated fashion and became a presence in Washington, DC. Over the past two decades, CS worked closely with its parent organization, the IEEE, in collaborating on public policy issues in various settings: state and federal in the United States, and in various countries, such as in Europe. These were not trivial efforts. The original policy committee established in the 1980s ended the decade of the 1980s with some 400 members and 12 subcommittees! Moving into a new headquarters building in Washington, DC in 1985 facilitated the public policy advocacy role [6].

CS grew up, so to speak, with the field. Over time, it influenced the lives of hundreds of thousands of individuals. It published over two dozen periodicals, held over a thousand conferences, and its online library contains well over a quarter of a million articles. Today, roughly half its members work outside the United States, which means that the network of experts in the field is an infrastructure diffusing information, formulating transnational worldviews, and implementing professional certification programs [7].

When a formal history of the society is someday written, that historian will tell us that CS always intended to shape the nature and use of computing. By 2004, CS had developed several multi-year strategic plans, beginning in 1991. It continuously took a service-oriented view of things. In its 2004 strategic plan, for instance, it described its intentions "to be the leading provider of technical information, community services, and personalized services for the world's computing professionals" [8]. CS expects to continue providing education, publishing outlets, and community for decades to come to an ever-growing population already living in 150 countries. Yet, its focus has centered largely on the professional technological/training needs of its members and less on issues of wider concern to the countries in which its members live or to some of the managerial issues touched by computing when compared to its technological activities. We will have more to say about those issues later in this chapter.

The ACM, established in 1947, always had a more narrowly focused membership, dominated largely by academic computer scientists and researchers. ACM counted among its members some of the builders of the earliest computers and, later, designers of programming languages. These included such luminaries as John H. Curtiss, John W. Mauchly, Harry D. Huskey, Allan J. Perlis, and Jean E. Sammet. ACM created local chapters and held conferences around the world. It also established and manages the Turing Award, arguably the most prestigious award one can receive for technological contributions to computing. Like CS, it also has published various journals, the most important of which is *Communications of the ACM* (launched 1958). It, too, hosts conferences. Similar stories could be told about other associations listed in table 6.1.

THEIR ROLE IN MODERN SOCIETY

Over the past eight decades, computer scientists and engineers have been a busy group. Their work can briefly be summarized. They developed multiple generations of mainframe computers and peripherals, mini systems, personal computers, and even smaller computational devices. Their work spanned components (e.g., integrated circuits), hardware, software, programming languages and utilities, architectures, information processing, materials science, physics, and chemistry. They contributed an enormous body of thinking about the collection, sorting, analysis, and use of data, and the interactions of various components of the technology with information, from silicon and electronics to how to engage in human–machine interactions (e.g., GUI and the World Wide Web). They took computers in rapid succession from highly unreliable, large, and expensive experimental machines and systems of machines to ubiquitous, tiny, inexpensive devices. In the 1960s, they began the historically profound process of merging telecommunications and computing. That very complex convergence of technologies, which is still underway, triggered the transformation of so many aspects of modern society that so often leads sociologists, economists, reporters, and pundits to declare that we live in the Information Age. As they drove down the cost of various technologies and both transformed them into easier to use systems and shrank their size, the number of people who could use these increased. Now it seems that anyone can have access to computing, and if we think of mobile telephones as little computers, then one could argue the case that over 3 billion people use computers today. It is a remarkable set of achievements created by only several million people backed up by tens of millions of government, business, and IT workers around the world.

Early accounts of the history of computing were largely written by members of this community. They naturally emphasized the role of engineers, machines, and technologies. The first wave of historians to examine the history of IT began telling a story that included as well the firms that made these technologies available to users and the institutions that supported their development (e.g., U.S., French, British, and Soviet governments). In the process, historians brought more types of individuals onto the stage to share the accolades with computer scientists. These included IBM executives, generals from the Pentagon, officials at the National Science Foundation (NSF), and IT professionals working as users in government and business from across the world. DP Managers became MIS Directors, then CIOs. Meanwhile whole new IT-based industries developed: software firms such as the mighty Microsoft, and hardware companies such as IBM, Apple, Hewlett Packard, Sun, Nixdorf, Hitachi, and Dell. In many of the more advanced economies, it was not uncommon for a nation to spend 6–8% of its gross national product on IT by the early 2000s. It was becoming crowded on the stage, as computer scientists were joined by others who were recognized for their achievements in the diffusion of computing.

Historians of computing also found themselves a bit crowded as well, beginning largely in the late 1980s, and extensively so in the 1990s, because as the Internet spread, thousands of commentators from many fields weighed in on the evolution, use, and consequences of computing. Now, instead of a stage to hold all the contributors to the creation and deployment of computers, we needed a stadium that could hold many times more people. We had to add journalists, sociologists, ex-CEOs writing their memoirs, corporate archivists and media relations people commenting on IT, and public officials keen on regulating or at least shaping the use and consequences of the technology. Economists argued about productivity paradoxes, business managers about Moore's Law, and public officials about censorship, intellectual capital protection, and effects on democracy, while sociologists and cultural anthropologists talked about networked societies.

Sometime between 2002 and 2004, the world reached a tipping point in the number of citizens in North America, Europe, East Asia, and the middle and upper classes in Latin America who became extensive users of the Internet for gathering information and conducting transactions [9]. We do not yet have composite statistics for the entire world but hundreds of surveys done in those years clearly demonstrate that now nearly a third of the planet was becoming engaged with the technology and, in the process, forming opinions about how it should be used and what shape it had to take. Computer scientists and then a tiny wave of historians and other commentators now had to share the limelight with the public at large, making even our allegorical stadium far too small. In short, whereas computer scientists and technologists served as the hinge of the technology, because they designed, built, and diffused most of the information technology, they were now outnumbered and outtalked. As the activities of the ACM and the CS attest, they were busy at work inventing new technologies and pushing the frontiers of knowledge about computer science, while economists and public administrators anguished over whether there were enough of these people to serve the needs of society. It is a remarkable situation if you are a computer scientist, or an expert of any sort on the technology in almost any part of the world.

There seems to be no end in sight to the demand for the technology. Studies conducted by economists at IBM and at the Economist Intelligence Unit (EIU) on how economic development was done observed that since the 1990s, hardly (if any) national economic development strategy omitted leveraging information technology as a critical part of the plan, an issue discussed more fully in Chapter 3 [10]. It has long been understood by economists that IT can either generate new jobs, firms, and industries or improve the capabilities and productivity of existing ones [11]. As national economies continue to plug into an increasingly integrated global economy, one characterized by industries that depend on workers and work being done around the world, one of the substrata that hold all that together is IT. Other infrastructures include laws protecting contracts and property, regulation of inappropriate practices, and education and training programs that make available competitive workforces. But back to the technology: public officials look to their local technologists to advise them on how best to use IT and largely to their economists on how to integrate those into national economic policies. Invariably, one sees officials reaching out to the technologists for advice or help, but we do not observe computer scientists and technologists overtly taking the initiative to reach out to officials. That situation really should change, because they can make a difference. One example will have to suffice to illustrate the point.

Professor Nicholas Negreponte at the Massachusetts Institute of Technology (MIT) has designed and is starting to manufacture a tiny laptop, if you can even call it that since it looks like a green plastic toy, that draws its data and software off a wireless Internet connection and currently costs about $200 per machine. It is designed to be used by children in an educational setting, ideally in poor countries, although we rich Westerners are beginning to wonder if they would not also make sense for our own children to use. He has shown the device to public officials all over the world and in some countries they are slowly now being adopted, most recently, for example, in Peru. The point is, he is a computer scientist who used his skills to help society in a proactive way by leveraging his technical and managerial capabilities.

African and Latin American countries need their local scientists to be just as creative in finding ways to apply the technology. Positive examples can be found everywhere, from what occurred in South Korea, which was a backward nation with a very low GDP twenty-five years ago, but is now a high-tech powerhouse whose population are among the most extensive users of broadband in the world, to Japan, with its national policy to become an information society. It seems that every coffee shop in Estonia is equipped with wireless Internet connections [12]. Our research clearly demonstrates that the use of IT by all levels of society is the most extensive that it has ever been and yet it seems that "everyone" still needs the advice and experience of the technologists to leverage IT properly.

WHEN SCIENTISTS AND TECH FOLK TAKE THINGS INTO THEIR OWN HANDS

Negreponte is only the latest in a long list of computer scientists and engineers taking matters into their own hands. They have done this as individuals, through their associations, and as members of corporations. Although we do not yet have even a one-volume history of their role, much has been written about it. MIT's Vannevar Bush, an early developer of analogue calculators as far back as the 1920s, lobbied and published on the role of science and computing in American society in the 1930s and 1940s. There is a long tradition of technologists publishing in each subsequent decade on what IT could or could not do and what society should do about it [13]. To be sure, one could argue that this community does not have the breadth of skills for such roles, if we recall earlier efforts by Howard Aiken in 1948 and John von Neumann in the late 1950s as examples. Yet we have the countervailing examples of the CS and IEEE in the United States, and also the practice of government officials in Washington, DC sustaining technical agencies to advise and support efforts in the rest of government, and to finance research and "think tanks." The European Union created forums in which computer scientists, and even historians of IT, could come together to advise national governments on how best to use IT. Of course, the EU itself is an institution with a pan-European policy of supporting IT. We will discuss further how best to proceed below, but suffice it to say that a more pro-active strategy calls for institutional initiatives rather than attempted heroic efforts by individuals.

Groups of engineers have long made a difference in the hallways and meeting rooms of corporations. In the late 1940s at IBM's laboratory in Poughkeepsie, New York, home of the company's research and manufacturing in the United States at that time, a number of engineers familiar with the most advanced electronics that surfaced during World War II began to think about computers. Lab directors started hiring more of these kinds of people and over the course of a decade called on various American government agencies to explore the possibilities of building computers funded by public officials. Their conversations were specific, with few people in the room in such places as the Bureau of the Census and at various military agencies. Other small groups of engineers from the Eckert-Mauchly Computer Company, which eventually built the Univac, did the same thing, as did others from Burroughs, ERA, and NCR [14]. These efforts often occurred before some companies had embraced the computer as the future technology platform. That was especially the case at IBM, a situation well documented by IBM's CEO, Thomas J. Watson, Jr., in his memoirs, in which he described the political and managerial wrangling that went on inside his firm for years as young computer scientists pushed for a greater commitment to the technology and general management either resisted because of the risk of losing revenue flows from tabulating equipment or simply tried to figure out if there was a commercial market for computers [15]. Historians who have looked at IBM's history from the late 1940s to the mid-1950s agree that the firm's electrical engineers and computer scientists pushed harder than any other constituency inside the company for the transition.

The advocacy role of this community extended outside of the firm. Peter Harsha, an IT industry watcher in Washington, DC, documented a number of these activities. After the Soviets launched Sputnik in 1957, the American government became energized around the need for more scientific initiatives far beyond what it already had promoted. Two by-products of that growing interest were the establishment in the Pentagon of the Advanced Research Projects Agency (ARPA) and the National Aeronautics and Space Administration (NASA). Both subsequently stimulated the advance of computer science for decades. But, in particular at ARPA (later called DARPA), a small group of computer scientists and engineers came in and out of the agency, usually on roughly two-year rotation assignments, to set and support national research agendas for computing that pushed the field forward by funneling research funds into corporations and academic institutions. Harsha concluded that this "agency was remarkably nimble for a federal entity, able to act and approve new research programs with minimal bureaucracy" [16]. We all know about DARPA because it funded development of what today we call the Internet.

Harsha also reminded us about the role of scientists and engineers during the American presidential elections of 1964, when Democratic Lyndon Johnson was running for reelection for president against Republican U.S. Senator Barry Goldwater. Up to that time, scientists from all disciplines and of all political stripes played hardly any role in national elections and rarely expressed opinions in public about the functions of science, technology, or national policy. Occasionally, someone might serve in a "brain trust" advisory capacity, but that was about it. However, that year a group who called themselves Scientists and Engineers for Johnson–Humphrey, came together out of fear that Goldwater would prove unsuitable to govern the nation at a time of heightened tensions over the possibility of nuclear war. This organization grew quickly into a community of nearly 50,000 members and ran a national publicity campaign in support of Johnson's candidacy. Political scientists and historians later credited this group for Goldwater losing the election because these scientists had created in the public's mind the perception that he was some sort of reckless "bomb-dropper" [17]. Although scientists and engineers had misgivings about their role, nonetheless they had influenced events. For scientists in all fields, their actions had set a precedent because of their increased involvement in national dialogues. It became a role they continued to play in a more subdued manner in subsequent years. Computer scientists were reflecting the broader pattern of behavior evident in the scientific community at large.

In more recent years, scientists from all fields, including computer science, began coalescing around a new issue—global warming. All through the 1980s and 1990s, experts in various fields had accumulated evidence that the world's environment and, specifically, its weather, was changing faster than they thought was normal and gradually but increasingly came to the conclusion that the problem was largely attributable to the expanded use of carbon fuels by humans in the twentieth century. The usual academic debates proceeded on the "pros" and "cons" of the evidence for years, but by the early 2000s, the community as a whole had reached consensus on the matter. Individual scientists in different parts of the world began advocating changes in national policies and economic practices to mitigate the effects of global warming, although there continues to be controversy over its causes. Nonetheless, scientists committed to the notion that humans were causing the world to heat up became increasingly vocal, led initially by climate scientists and later supported by resolutions passed by over 30 scientific associations, including all the leading ones around the world, such as the American Association for the Advancement of Science, Britain's Royal Meteorological Society, and the European Academy of Sciences and Arts. By 2007, it had become routine for large groups of scientists representing colleagues around the world and across multiple disciplines to issue reports and warnings, typically before world leaders met at their annual G8 summits. It is a process still under way.

Individual computer scientists, as members of any of the associations that grappled with the problem, were, in effect, part of the debate. What has not yet happened is the formal institutional taking of sides in the discussion by the Computer Society or the IEEE. Maybe they should not. However, what has been made clear from the role of meteorological scientists and geologists in the debate is that there may be a role for computer scientists and other information technologists to play more forcefully in influencing public policy and corporate practice, a role that they seem to have already begun playing.

WHEN TECHNOLOGISTS GO GREEN

No socially charged topic has so caught the imagination and attention of the IT community as green issues. CIOs, programmers, systems analysts, computer scientists, engineers, IT vendors, their industry and academic associations, and the technical press and media have generally jumped on the bandwagon to address the world's environmental problems with greener technologies. This happened almost overnight, essentially since around 2005, as the scientific evidence for global warming and the role of humans in the process mounted and made its way into the lives and reading practices of technologists. The interest in green themes seen within the IT ecosystem can be described as a social movement with all the attributes of noble, selfless causes. It also happens to be very good business and, from a research perspective, a "hot" topic. For example, IBM periodically hosts company-wide jams to engage hundreds of thousands of employees in dialogues about issues within the firm. Green practices has made the short list of issues of most interest to employees. As the company began paying increased attention to IT green issues, one was hard put to find anyone in the firm who did not want to contribute to the cause. It was a truly remarkable occurrence, one replicated in one company after another. This level of interest represented a departure from past passivity when it came to social issues influencing the nature of computing. It made most prior social topics and issues pale into insignificance. While it is difficult to forecast whether this enthusiasm will last or not, since it also represents an opportunity to de-

sign whole new classes of systems and because there is an economic appetite to replace machines that consume more energy
with more efficient ones, one could reasonably expect the momentum to last at least for as long as this book stays in print.

From a practical business managerial perspective, IT interest
began with the specific issue of energy efficiency. It had actually
been a longstanding issue. In the 1960s and 1970s, engineers and
computer scientists explored how to channel the BTUs spun off
mainframes to heat buildings that housed data centers. Air conditioning manufacturers participated in the effort all through the
second half of the twentieth century as they too sought to lower
the cost of their products by diverting heat away rather than having to cool it. The cost of electrical power rose over the past four
decades, beginning in the early1970s, in part because oil prices
went up, as did the expense of constructing electrical generating
plants, mining coal, and using nuclear energy. The problem came
back in the early 2000s again with rising costs of energy, and with
the added concern about reducing carbon footprints that, in turn,
affected pollution and global warming. Some public officials became concerned that the use of electricity was rising so fast in
large cities due specifically to increased use of IT that they might
not be able to meet demand. London, for example, sought to encourage local data centers to find ways to lower use of electricity.
Meanwhile, CIOs all over the world continued to add servers to
their networks to satisfy end-user demands for increased computing power. All the key surveys on demand for computing conducted in the past several years suggested, however, that the need for
additional computing would remain intense over the next decade;
that should be of no surprise.

Almost every survey of green IT during the same period also
confirms that the most intense interest in curbing use of power
and cooling is focusing on data centers. New software tools to
track consumption appear continuously; every major hardware
vendor is introducing products that use less electricity and run
cooler. To some extent, this is a normal evolution as computing
continues its seven-decade-long trend of miniaturization and less
moving parts, one with no end in sight. Tucked under the covers
of that trend is another one: the reduction in power and cooling
required of new generations of computer chips, thanks to the work
of computer scientists and engineers. Yet, they have not solved
the problem. One study recently pointed out that data centers con-

sume up to 100 times more energy per square foot than any other function in a business building, largely caused by energy consumption still increasing per server, in some instances fourfold between 2001 and 2006 [18]. This is an unacceptable situation that the IT scientific and engineering community has to fix. In addition, it drives continuing increases in operating expenses. A recent survey of small and mid-sized companies in Europe conducted by IBM revealed that energy cost in general was the largest growing line item in the budgets of half the firms, surpassing such traditional sources of rising costs as healthcare and routine salary increases [19]. So, in addition to IT managers becoming involved, now we have general management in firms and government agencies putting pressure on their IT staffs and vendors to address the problem.

CIOs are beginning to understand how much power they are consuming [20]. Second, they are taking into account green features of IT products as they decide what new hardware to acquire. Third, they are upgrading existing infrastructures and factoring in green considerations, as, for example, where in an organization they should move IT work, such as to data centers that use less electricity. Since hardware turns over fairly quickly, on average every two to four years, CIOs know they can rapidly lower their energy consumption because their suppliers will continue to improve the energy efficiency of newer products. Fourth, as they build new data centers, they are implementing energy reduction and environmentally efficient strategies, such as shrinking the size of glass houses and using building materials friendly to the environment. When combined with newer hardware, the effects can be impressive. For example, the Georgia Institute of Technology Center for the Study of Systems Biology collaborated with IBM on the configuration of a supercomputer, reaching back to an old idea from the 1960s and 1970s of building into the equipment a rear-door heat exchanger, which cut air conditioning required for the machine by just over half. That, in turn, lowered operating costs at the center by over 10%, translating into a savings of some $780,000 [21]. As stories like these spread throughout the IT community, management will have more specific ideas about what to do and will be able to set realistic objectives [22].

This trend also extends to small systems. For example, in 2008 Dell took great pains to explain to its customers how it had reduced energy consumption of its products and by implementing green practices within the firm, such as the recycling of old and returned products and lowering energy consumption in their manufacturing processes. In Dell's products of 2008, its engineers and vendors had redesigned power supplies to reduce use of wasted power at lower workloads, introduced variable-speed, temperature-controlled fans that spun at lower speeds when the rooms they were operating in were cooler, used smaller form-factor hard drives that could save up to 7 watts per drive over the more conventional 3.5″ versions, and lower voltage processors [23]. Some parts are still energy hogs that need redesigning, such as a fast GPU video card present in so many PCs and laptops, which probably will have to go the way of the large disk drives of the past and be replaced by motherboard video-output techniques, for instance.

Now, all of this may sound like a foreign language to many readers, but there is a point to be made here. All computing systems, like automobiles or other complex objects, are made up of various parts and subsystems. Historically, improvements in large devices occur incrementally over time. That is a direct lesson from history. Real improvements in green computing will occur through incremental enhancements in the performance, parts, and configuration of equipment over time. That is where computer scientists and engineers come into the picture. They design those subsystems and components, and determine how they will work together. It is an incremental process. To be sure, on occasion a spectacular improvement comes along. When some unanticipated innovation becomes part of the technological mix, most technologists know that is an exception. So when we read about future systems that may be biological, or use something other than silicon, they seem interesting and may come into existence, but, in the meantime, we need to navigate quickly to more efficient systems the old fashioned way, by applying good science and engineering practices to improving existing technologies.

Environmental regulations and government policies are spurring the computing community along as well. In 1992, the U.S. Environmental Protection Agency began encouraging vendors to focus on greening their products, which, in turn, evolved into specific environmental regulations in North America and in Western Europe. In the 1990s, the European Union implementing regulations governing the use and disposal of hazardous substances, and on the disposal of old electronic equipment, a series of mandates that continue to appear. Today in Europe, vendors must accept their old products that are returned for recycling. Simultaneously, standards appeared for controlling use of heavy metals and flame retardants. Environmentalists, often including computer scientists and engineers, have become active in setting standards, such as those of the Climate Savers Computing Initiative (CSCI) that encourage reduced energy consumption of PCs, the Wildlife Fund's Climate Savers program, the Green Computing Impact Organization, Inc., the Green Electronics Council, and the Green Grid; the list of organizations grows every year. Green Grid is interesting. Founded in February 2007, it has many supporters such as key IT vendors AMD, Dell, Hewlett Packard, IBM, Intel, APC, Microsoft, Rackable Systems, SprayCool, Sun Microsystems, and VMware, and several hundred other suppliers. In short, these organizations employ tens of thousands of IT experts, providing them the institutional channel through which to make a difference. So far, Green Grid is focused on improving energy efficiency, but that will change as that problem is solved and the bigger issues of environmental impacts are addressed next.

Environmental discussions have been expanding since about 2005 in a wide variety of fields, more than can be discussed in this chapter. Two of increasing concern, and that IT organizations should weigh in on, involve environmental impacts of the manufacture of computer products and disposal of discarded items. Manufacturing has the well-known challenge of trying to keep chip manufacturing as pollution free as possible, on which much progress has been made over the past decade, but still has far to go, and which has the added problem of legacy pollution left over from manufacturing activities of prior decades. One by-product still to be fully conquered, of course, is seepage into underground water, but there are other related concerns, too. With respect to e-trash, the issue has a long history. For decades, there have been firms all around the world that extracted gold and platinum from older machines. Today, that work has extended to dismantling equipment for additional metals (such as lead) and other components that in the process create environmental and health problems in Asia, Latin America, and, increasingly, in various African countries. There is much discussion in the press and by environmental activists about these various issues, but they are not in any position to address them. They do not run manufacturing facilities or dispose of old CRTs; members of the larger IT community do that and so it will have to be that group, comprised of companies, scientists, and engineers, and their industry associations that will have to find greener ways to make and dispose of IT equipment. Regulators in Europe and increasingly in North America have spurred on manufacturers and retailers to do more through stringent regulations, which is a good start, but ultimately it will be the computer scientists and engineers who will have to develop and implement solutions to these problems. So far, computer scientists and engineers have only just started to frame the issues, define the challenges, and pay attention to these problems. And, of course, these problems are compounded by the fact that IT is embedded in all manner of machinery and consumer goods, so whatever environmental problems technology creates are spread in various proportions to other industries and things, from automobiles to flat screen TVs, to iPods and iPhones, microwave ovens and lawn mowers, even to household heating and air conditioning systems, and children's automata toys.

Negreponte's laptop, which has received positive exposure throughout this book, illustrates the problem. As interesting as these laptops are, look at them from a green perspective by thinking about what happens someday when hundreds of thousands, if not millions, are replaced with a new generation of equipment. Then we face a not-so-positive issue. The fact is, they are a potentially excessive polluter based on the components and metals that comprise the devices, as wonderful as this technology is for children. What will be done to protect the children's environments when these have to be disposed of? How will that be done in practice? Will they simply be tossed into landfills or pilled on top of all the CRTs and PCs coming out of the developed economies and shipped to poor countries with minimal environmental regulations? Professor Negreponte will not be able to answer those questions because the decisions will be made by officials and individuals over whom he has no control. Perhaps the community he works with at MIT and others will be able to develop greener second-generation laptops, but we are still left with the real problem of what to do with the ones already in existence. The problem is also compounded by the fact that his are not the only laptops being manufactured that are intended for poor children in underdeveloped economies. So, we have a long way to go as an IT community in addressing e-pollution.

In addition to these environmental issues, software developers are another community playing a growing role in the greening of the world. The following list of the current roles of software is both obvious but not always implemented:

- Using collaborative communications tools to reduce commuting from home to office
- Moving processing work to underutilized servers to lower the demand for more machines
- Managing inventories of equipment using life cycle management practices
- Optimizing HVAC [24] for hot spots
- Optimizing data storage uses and demand
- Designing processes that reduce carbon footprints, such as is happening with supply chain management
- Implementing intelligent traffic management systems to reduce engine idling, inefficient automotive travel, and traffic congestion
- Modeling tools for the design of airplane and automotive engines
- Deploying more online applications and use of electronic forms to reduce paper consumption

Programmers and systems analysts are leading the charge in collaboration with end users. At IBM, for instance, all divisions have been able to reduce the demand for office space, spinning off a multibillion-dollar savings by making it possible for over 40% of its employees to work remotely, either at clients or at home. Software made that possible, along with changes in the processes and culture of our work practices. It was a long journey, however, one that began about 1990. I say "about," because various locations in the company had been experimenting with mobile work once laptops and their predecessors came into existence, starting in the 1980s. As more versatile, smaller devices such as netbooks, and more useful software come to market, people will find new ways to reduce their personal carbon footprints.

Academics are addressing green issues as well. Their universities are doing more than just producing a stream of patent applications and press releases. For instance, there is the National Energy Research Scientific Computer Center at Berkeley Lab, with its Computational Research Division, both parts of the Lawrence Berkeley National Laboratory at the University of California—

Berkeley. Researchers there are working on how to reduce energy consumption in next-generation computers and storage technologies used in scientific computations. Part of their work focuses on the development of multicore chips to lower energy use. Today's basic strategy of computer vendors to lower energy consumption is by improving the performance of their chips. Other scientists are developing algorithms to optimize use of computing by colleagues as they do their research. Still others at Berkeley are examining how to optimize storage within disk drives, reducing the physical spinning of these devices while optimizing utilization [26].

Advocacy within the IT community is a natural follow-on to much of these activities. The major organizations of computer scientists and engineers are just beginning to engage in the issue, a reflection of growing interest expressed by their members. The IEEE's Xplore® digital library is becoming a source of information on green computing, but the pickings are sparse at the moment. The IEEE Computer Society has also started to pay attention to the issue. As this chapter was being written, it hosted the twenty-sixth annual IEEE International Conference on Computer Design, with green computing as its theme for 2008. This is an important milestone for computer scientists and their associations because it is institutional recognition that this is an important issue and from a practical perspective, an opportunity for scientists and engineers to come together to share ideas and formulate collaborative initiatives. Theory and practice come together at conferences hosted by the IT communities' institutions. Their interests span the breadth of computer science: computer systems, processor architecture, logic and circuit design, electronic design automation, verification and testing, modeling and performance analysis, operating systems, programming languages, memory hierarchies, and parallel processors; the list is long. These are areas of interest to the technologists and they are given an opportunity to work with like-minded people down in the bowels of IT on green issues [26]. This particular event is much like other conferences in that it is international in scope, with participants from scores of countries. For example, while this conference was being held in the United States, another IEEE conference took place in Tsukuba, Japan, home to a large high-tech community, on the general theme of cluster computing. Green themes became part of that program's agenda too [27].

What does the future hold for green advocates within the IT community? In addition to more of the same, and a louder voice through their associations, is a vast area of opportunity in the field of energy and for the utility industry providers themselves. Additionally, since so many products are intelligent, the work of technologists in reducing the carbon footprints of computing, such as chips, will be embedded in automobiles, papermaking machines, aircraft engines, and so forth. But it will have to be the IT professionals who show others how to leverage any advances made in the greening of computing, just as they always did whenever they invented something new. Second, there is a rapidly growing interest in measuring consumption of energy in devices, offices, and homes. Somebody has to invent the sensors and the software to do the work for a new generation of energy management tools useful to a major electrical utility, or in one's home, such as tracking energy consumption by the refrigerator. Add in the growing market for clean energy and the opportunity appears massive. In 2007 alone, venture capitalists invested $3.4 billion in clean-energy projects, what many venture capitalists argued was nothing less than a burst of energy on their part. So the funding and support to take IT into new fields is impressive and increasing. The concept of green energy is also spilling over into other areas, such as water management and conservation all over the world, made possible by use of meters, modeling, and modulation of consumption. It is no accident that a technology company, IBM, established two centers of excellence in the field of water management, one in the Netherlands and the other in Ireland, to start working on the issue. The majority of the staffs at both sites are not hydrologists but computer experts.

THEIR FUTURE WORLD

The world is growing and changing around us. There has long been a debate about the supply of computer scientists and engineers, going back to the birth of the computer in the 1940s. By the end of the 1980s, the debate turned on the issue of the perceived inadequate supply of programmers, a concern that surfaced again with the need for COBOL programmers at the end of the century to remediate Y2K concerns. As recently as 2004, William Aspray, a highly respected expert on IT issues and history, brought together public policy experts and others from academia, in part to discuss what the United States should consider doing in the years to come to ensure that there will be enough computer scientists and technicians to serve an increasingly technology-dependent society, evidence that the concern remains alive and important. Meanwhile, American software firms were pressuring the U.S. Congress to let more foreign programmers into the country, with an eye cast on the large supply available from Eastern Europe, Russia, and Asia. Technical societies, like the IEEE, tended to be uncomfortable with such debates about visas since it had members from all over the world, and was reluctant to get into the middle of the debate, although pulled by one side or the other into it [28]. Meanwhile, India had built a powerhouse software industry in the 1980s and 1990s that had become the envy of many countries, and, under the radar, the Irish had done the same for hardware and computing components, sparking a remarkable local economic renaissance in one generation. And who can ignore the transformation of New Zealand's agricultural economy, which is best known for mutton but that became a center for some of the most advanced movie production techniques in the world, and, of course, for its film industry, making the trilogy, *Lord of the Rings*? The country rapidly became a magnet for programmers, computer engineers, and video game designers. The point is, computer scientists and engineers, and other IT professionals, are experiencing a renaissance of their own that reflects several features.

First, their numbers are increasing all over the world; labor forecasts suggest that this trend will continue. It is now a fluid, nearly global community, one often cited by sociologists as an example of a new elite international class that roams the world for good places to live and interesting work to do [29]. Old measures of how many graduates of universities are being produced, while useful benchmarks, may either simply be inaccurate, as is the case with estimates about the number of graduates coming out of China, Russia, and old Soviet Bloc nations, because these do not reflect the fact that computing can be learned in a variety of settings not well tracked. For another example, graduates with M.B.A. degrees in many American universities learn to program, build, manage, and use databases, and to perform simulation and operations research, all while studying for a business degree. There is no advanced science degree program ignoring computing, its tools, or even its methods of transformation, since often it must be scientists working with IT experts who invent new digital tools, as occurs routinely now in biotechnology, pharmacology, and medicine, for example.

Second, where these people perch in an economy has been changing for decades, a facet of their field not yet well documented. During the first several decades of computers, the technologists, for the most part lodged in computer departments in companies and governments, and computer science and engineering departments in universities, and were scattered across the entire spectrum of jobs in IT firms, from CEOs to entry-level programmers. During the past twenty years, however, an undocumented pattern became evident to those who lived in the world of information technology in which programmers, computer scientists, managers, and executives with IT backgrounds began seeping into noncomputer jobs, such as vice presidents of manufacturing, retail, telecommunciations, and marketing, and later even as CEOs of companies. To be sure, that was inevitable as people moved through their careers and circumstances played out.

In addition, as the work of non-IT organizations became more computer-intensive, technologists appeared in those departments. For example, as computer chips were built into automotive engines, the number of programmers in companies like General Motors skyrocketed. In the case of GM, recall that it needed so many of these skills that it bought Ross Perot's IT company, EDS, in the early 1980s. One would be hard pressed to find any midsized agency or firm that did not have engineers, programmers, systems analysts, and other technologists working outside the glass house. In short, there are so many experts on IT that official employment data understate consistently where these people work. This circumstance applies all over the world. In China, for example, over 600,000 new engineers graduate annually from its universities, the majority having been heavily exposed to computing. The Indian results are similar. As a consequence, we can reasonably conclude that much information about computing and its scientific and technical underpinnings are broadly diffused across the majority of national economies. Gerard Jay Sussman, of MIT, described the ultimate consequence of this diffusion of knowledge:

> At this moment in history we are only at the beginning of an intellectual revolution based on the assimilation of computational ideas. The previous revolutions took a long time for the consequences to actualize. It is hard to predict where this one

will lead. I see one of the deepest consequences of computational thinking entering our society in the transformation of
our view of ourselves. [30]

Besides acknowledging the effects of computing on how we
speak and what words we use, he observed that "my experience as
a computer programmer has made me aware that many of my own
problems are bugs that can be analyzed and debugged, often with
great effort, and sometimes patched" [31].

Third, we have now entered a period in the adoption of computing that cannot be described as anything less than profoundly
historic. I already mentioned a few numbers about machines and
technologists, but all the evidence indicates that computing is so
extensive that in most countries it can be described as pervasive,
except in the poorest nations. One set of numbers reinforces the
notion of diversity in the diffusion of these technologies. The
World Bank, which has as its mission to help the poorest nations
rise out of poverty through economic development, reported that
as of 2004 in Sub-Saharan Africa, demonstrably the poorest region
on Earth, 15 out every one thousand residents already had access
to a personal computer; 80 people out of a thousand to a cellular
phone. At the other extreme—Europe—98 people out of a thousand had access to a PC; 440 people to cell phones. But what is
most interesting is that the rates of adoption of these emblematic
technologies had actually increased between 1997 and 2004 all
over the world, including in all poor regions [32].

If we put a historian's hat on, one would have to argue that what
societies are experiencing is the emergence of an era in which
computer science is seeping into almost all other technologies, regardless of what name we give to it. Carlota Perez, who attracted
the attention of many business executives in the early 2000s with
her historical analysis of where computing fitted into the bigger
picture of human adoption of all manner of technologies, while
perhaps simplifying the message, got it right. She argued that from
the 1700s to the present, five technological revolutions occurred,
most of which are reasonably obvious: the Industrial Revolution;
the Age of Steam and Railways; the Age of Steel, Electricity, and
Heavy Engineering; the Age of Oil; Age of the Automobile and
Mass Production; and the Age of Information and Telecommunications [33]. The reader is undoubtedly familiar with the key elements of the last one: computer chips, telecommunications, control instrumentation, cable, Internet, e-mail, and so forth. But,

almost brushing close to Sussman's idea, she noted that over the next half century or so, humankind will embed more computing into their lives and work, much as the earlier technologies took time to diffuse throughout societies and affect the way worked and played. Perez's list of what gets done next is useful for our purposes:

- Information intensity (microelectronics-based ICT)
- Decentralized integration/network structures
- Knowledge as capital/intangible value added
- Heterogeneity, diversity, adaptability
- Segmentation of markets/proliferation of niches
- Economies of scope and specialization combined with scale
- Globalization/interaction between the global and the local
- Inward and outward cooperation/clusters
- Instant contact and action/instant global communications [34]

We will leave it to others to debate the merits of the list and the contours of each feature. The point to make is that these are widely recognized as the kinds of changes computing will bring about in the years to come, indeed, over the course of the lives of everyone reading this book in the early 2000s.

What does this mean for computer scientists, engineers, and IT specialists at large? We discuss below the leadership role they could play outside their computer world and some key needs and roles in support of their daily work. While forecasting is at best a relatively unscientific, perhaps iffy, activity, some trends are evident already and, thus, serve less as a view at the crystal ball than as observations about processes under way. In some ways, the future is more of the present. For a half-century, anybody working with information technology has faced the need to find ways to stay current, to learn about the evolving technology and how best to use it. That requirement remains, because the evolution of technology and the introduction of a continuous flow of hardware and software products proceed with no abatement either in speed or volume. So, training a new generation of computer scientists, along with keeping all the other technologists current in their skills, will remain an important feature of their work for years to come. This will be complicated by the fact that innovations now surface all over the world. Korean R&D on integrated circuits, social networking software and applications in the United States, and new software packages coming out of Europe and India are examples. Those doing such things represent an ever growing community. If the Computer Society worries about training and educating 100,000 members, a core mission it always had, in the years to come it will have to think about how to support 200,000 or even over a million technologists, while sustaining innovative activities in all phases of its members' work.

An additional development involves "networking with other professionals," to quote a strategic planning document prepared by the Computer Society itself, reinforced by the epigram at the start of this chapter, also from the same report [35]. Will the professionals need to develop tools to help them network within an ever-larger community, or will they use existing and emerging ones? History teaches us that they will use tools colleagues develop as part of their work in corporations and university communities. Many are appearing right now so the inevitable shakeout will have to occur to get down to the few, the best, and the most widely used facilitative software tools. Along the way, technologists will deal with such technical and nontechnical issues as data security and privacy as more information about individuals goes online, along with software to mine that information for socially and legally acceptable, and, undoubtedly, unacceptable, purposes. It will be the IT community that will ultimately have to develop the tools and techniques that their individual national societies ask of them.

A third long-standing trend that will continue to unfold is the migration of technologists to all manner of leadership roles in every industry and country. I mentioned this trend earlier in this chapter, but we need to discuss further some of the implications. For one thing, it will increasingly be difficult for someone to build a career within IT without having other skills: managerial, process, leadership, business, industry-specific understanding, and so forth. Historically, technologists worried about keeping up to date with computing technology, or focused their time on creating new forms, but in the years to come they will need to play a larger role in their nations, economies, and enterprises, so they must learn new things. Can their technical societies help with that? Absolutely, and they should. Individuals will need to define their careers differently as well, which means they will have to take individual initiatives to keep up with others sets of ideas and facts, including managerial, nontechnical operational processes and social and political developments. Having an MBA in business administration with a heavy dose of IT is already becoming a fashionable combination of training, suggesting that perhaps the trend is already taking long-term root. The book you are holding exemplifies that blend as it is more about nontechnical issues, yet was published by a highly respected computer society. It is a book that can be read by computer scientists and political scientists, by CIOs and economists. This broadening of issues mixed with technology is becoming a new knowledge for technologists.

AN OLD ROLE MADE NEW

This discussion begs the question: Is there an evolving role for computer scientists, engineers, and other IT professionals in the years to come beyond the daily tasks of inventing, building, deploying, training, and using information technologies? To be sure, these are five core functions that have occupied much of the time of computing technologists over the past six to seven decades and there is no indication that these will go away. But, in answer to the question, the response is yes. As computer technology spread throughout societies all over the world, so too did the requirement for insights on how best to use it.

This issue has two edges. On the one side, there is the role of computer scientists, for example, in educating society on its best uses, combining development of technologies, and advocating how best to deploy their use. IBM engineers in the early 1950s and Professor Negreponte in the early 2000s exemplify this role, largely because at the cutting edge of new technologies they are often the first people to sense the possibilities. In developing economies, such as in parts of Africa and Latin America and across all of Eastern Europe, there is an urgent need to have computer experts explain how best to use their technologies in the economic and social evolution of their individual countries. This advice can take a wide variety of forms: advocating use of technology in preventive health care, how best to use IT in a responsible way to protect financial systems, or assuring voting accuracy; the list can be extensive and needs to be tailored to each society. This is more of an informative advisory role for computer scientists to play than pure advocacy of their own agenda, and focus largely on applications, not social or political agendas. The other edge, however, is one of advocacy, involving computer scientists, engineers, and other technology experts influencing the course of events, as we saw with the American presidential election of 1964. This is where IT experts can advocate for better environmental policies, by participating individually in social and political movements and demonstrating how computing can help, or together as large interest groups reflecting the values and concerns of their time and place through their network of associations, such as the ACM, IEEE at large, or the Computer Society. As a member of their IT world, I favor a more activist role for technologists, because they are both a product of their time and place and are knowledgeable about how technology could be used to further their priorities or accomplish proposed tasks in the best interests of a society.

If one is inclined toward a more activist role of advocacy, then a number of actions could be taken. Here is my short list to engage the IT community:

1. Populate various governmental and other advisory boards and councils with IT experts dealing with such issues as economic development, environmental protection, and health in a systematic way.

2. Expand education of IT professionals to include such soft issues as management, personnel, public policy, economic development, and personal communications, maybe even writing.

3. Energize organizations to articulate points of view and lobby for them, such as on the use of IT in education, improvements in preventive medicine, and public policy.

4. Computer scientists and other technologists should personally do the same, leveraging the respect and gravitas that they enjoy in their societies.

5. Educate the public, and their officials and other leaders, about the possibilities and limitations of information technology to keep expectations realistic.

6. Introduce social and values-driven considerations in their work to influence evolution of the technologies they develop, as they have done for decades with IT for handicapped users, and for centuries for all manner of other technologies.

The list could be extended, but these six activities can serve as an effective starting set of actions going forward. History teaches us that when computer scientists talk, people listen to them, and they influence the course of events. They do not have to limit their impact to the daily work of creating and using IT. Today, they represent too large a community of experts vital to the welfare of their societies in most countries to remain silent and not be influential. Imagine the impact a computer scientist would have should he or she ever serve as a cabinet official or even the president of a country. We will soon learn about the effectiveness of such a leader because in January 2009, American President Obama appointed a recipient of the Nobel Prize in physics, Steven Chu, to be his Secretary of Energy. His appointment, however, is not the first; just rare for a scientist or technologist. Another example came from business when a career IBM executive, who had served as chairman of the board of IBM's World Trade Organization in Europe, Jacques Maisonrouge, after retiring from the company in 1984, served briefly in the cabinet of the French government. Doctors have, as have economists and even historians. In each instance, they brought the values and special insights of their profession and discipline to bear on managing public agencies, so it is not an unreasonable possibility for members of the IT community.

Never have we lived in a time when scientists and engineers have been so valued and respected, so essential and desired, as we do today. It is both a position of privilege and responsibility, one in which what we think and how we act makes a difference. It is why an expanded role for this community makes sense, particularly since they will say grace over the kinds of issues and developments described in the book's last chapter. There we will also discuss matters of personal and institutional leadership that can make the voice of the scientific and technical community a valued one in our society.

NOTES AND REFERENCES

1. Services science is a new field, a combination of thinking from IT, process management, operations research, sociology, and anthropology looking to transform services of all types into a rigorous science-like field, much as electrical engineering and other disciplines came together in the 1950s to form what eventually became known as computer science. For a definition and description of this concept, now about a decade in development, see Jim Spohrer, Douglas McDavid, Paul P. Maglio, and James W. Cortada, "NBIC

Convergence and Technology-Business Coevolution: Towards a Services Science to Increase Productivity Capacity," in William S. Bainbridge and Mihail C. Roco (Eds.), *Managing Nano-Bio-Info-Cogno Innovations: Converging Technologies in Society*, Dordrecht, Netherlands: Springer, 2006, pp. 227–253.

2. The *IEEE Annals of the History of Computing* regularly publishes studies of computing projects that developed in various countries.

3. U.S. Census Bureau, *Statistical Abstract of the United States: 2006*, Washington, DC: U.S. Government Printing Office, 2006, p. 187.

4. Ibid., p. 188.

5. Ibid., p. 401.

6. History of CS for this and previous paragraph drawn from Merlin G. Smith, "Four Decades of Service, 1951–1991," *Computer*, (September 1991): 6–12.

7. Information drawn from http://www.computer.org (last accessed 11/5/2008).

8. *Evolving the World with the World's Computer Society: Strategic Plan for the IEEE Computer Society, 2004 Edition*, IEEE Computer Society, 2004, p. 1.

9. World Bank, *Global Trends and Policies: 2006 Information and Communications for Development*, Washington, DC: World Bank, 2006.

10. For a summary of the findings of nearly a dozen reports, see James W. Cortada, Ashish M. Gupta, and Marc Le Noir, *How Nations Thrive in the Information Age: Leveraging Information and Communications Technologies for National Economic Development*, Somers, NY: IBM Corporation, 2007.

11. For a useful introduction to the key themes with examples, see Maximo Torero and Joachim von Braun (Eds.), *Information and Communication Technologies for Development and Poverty Reduction*, Baltimore, MD: Johns Hopkins University Press, 2006; and the classic work on the subject, Richard R. Nelson, *The Sources of Economic Growth*, Cambridge, MA: Harvard University Press, 1996.

12. The Asian experience is of particular interest because so many countries have borrowed from it. For an introduction, see Henry S. Rowen, Marguerite Gong Hancock, and William F. Miller (Eds.), *Making IT: The Rise of Asia in High Tech*, Stanford, CA: Stanford University Press, 2007.

13. For citations, see James W. Cortada, *Second Bibliographic Guide to the History of Computing, Computers, and the Information Processing Industry*, Westport, CT: Greenwood Press, 1996.

14. Arthur L. Norberg, *Computers and Commerce: A Study of Technology and Commerce at Eckert-Mauchly Computer Company, Engineering Research Associates, and Remington Rand, 1946–1957*, Cambridge, MA: MIT Press, 2005.

15. Thomas J. Watson Jr. and Peter Petre, *Father Son & Co.: My Life at IBM and Beyond*, New York: Bantam, 1990, pp. 188–207.

16. Quoted in William Aspray, *Chasing Moore's Law: Information Technology Policy in the United States,* Raleigh, NC: SciTech Publishing, 2004, pp. 9–10.

17. Ibid., pp. 11–13.

18. David Cappuccio and Lynn Craver, *The Data Center Power and Cooling Challenge*, Gartner, November 2007.

19. IBM, *IT Energy Efficiency for Small and Mid-sized Businesses: Good for Business and the Environment*, Somers, NY: IBM Corporation, December 2007.

20. Richard Keiser et al., *Technology Sector Strategy: CFOs Cautious on End Market Growth in CY08, But Support ForCapEx/IT Spending Remains Positive: Will It Materialize?*, Bernstein Research, November 26, 2007.

21. IBM, *Georgia Tech Implements A Cool Solution for Green HPC with IBM*, Somers, NY: IBM Corporation, October 2007.

22. IBM, *Creating a Green Data Center to Help Reduce Energy Costs and Gain a Competitive Advantage*, Somers, NY: IBM Corporation, May 2008.

23. "Energy Efficiency," http://www.dell.com/content/topics/global.aspx/corp/environmental/en/energy?c=us&l=en&s (last accessed 11/2/2008).

24. HVAC means heating, ventilating, and air conditioning.

25. For details, see http://www.newscenter.lbl.gov/feature-stories/2008/04/14/green-computing/ (last accessed 10/26/2008).

26. "ICCD 2008," http://iccd.et.tudelft.nl/ (last accessed 10/26/2008).

27. http://www.cluster2008.org/cfp.html (last accessed 10/26/2008).

28. William Aspray (Ed.), *Chasing Moore's Law: Information Technology Policy in the United States*, Raleigh, N.C.: SciTech Publishing, 2004.

29. For a recent example, see the work of Richard Florida, *The Rise of the Creative Class*, New York: Basic Books, 2002; *The Flight of the Creative Class*, New York: Harper Business, 2005; *Who's Your City?* New York: Basic Books, 2008.

30. Gerald Jay Sussman, "The Legacy of Computer Science," in National Research Council, *Computer Science: Reflections on the Field, Reflections from the Field*, Washington, DC: National Academy Press, 2004, p. 183.

31. Ibid.

32. International Bank for Reconstruction and Development, *Global Economic Prospects: Technology Diffusion in the Developing World*, Washington, DC: World Bank, 2008, p. 72.

33. Carlota Perez, *Technological Revolutions and Financial Capital: The Dynamics of Bubbles and Golden Ages*, Cheltenham, UK: Edward Elgar, 2002, pp. 8–21.

34. Ibid., p. 14.

35. Computer Society, *Evolving the World with the World's Computer Society*, 9.

7

LOOKING DOWN THE ROAD INTO THE TWENTY-FIRST CENTURY

Prediction is difficult, especially about the future.

—Yogi Berra

Is there anybody who does not want to have at least a quick glance at the future? How long will we live? Will we be healthy? What will be the destiny of our children? Who will win the lottery? Who will win the next election? Where and when will the next crisis strike my nation? When will the next ice age cover Berlin? How will my business do in the next quarter? How is IT evolving? What is the next growth market? Who will be my competitors tomorrow? Managers of companies and public officials can be accused of being even more curious than their customers and citizens, because their professional success depends in part on understanding unfolding events. It seems that everyone thinks they can optimize their chances for prosperity if they just knew what was going to happen before their rivals did. Moreover, generations of managers and leaders have been trained to seek out the future as part of the best practices of management. In ancient Greece, generals went up to the temple to have local priests interpret the future; every society has had futurists. As in ancient times, today's leaders in all manner of institutions and professions have resources to pay someone to divine the future. The Greek general may have left a goat as an offering at the temple, but today's manager subscribes to a service from IDG or Forrester to predict what Oracle or Microsoft will do next, or what technological wizardry will come out of an IBM laboratory or from the mind of Steve Jobs at Apple. In short, nothing about our appetite for the future has changed in a very long time, or has it?

It turns out that in the twentieth century, science, mathematics, and statistics have improved our ability to look forward in ways that build positively upon the techniques of the temple's priests or some village witch doctor. Whether management acts upon what they learn is another matter for discussion outside the scope of this book [1]. However, managers in business and government have long displayed an appetite for forecasts, to such a point that many hundreds, if not thousands, of consulting firms and IT industry watch groups, think tanks, and research firms have thrived for decades serving a growing clientele around the world by providing predictions and "futurecasts" to their clients [2]. Whenever a technology or industry experiences greater change than others, demand increases sharply for forecasts of events, sales volumes, changes in laws and regulations, new uses, and transformations in how businesses are (or will be) managed or government agencies run. Computer and telecommunications technologies have experienced substantial and continuous changes in reliability, function, price, terms and conditions for their acquisition, and use since the 1940s. There are many ways to defend that statement: tracking the number of patents, product introductions, turnover of installed equipment, and pricing. The literature on these issues is nothing less than massive [3]. For our purposes, it is enough to recognize that churn. How that occurred is outside our scope of discussion but has been well documented by others [4].

Because technology is influencing how all manner of work is done and how whole industries are transforming, it is actually more important today to understand how to look at the future of industries than to the specific details of the next evolution of some technology. That is why we need to turn immediately to a discussion of futures, asking: How does one forecast future trends in an industry, particularly one that is being changed rapidly by the evolution of either science or technology? Next we should look at megatrends in information technology that are relatively long term, not so much to displace the work of firms that do such analysis, but to suggest the driving forces underneath many of their forecasts. Their's are usually focused on the volume of exist-ing products that will be bought or sold, and not necessarily con-cerned with underlying technologies that have made possible, for example, the Nano iPod, which is tiny and remarkable in its ca-pacity. To make the point: the Nano is about the size of a book of matches and weighs only slightly more. The Nano has more com-puting power, storage for data, and is far more reliable and faster operating than a $1 million computer sold by IBM thirty years be-fore it was introduced [5].

Next, I want to step back from all the previous chapters and draw out recommendations about how managers and public offi-cials should act in the years to come, particularly between now and roughly 2025, when so much will have changed that this book may then be seen as quaint and naive. There is also a crucial role to be played by technologists to describe as well.

HOW TO SEE THE FUTURE OF AN INDUSTRY

Traditional forecasting tools, such as those used by economists, the creation of scenarios, and methods used by economists, con-sultants, and futurists are limited by the quality of their inputs and can be quickly discredited by an unanticipated event, such as a natural disaster or some human activity (e.g., 9/11) or the bank-ing crisis of 2008–2009 [6]. The rapid dispersion of IT into some aspects of an industry's ecosystem also calls for revisiting a few traditional methods of predicting the future developed by econo-mists and others as far back as the 1930s. Increasingly, managers and public officials are taking into consideration the effects of technologies of all kinds, not simply IT [7]. This is so much the case that hardly any serious institution-wide strategy develop-ment occurs without considering the role of IT. Most analytical models today routinely take into account some combination of four specific dimensions, all mentioned at various times in earlier chapters: political/legal, economic, social/cultural, and technolog-ical (PEST). Such PEST analysis models include all four elements, and are widely used by business schools and strategy consultants to help define potential opportunities and threats that a company, industry, or government agency might face [8].

Futurists favor using processes that pull together strategic and operating plans that include monitoring of industry trends and a continuous scanning of the environment for changes, because so little seems static today. They seek to identify driving forces, such as demographic changes or components of economic globalization, while remaining aware that contingency planning is always needed to accommodate unpredictable events. These kinds of considerations can then feed traditional planning activities that include articulating visions, missions, goals, and short- and long-term strategies of individual companies and public agencies [9].

However, one must go one step further by developing a point of view that extends beyond the normal planning horizon used today. Futurists will routinely look out 10, 20, even 40 years, while management normally thinks in terms of 1, 2, or 3 years ahead. The longer view is increasingly justified by our growing knowledge that technologies fundamentally affecting an organization take longer to evolve into products, to be deployed, and to generate results and consequences. The same is true regarding societal changes. In other words, the longer-term influences on an organization often manifest themselves over a greater period of time than the normal quarter-to-quarter horizons of corporations and the year-to-year time lines embraced by public officials. Thus, planning exercises need to conform more tightly to those timelines than might otherwise be the case. In short, as the role of IT increases, it calls the tune for how traditional planning has to be conducted. At the same time, there are enormous changes that occur very quickly, such as in telecommunications, which since the early 1990s has undergone a massive explosion of technological innovations and effects, many of which, however, had been predicted as far back as 1970 by futurist Alvin Toffler; he was not alone in predicting such changes [10]. This is all well and good, but the fact remains that if someone is working in a high-tech industry, or one affected sharply by changes in science and technology, new methods will be needed, because the role of technology in planning is just now receiving serious attention.

To improve the quality of its view of the future, a company or government agency must have a solid perspective on how its ecosystem is changing, so that the actions and strategies of the organization can optimize its performance. What should be done that is different? Although the benefits of any approach are obvious to management and, thus, need not distract us here [11], it is important to point out that longer-term planning horizons give an industry or organization a greater ability to deal with inevitable surprises, such as the arrival of a leapfrogging innovation from outside a given industry that leads to new forms of competition. Using multidisciplinary approaches to understand the future and then that same diversity to respond to specific events constitute best practices. In the public sector, the case studies presented by Richard E. Neustadt and Ernest R. May on how the American government reacted to the Cuban Missile Crisis represent a textbook example of the process at work [12]. Sometimes, the need for a better way takes on a great sense of urgency. In the pharmaceutical industry, the science of medicine is undergoing fundamental changes to an extent not seen in over a century. Al-Queda, the Taliban, and other armed groups considered backward by military forces can hold large, advanced, modern armies at bay by the deployment of small consumer electronics, cell phones, and laptops. The list is endless.

Table 7.1 lists the characteristics of science- and technology-based industries and government agencies that account for the volatility and difficulty in forecasting the future that one must take into account. The first step is to see if there are some financial structural changes that have been occurring over the previous decade or so and understand what caused these, because such trends may extend well into the future. For example, the long-term decline in the value of the stock of a firm or of a group of companies in an industry is a sure sign of a megatrend at work. In

Table 7.1. Issues that make forecasting the future difficult for industries and governments

Shifts in underlying science or technology
Relentless innovation in a technology
Changes in regulatory practices
Changes in business models or inputs
Emergence of new competitors
Changing demographics
Changing geopolitical environments
Increasing pressures on pricing and profits by governments and other customers
Pressure to speed up product introductions
Shorter exclusivity of effective patent protection for new products and prices
Increased public pressures on an industry, reflecting changing expectations of customers and stakeholders

Source: Adapted from James W. Cortada and Heather E. Fraser, "Mapping the Future in Science-Intensive Industries: Lessons from the Pharmaceutical Industry," *IBM Systems Journal* 44, no. 1 (2005): 167–168.

government, it could be the shifting of budgets away from or to some agency, or changes in a department's staffing caused by retirements, inability to hire, or budget cuts, or to some societal trend, such as changing demographics. It is not enough to see declines in productivity; it is necessary to understand the causes of that decline and then to ask, "If unchanged, what could/will happen over the next decade or longer?" The answer begins to provide a sense of urgency to take action and is the economic/budgetary justification.

The second step is to ask what technologies are affecting the firm, agency, or industry and then trace their long-term evolution back a decade and project them forward 10 to 15 years. (The next section provides an introduction to the issue.) Also appreciate what is causing the technological changes to speed up or slow down, as often this is not due to the miracle of some newly emerging technology, but rather to more mundane causes, such as changes in tax laws or government regulations. Not all of those may occur in the country that is home to a firm or agency; they can surface anywhere in the world. A Japanese pharmaceutical company has to worry about the actions of the U.S. Food and Drug Administration, while American firms increasingly have to pay attention to the environmental regulations of the European Union if they want to sell products in Europe, a market now larger than that of all North America. On occasion, the U.S. Congress has been forced to change American law due to rulings of the WTO [13]. Such lists of transnational effects on the form, use, and deployment of technology and other operational practices is actually increasing. The most recent example came from the banking crisis of 2008–2009. One rarely sees a corporate or government strategy that takes into account these transnational influences on local operations. That has to change.

The tasks to map the future are straightforward. Define it at very high levels and project it into a period beyond one's normal planning horizon. Include today's trends so that they are not lost in the subsequent dialogue. Use standard scenario planning methods but extend these out by 10 to 15 years and include the technological and regulatory factors mentioned above. Do not be tempted to do what is normal, namely, looking out only 2 to 3 years, because that will not expose the root drivers affecting one's organization. Select a few, not many, potential drivers and focus on exploring those in depth. These can be changes in science (as in pharmaceuticals), communications technologies (as in the telephone industry), or database management tools (as in social services). Other areas of interest can be added as it becomes evident that they increasingly will affect the future. By looking at a few important influences, one can begin to plot out a set of recommendations that can be implemented in phases over time that address the impact of the predictions across all of the value or service chain of an organization. When studying long-term issues, describe the driver, how it is manifesting itself now and could (will) in the future, the implications of those manifestations for one's own enterprise or agency, and only then begin to create strategies that are either in response to those or take advantage of them, along with the routine cost/benefit business cases for action. Since scenario planning is used, low-, medium-, and high-probability cases should be defined so that a decision maker can take a variety of possible actions with some measurable expectation of results and consequences.

Once the initial work has been done, it should be socialized across the organization and among experts, of course; this is a business-as-usual step. However, since it involves a longer period and includes a greater emphasis on the role of technology, for example, it is crucial to do because something might have been left out and, probably more true, people who will have to implement proposed actions need time and dialogue to accept and embrace what will probably be a new disruptive and, thus, uncomfortable view of the future.

A second phase is to take this view of the future and build individual strategies for each agency, department, or unit within an organization, for what professors and consultants like to call key elements of the value chain, in conformance with the megaview of the future. This view is not an absolute dogmatic one, but rather a perspective that changes iteratively and needs to be "loose enough" to allow continuous adjustments to evolving realities. Column one of Table 7.2 lists the results of such an analysis involving the global pharmaceutical industry and how it affects its supply chain. In this example, the massive and growing availability of computing power used and predicted by computer scientists made it possible to map the human genome, and led to the start of a long process by which researchers could unravel the subcellular mysteries of human life. The greater use of computers to do R&D for drugs is also influencing what kinds of cures are being explored by scientists [14]. In the

Table 7.2. Issues affecting pharmaceutical companies over a decade: study results

Major industry-wide findings	Effects on future supply chains
Drivers of Change	Challenges affecting all pharmaceutical firms
• Tough times	Supply chains are creaking apart
• Old ways do not work	Strategic vision for the future
Road to the Future	• Demand synchronization
• Rise of targeted treatments	• Strategic sourcing
Recommendations	• Scientific manufacturing
• Disease-driven drug discovery	• New product development
• Transform drug development	• Restructuring
• Identify global blockbuster drugs	• New asset allocation
• Target marketing for targeted treatments	• New techniques to reach customers
Summary and Implications	
• Need new business models	

Source: Adapted from James W. Cortada and Heather E. Fraser, "Mapping the Future in Science-Intensive Industries: Lessons from the Pharmaceutical Industry," *IBM Systems Journal* 44, no. 1 (2005): 173.

case of social services, technologies are making it easier to create case approaches for providing citizens with services without having fundamentally to reorganize government agencies so far, although the long-term effects of computing will undoubtedly lead to the restructuring of many government agencies. This began in the United States with the creation of the Department of Homeland Security after 9/11 and with some of the less dramatic reorganizations under way during the same period among social service agencies in various European national governments.

Conversely, such changes are also causing changes in the technology. Pharmaceutical firms want better-managed and larger databases and computer memories, video game producers are affecting the type and rate of development of computer-based graphics, the military is furthering the evolution of networked-based management of complex interactions (e.g., the battlefield), and airlines and the military are active in the development of more integrated, faster situational awareness and control software to manage air traffic. The list is long. But the phenomenon of one's industry or firm affecting the evolution of science and technology should be taken into account and action items and strategies should be articulated as part of any organization's long-term plan of action. It is an enduring pattern of behavior that has existed in its modern form since the late nineteenth century.

Much of how all of this occurs is basic project management, skills most firms and public agencies have today. But there are also some interesting by-products that are not so obvious. For example, as an organization increasingly does this kind of long-term planning, its management team comes to believe in the forecasts and a few key members become willing to take actions based on their emerging worldview. Additionally, the majority are less likely to feel the ebb and flow of current events as being beyond their understanding let alone their control. It is one of the reasons, for example, why every spring at IBM, computer scientists prepare a presentation that they make to the most senior executives about the future of IT and why line management across the same corporation also articulates the impact of those changes on their sector of the world's market for products and services. When well done, management optimizes their work, taking advantage of such insights. Effective execution creates an internal appetite for information beyond what might have existed before, and it becomes a more focused interest. The public, customers, and other interested parties become interested in the organization's perspective on the future, thereby affecting it as well, perhaps as a variant of the Pygmalion effect at an institutional level.

Of course, this approach for accommodating the influence of IT has its strengths and weaknesses, although its virtues outweigh the limitations. This kind of forecasting works across many industries and government agencies. This strength is important since, increasingly, firms, industries, agencies, and entire governments are interacting more closely together, in part thanks to the conveniences made possible by IT. Thus, crossing traditional lines of strategic planning will become increasingly necessary. In such industries as telecommunications and media, this is an essential finding because many firms in those two industries cross over to each other's area of business in their development of new business models. In the instance of governments, we have the case of the EU stimulating closer interactions among 25 governments, while the WTO is doing so globally, if less intensely. Science, technology, and regulatory activities are thus creating increasing forms of homogenization across agencies, firms, industries, and regulations, one of the key megatrends discussed in the first two chapters of this book.

As the pressure to innovate in offerings, services, and products also increases, firms can find inspiration and collaborators across multiple industries, meaning that strategies and forecasts created in one industry or by one government can be tapped into as good sources of insights for one's use in another industry or agency. The EU has even made the hunt for innovation a strategic imperative for all its industries, governments, and member nations [15]. As companies and governments increasingly organize their operations into components, complete with their own processes, organizations, and IT infrastructure, and move them about quickly within their larger organization or to some other institution or firm, one can create criteria for change based on these kinds of forecasts.

Ultimately, the key advantage of this approach over traditional scenario-planning techniques is that a company or agency is not extrapolating purely from today's environment. By stepping outside its current horizon, management is given the freedom to think beyond traditional views about its environment, industry or society. The future does not necessarily need to be a small variant of today's model. For those working in an industry that has been around a long time, such as pharmaceuticals, IT, telecommunications, banking, or government, this can be unnerving, but also rewarding for those willing to explore new possibilities.

This method has its limits too. Approaching any analysis of the future with discipline is very difficult to do. It requires help from futurists, consultants, academics, and industry experts, and is not to be done by a roomful of managers from one organization over a long afternoon. This takes months of hard work, a commitment many are not willing to make because of the greater value they place on near-term trends and actions. It is also an art, with no guarantees of absolute certainty. It will not predict the arrival dates of the next four economic recessions or the success of five new start-up companies by name. But it will give management confidence that they have a better perspective of the future than those who have not gone through this kind of an exercise. It does have a bias toward an insular view because it works best when focused on a single industry; futurists and managers have not yet learned how to do this across multiple industries simultaneously.

Finally, one can ask, can such a technique be applied to a whole society? In theory, the answer is yes, although most forecasts of future behavior in a society are limited to the near term (e.g., 2–5 years) and often to some clever writer's clear-thinking but less-disciplined approach to the topic. So, we really do not know if this can be done effectively. What we do know is that experts on a society normally shy away from such exercises, most notably historians, political scientists, and, to a certain extent, economists. Governments, however, do look out constantly to the future of narrower themes, such as the costs of providing healthcare to an aging population in their country, the number of which they even know by name and age because everyone who comprises the data for their study is alive today.

KNOWING HOW INFORMATION TECHNOLOGY IS EVOLVING

The American baseball player quoted at the start of this chapter understood perfectly well the central problem with forecasting. However, what many managers do not always realize is that everyone has some say about how the future will evolve, and this includes those who do research on computing's technologies, if for no other reason than because someone chooses what to develop, and those who fund the development of IT, such as corporations and government agencies that also shape the direction of innovations. Then there is an R&D and product development aspect of *path dependency* by which one builds on prior work. There is hardly any example of an IT product that has appeared in the past century that did not grow out of some preexisting technology. The first generation of computer chips, developed in the late 1950s and early 1960s, grew out of insights acquired in the 1950s from the development of the transistor, which first appeared in the late 1940s and that, in turn, emerged as a by-product of research done on the electrical properties of silicon conducted in the 1930s. In each instance, it took some ten years to move from one technology to another in the laboratories and, subsequently, another few years to reach the marketplace, and then continued to evolve for decades.

Tracking path dependencies, therefore, is a way of understanding the evolution of technology from concept to product used in someone's organization. It is a process that continues [16]. For example, concepts behind pervasive computing—the idea that anything can have computing embedded in it and, in turn, is connected to the Internet or to some other network, from coffee

machines to one's clothing, not just industrial equipment or vehicles and medical machinery—were well honed theoretically in
the 1980s and 1990s, and by about 2002 were reflected in actual
computer components and architectures. Just between 2003 and
2008, computer scientists took a next step of developing embedded software in systems designed to stay running all over a network, followed by pervasive connectivity as a follow-on research
topic, which is now evolving into a development initiative to
create reliable hardware and software working in business enterprises that are becoming highly modular and support quick evolution. Examples are the various RFID tags and software that
track inventory and wayward pets and patients, but could also
help spur evolution of corporations into what many are calling
integrated global enterprises. In the world of computer architectures—the fundamental design of how hardware and software
work together—one version evolves into another with significant
overlap: large systems architectures are redesigned to support the
massive Internet networks that exist around the world, new vari-
ants support communities of users, and so forth. Even Microsoft's
ubiquitous Windows, itself a computer architecture, continues to
evolve out of previous versions dating back to the 1980s, with
design points for future versions well understood not just in software laboratories, but also by a demanding public continuously
asking for changes.

It would not be productive in this chapter to catalog the many
lines of investigation into IT, because there are too many and the
specifics change so quickly. It is more fruitful to understand how
best to learn about changing technologies that affect the work of
organizations. As one looks at various technologies, it is less important to be concerned about the technical details because engineers will quibble a great deal over those; it is more important to
link results, because the demand (or lack thereof) for a technical
evolution often drives the speed with which it occurs. For example, today there is a massive world-wide demand for mobile, lightweight, physically small computing devices, which, in turn, is
causing the manufacturers of mobile phones to develop products
that have become a viable alternative to PCs and laptops for ac-
cessing the Internet using broadband wireless networks. Apple's
iPhone is the tip of the iceberg that already has caused competitors to bring out both copycat knockoffs and devices with new
functions. But going a step further, with high speed broadband

connections via cell phones, use of multimedia and social networks will expand rapidly.

What does that possibility portend for a business? For one thing, if you were an Internet service provider (ISP), you would likely move into that market, offering to create services for other firms, to manage distribution of content, and so forth. Providers of content on the Internet, such as Google or news organizations, and music producers, would be congratulating themselves, because they would now have a vast new market and the opportunity to use their novel ways of distributing their materials to the public, building on existing ways of doing business. Retailers, bankers, and social services agencies in governments would (indeed will) start delivering their goods and services more extensively that way. Mobile workers are already creating greater specialized networks, such as special-operations soldiers in a guerrilla war or consultants scattered across a country working on one project. Mobile broadband services would also mean a major refurbishing of an organization's computer systems, also networks, of course, and even what applications are accessed by employees. Mobile communications is an example of a technology used here because it is a major beehive of R&D going on around the world, which is central to what computing will look like over the next decade or two.

Wikipedia taught us that whole communities of strangers can come together whenever they want to interact, creating a new body of knowledge. Blogs are now doing the same thing for discussions of specific issues, while other communities are forming over the Internet. As managers observe such a pattern, and this one is so obvious, they can turn the IT trend issue on its head and ask such questions as, "What are these users doing?" and "Consequently, what kind of research and development is going on in support of this megatrend?" In response to the first question, it becomes quickly evident that new users are joining the trend, contributing information (data) and doing things, often for free; thereby, they enhance the overall value of something, such as Wikipedia, as it acquires more entries and better informed existing ones. That phenomenon increases its value as more people participate, an occurrence that had long been evident in telecommunications with telephony and even as an economic principle. Talk to computer engineers and they can answer the second question, telling you that they are developing easier-to-use software tools, collaborative mechanisms and intelligence gathering, creating integrative tools to connect new and old software systems together, and making it possible for massive quantities of people to come in and out of Web-based sites and applications. These activities put a premium on open systems, reliable software, and massive data storage functions as people organize themselves around specific sets of information or subjects, not software or organizations.

What about paying attention to highly traditional questions about the future of IT? Is there no value in that? First, what are some of these "traditional questions"? For a half-century, computer chips have become faster, more reliable, less expensive, and acquired greater horsepower and flexibility. In fact, this is so much the case that there have been near-scientific laws formulated to describe this trend, most notably Moore's Law [17]. What this historical evolution has done is drive down the cost of computing while increasing the power. Advertisements have pointed this out, such as those that occasionally claim that if automobiles had become as productive as computer chips, a Ferrari would only cost $5!! Most industry watchers pay attention to the cost and functionality of computer chips; indeed, Intel's business plan, and how the stock market judges it, is often based largely on the concept of Moore's Law. In time, that meant one could have a $400 laptop (2008) instead of a $5000 clunky PC (1985), with the newer one doing more work, with greater reliability, than the older device. The portable telephones one saw in movies made in the 1980s look incredibly huge because today we have tiny cell phones, with embedded, very small physical integrated circuits that also use less power, hence require smaller batteries. So, what goes on with computer chips is important.

They continue to shrink in size and cost, although some computer scientists are beginning to wonder how close they are in reaching the technical and physical limits of what can be done with silicon. Current thinking holds that this class of integrated circuits will continue to evolve for another 10 to 15 years, by which time newer technologies will begin to appear as possible replacements that could become important by the mid-2020s. One would want to know what the replacement technologies might be in roughly ten years. Will they be something made out of gas, a biological material, or some nanotechnology? Nanotechnology can be used in computers, to be sure, or in tiny machines embedded in one's heart to keep it working. The possibilities are endless and certainly will be emerging over the first half of the twenty-first century.

Queries about the cost of laptops and consumer electronics continues, of course, as do inquiries about when the Internet will run faster so that one can download a movie to a TV, mobile phone, or other "platform" in seconds instead of in dozens of minutes. As that happens, whole industries and companies will be transformed, not the least of which is television and movie making and distribution. With nearly 20 years of wide experience with the Internet, customers, citizens, managers, and public officials have also learned to ask other questions as a consequence of many technologies having been in place for a long time. These concern patent and copyright permissions, royalties for downloaded music, how to control pornography, and the spread of political information deemed inappropriate by a government. In short, much about looking at the future of technology really needs to focus on the slower evolving trends of how IT is used and resulting consequences.

Yet, it seems that no editor of an industry or professional magazine can resist for long the annual urge to have some expert on computing write an article on the "Five Technologies to Watch for Next Year." That article has been written by thousands of people and published in hundreds of magazines and journals over the past six decades. Everyone participates: technology journalists, magazine writers, engineers, consultants, professors, scientists, public officials, and business executives, even your author. Are there a half-dozen trends one should pay attention to over the period from roughly 2009 to 2025 that can be expected to play important roles in how people work and play? Notice, that I did not say play *dramatic roles* because that implies that some new technology bursts on the scene; that kind of event is as rare as hen's teeth. Rather, some technologies finally mature to the point at which they are practical to apply, such as might be happening now with alternative fuel automobiles, but not electric cars. Everyone has their list; mine is in Table 7.3. It is short, to be sure, and one should probably keep a short one relevant to their work or play, casting an eye on developments in the technology and on how people are beginning to use it. That is a skill every manager, leader, and influencer needs to develop. The exotic possibilities remain ensconced in research laboratories and, thus, need not detain us here, as much fun as they might be to describe, such as ma-

Table 7.3. Six information technologies to watch that will affect work and play, 2010–2025

Technology	Possible effects or uses
Nanotechnology	Better monitoring, especially in medicine
Database software	More data collection, analysis
Sensors	For medicine, security, inventory tracking
Computer chips	Drives down costs, increases capacity, new uses
Batteries	Smaller, more places to use electricity, cheaper
Internet communications	Affects social relationships, use of other ITs

chines as smart as humans, which some computer scientists think we will have by mid-century [18].

However, Table 7.3 speaks to the underlying technologies, not to the trends of what all that means. Although it is always risky to predict what is going to happen, several trends are so evident today that most forecasters agree that there is a high probability of their occurring. So, they too are worth keeping an eye on as one goes about the business of running an enterprise and developing plans for its future. The most pervasive, and the one which will give more voice to those who think the computer revolution is in its infancy, is convergence. Almost every major technology is slowly merging with other technologies. The glue, or magnetism, facilitating that megatrend is IT. Most specifically, between now and the mid-2020s the major areas of convergence involve biotechnologies, nanotechnologies, materials technologies, and information technologies (components, devices, and software). Furthermore, if one inspects each of them for trends, actual accomplishments (e.g., patents filed), and the experts involved with them, there is almost universal agreement that the *pace* at which developments in these technologies is occurring is actually *increasing*. The *volume* of activity, is also expanding such as the number of research projects and implementations of existing technologies.

As integration of these various technologies occurs, they will continuously, yet incrementally, spin off. There will be profound implications for societies, governments, and corporations. One RAND Corporation study of possible uses of converged technologies makes for interesting reading [19]. Table 7.4 lists some of these. But as most economists will argue, and as I did in chapter three, the most advanced economies will benefit the earliest from these trends, and at the other end of the economic spectrum, those

Table 7.4. Examples of uses of converged technology, circa mid-2020s

Personalized medicine
Targeted drug delivery
Embedded sensors in consumer goods
Tiny electric power systems
Organic electronics
Pervasive (undetectable) cameras
Massive databases of information
Wireless Internet with bundled information
Extensively improved cryptography

Source: Richard Silberglitt, Philip S. Antón, David R. Howell, and Anny Wong, *The Global Technology 2020, In-Depth Analyses* (Santa Monica, CA: RAND National Security Research Division, 2006), pp. xvii–xxi.

least developed will not benefit from them as much. The reason is that it takes so many other environmental factors to facilitate deployment, such as availability of electricity, sufficient levels of literacy, and economic wherewithal. In turn, that leads to diversity of uses. Equally varied are the possible implications for society. These range from the ability to grow more genetically altered crops to vastly extended uses of solar energy, to better health due to improved methods for assessing and monitoring health, then responding with "made-to-order" drugs, what scientists and doctors elegantly call targeted treatments. By then, green manufacturing will have become a reality with positive implications for cleaner air and water. Wearable computers could improve health through high-tech clothing that monitors body temperature and, possibly, heartbeats.

With continued miniaturization of all manner of technologies, human populations will be able to spread out further into areas of the Earth that previously were not realistically inhabitable. For example, inexpensive solar energy and wireless Internet would make the great plains of North America or the Savannas of South America and Africa more comfortable and safe to live in for those people who are used to inhabiting cities. They still will need consumer goods, food, law enforcement, education, and medical facilities, albeit increasingly in different ways than provided today.

Permeating many of the uses of converging technologies are issues already playing out in societies all over the world. The most important involve privacy and anonymity because there will be exponential increases in the amount of data that becomes available in massive databases equipped with increasingly useful software to analyze this flood of new information. This is not so difficult to forecast because it has already started with the deployment of sensors, use of biometrics, installation of cameras, and expanded use of GPS. We have all personally seen these already at work. What most individuals may not realize is that for each of those uses of high-tech devices, the underlying technologies making them possible are all in early stages of development; in other words, they remain crude. Yet all are currently the subject of intense additional development, which is why by the mid-2020s one can reasonably expect further and more intensely used versions of all these and why there will be more need to address such issues as how privacy will be handled. In short, there is much for a policy maker or a business manager to watch for coming over the horizon. Because these changes come at us incrementally, in a piecemeal fashion, yet massively over time, no responsible leader or observer of contemporary events can avoid paying attention to them.

Complicating the discussion about looking at the future is that many forecasts are inaccurate—a point made throughout this book—so everything must be taken with the proverbial "grain of salt." What gives confidence to experts on technology about these trends is that they emerge so slowly that one can see them coming from a distance. The real challenge is to resist the hyperbole that comes so often with such forecasts. The world is amazingly filled with enthusiasts for new technologies. The voices of critics who caution against the negative potential consequences of new technologies are routinely drowned out in the process. Historical experience also suggests changes come slower than the enthusiasts would argue, but they come nonetheless.

So what is one to do?

A STRATEGY FOR MANAGERS AND PUBLIC OFFICIALS

First, do not abandon the immediate future. There is still a requirement to understand current macro issues involving whole societies, economies, and industries, not just demand for particular goods and services. Understanding what is going on today, this quarter, this year, and predicting trends for next year, remains as urgent a task as ever. To be sure, the results are also going to be quite different than when looking farther out. For example, compare what mega-IT issues are listed in Tables 7.3 and 7.4 with those listed in Table 7.5. The third table is a partial list of IT-related trends that I watched as I was writing this book in 2008–2009. Notice that the list is more focused on IT components than on base technologies. It does not include forecasts of how many iPods are going to be bought or when IBM is going to announce the availability of some new service or product. Some of them are interesting because of general societal trends causing these to be of interest, such as economic uncertainties caused by rising cost of energy, climatic changes, globalization of economic activities, continued rising power of the consumer over suppliers, viral marketing, and mobility of work and play. Industries also draw attention because of their effects on IT developments, such as healthcare, pharmaceuticals, communications, media and entertainment, and, to a lesser extent but not to be ignored, the military (stimulated by network-centric operations) and government (due to identity management initiatives). Hot spots in science also have to be watched because of the convergence of specific areas of development with IT, most notably nanotechnology, which seems to have finally taken off, medicine based on the understanding of DNA's activities, and other developments rapidly appearing in neuroscience and quantum physics.

We have not discussed the consumer to any extent in this book, which may seem odd, but is due to the fact that other players actually convert technologies into products and offerings, or regulate what one can do. However, the consumer is not to be dismissed. With respect to IT, ever since they learned to use the Internet in

Table 7.5. Tactical IT trends, circa 2008–2009

Energy use of data centers
Cloud computing
Information managing
Unified communications
Semantic webs
Security
Speech technologies
Virtualization
Social networking

the mid-1990s they have gained access to so much information about everything that they have tipped the scales of market negotiating power in favor toward them, in effect now telling vendors what to provide in the way of goods and services, and at what prices and terms and conditions. Since the early 2000s, they have also engaged in a rapidly expanding new form of social networking dependent on the Internet (e.g., Facebook, e-Harmony.com, blogs, wikis), to such an extent that they are altering how humans interact with each other. Of course, selling over the Internet is maturing as a practice, leading to such things as viral marketing, new forms of market prediction, and mobility of customers and suppliers [20]. All of that has to be placed in the context of globalization, most notably in emerging markets for IT in Central and Eastern Europe, and in Africa.

The one area of IT usage that perhaps is least appreciated by business and government leaders, because of its recent emergence, involves the use of IT in social networks. It seems that overnight new names of social communities became familiar: MySpace, Facebook, You Tube, Orkut, Flicker, and Dailymotion to mention a few. These are not small either. One simple set of statistics makes the point. As early in the life of this new class of IT applications as the spring of 2007, 350,000 new members were joining MySpace every day. Every second, 150,000 requests for some activity took place, involving 4.5 million people who were online at the site at all times! [21] This kind of activity parallels the huge surge that took place in worldwide participation in online video games in the late 1990s, when it became normal for millions of players to be online. Many senior managers and public officials still do not understand how massive these kinds of social networks have become, or how global, although many of their young and midcareer employees are active participants in this alternative reality. Thus, it is worth a few comments because this development will affect short- and long-term patterns of IT usage.

Social networks are webs made up of people who share common interests, like members of a club. On the Internet, one can now find a rapidly growing collection of social networking services that allow people to connect, as in a club, without physically being in the same town or building; they do it electronically over the Internet. That makes it possible to have much larger communities and to create and dismantle small and large webs of like-minded individuals, often very quickly and inexpensively. They share videos, information, and opinions; they trade ideas; collaborate on projects; and political and social causes as well. All of these activities raise interesting questions: Are there new markets emerging? If so, what are they? Are there behaviors going on in violation of social standards or laws? What regulations are needed? Should a company or government agency find value in facilitating conversations among customers and citizens? For each trend, one could drill down for volumes of activities and implications. For the short-term trends, many industry watchers do that already, so their studies can be used; one does not need to reinvent the wheel here.

Second, the restructuring of companies into globally integrated enterprises that is going on at the moment, more so than any emergence of new public administrative agencies, is something for both public- and private-sector leaders to pay attention to over the next few years. This trend is a harbinger of forthcoming enterprise structures that may well spill over into how whole industries are organized over the next couple of decades, followed by public institutions. As the chairman of one large company pointed out, "when everything is connected . . . work flows to the places where it can be done best" [22]. To be sure, we are in the very early stages of this kind of transformation, so the evidence of results are tentative, but it appears to be similar to what happened when companies first embraced computers in the 1950s. They looked to operational savings and to enhanced presence in their chosen markets for results. In both periods, those occurred [23].

Third, pay attention to operational and technical standards because they are critical to bringing together various issues: long-term and short-term IT trends, others involving business (e.g., globalization, globally integrated enterprise), and how governments deal with each other (e.g., increased and varied forms of collaboration). If one is going to pay attention to standards, one must recognize that they are not limited to some software discussion. Increasingly, these must involve standard financial charts of accounts and accounting practices so that one can measure the performance of multiple parts of an enterprise through a common system, or respond to the growing standardization of accounting practices imposed by governments. Another very IT-intensive type of standard involves having common forms of data and shared definitions of what makes up those data, so that one can support such things as standard financial charts of accounts across all corners of an enterprise and compare costs and sales results from many countries. Common processes represent an obvious third set of standards essential for operating a multinational firm, having business partners work with each other, and for governments to deal with each other. Finally, back to a topic mentioned repeatedly in this book: there is a growing trend of globally mandated standards that are created by law, by edict of an executive, or that emerge de facto from some technical or professional standards board or best practice. With respect to all four types of standards, enterprises that are farthest along in operating in a global market are also the organizations that most prize standardization along these four dimensions. What little statistical data there is on the subject indicates that governments in general lag behind the private sector's largest enterprises in each dimension by a third or more [24].

Besides saving operating costs, where these standards are implemented there are now reports of other positive consequences of their implementation. They are causing technology footprints to simplify. For example, companies are reducing the number of enterprise resource planning (ERP) software tools, which represent important reductions in operational complexity. The number of data centers is also coming down, along with the number of redundant software systems, even in financial reporting and accounting. Use of shared services across departments, divisions, and country organizations is incremental, except generally by governments, which still find it attractive to maintain their organizational silos, although that behavior seems to be now just starting to change, due to the need to integrate more closely law enforcement and various social services. Outsourcing to wherever and to whomever can do the work most effectively and inexpensively is again attracting attention. Improving the quality of data collected is increasingly being done quicker, particularly the consolidation of activities necessary, for example, to produce a corporate-wide balance sheet. On the flip side, the process of implementing all four types of standards has been slow, often taking more than a decade to accomplish and even then not completed, because firms have had to meet many regulatory requirements and market speeds of operating have dictated the cadence of such migrations to common standards.

The list of recommendations about how to leverage IT is clearly leading to a future in which a half-century of developments in the technology will finally have accumulated to a point where one can confidently expect the next two decades to be significantly different in feel and function than the last four of the twentieth century. It is that reality that govern the issues discussed in this book.

Those responsible for organizing and performing the work of governments and companies are positioned at those points in a society in which decisions and actions are taken that will shape many of the characteristics of life in the first half of the twenty-first century. To be sure, technological developments in computing and telecommunications have already made it quite clear that individuals will also play a profound role, whether they be a lone terrorist who figures out how to use a garage opener in combination with a cell phone to blow up an army vehicle, an environmentalist or grass roots political group that creates social networking Internet sites in support of a national presidential candidate, or a nonprofit organization that leverages computing and GPS tracking software to block the hunting of whales or to call attention to the fighting in Darfur. In a sense, IT is making it possible for people to participate in the affairs of the world in a democratic fashion, regardless of what culture they live in or form of government they have. It is a new reality that extends far beyond simple notions of a flat world.

Yet, managers and public officials still control the vast majority of the world's resources, such as budgets, buildings, inventories, employees, laws, and regulations. Their job is to use these to carry out the mission of their respective enterprises. That does not change. They are the ones who fund research projects in computer science carried out by professors and pay the salaries of engineers in corporations that turn scientific knowledge and engineering know-how into "high-tech" products. These are the people who pass laws and mandate regulations that mold the features of a nation's economy. Much has been made about how individuals have gained power over their lives thanks to the use of IT—we have commented about the growing authority of consumers due to their access to information on the Internet—but companies and governments still constitute key components of all societies and they are going to be run by employees of those organizations for the foreseeable future.

Developments in IT over the past half-century have emerged that begin to give those leaders a sense of how things will unfold.

Chapter one, which discussed megatrends, spoke about the landscape upon which these managers and leaders step today and upon which they will continue to walk for years to come. Chapter two made the point that how this important class of technologies has been spreading seems to have a pattern of its own that transcends any particular technological innovation or economic dynamic. Many of these will continue to be the patterns of deployment one will see in the years to come because, as I have suggested in this final chapter, the computer wizards actually see more innovation and new uses of IT in the years ahead than we have had in the past. There is no evidence to suggest that the way these innovations seep into a society are going to change radically from those that exist today.

Chapter three reminded us that public officials and the leading business and social institutions of a society have embraced the use of IT to improve the security, quality of life, and economic well-being of their customers and citizens. Perhaps political scientist Samuel P. Huntington is right when he says that the world is moving toward a technological balance of power. If so, what officials do to leverage IT to improve their economies would be specific steps in the direction he says we are headed. That is why the patterns described in Chapter three are so important, because, ultimately, those are the strategies that will lead us to that technological balance of power. Then the actions described in Chapter four—the way organizations decide how to acquire and use IT—is the next level down in this process, demonstrating that for over a half-century common patterns of behavior have prevailed in the adoption of IT. Like the findings presented in the prior two chapters, there are emerging common practices that societies have found effective in embracing information technologies, regardless of whether we are looking at megatrends, public policies, or the actions of individual managers. Moreover, these practices are enduring, appearing again and again from one year to the next to such an extent that in looking at the future role of technologies one can turn to these patterns for insight on what to do and how to respond to new uses of IT. Moreover, one can also use such patterns to identify early on when new opportunities for progress or profit are presented by some new technological innovation.

That ultimately may be the greatest lesson of this book. In which case, our discussion about the Information Age in Chapter five can be seen more as a way of determining the extent and nature of the deployment and affects this particular technology is having on a society. In turn, those insights can influence the actions of organizations, businesses, and governments as they develop products, lay down strategies, implement tactics, carry out tasks, and develop points of view about all manner of social, religious, political, and economic issues affected by the pervasiveness of IT in their lives. Ultimately, it is that evolution in values and practices that will allow historians in the twenty-second or twenty-third centuries to determine if, in fact, we had lived in the Information Age.

SPECIAL ROLE OF THE COMPUTER SCIENCE COMMUNITY

If one were to total up the number of computer scientists, programmers, systems analysts, IT managemers, sales and consulting professionals, and observers of the IT world, the number would run into the millions of workers. These are not small communities. The Computer Society has roughly 100,000 members and IBM employees number approximately 400,000; in short, there is a long list of people who work with information technology. They also work and live in nearly 200 countries. Yet, this community is rarely called upon to set the direction for the use of information technology beyond the scope of their immediate jobs. The closest one routinely gets to any discussion about managerial roles are those concerning the functions of chief information officers (CIOs), a tiny percentage of this larger community. Every year, one or two business books are published that address the role of the CIO as a business manager responsible for advising senior line management about the role and value of IT, and about how to integrate the technology into the strategy of a firm or agency [25]. All the other millions of IT workers are expected to read manuals on open-source software, others related to database management, Internet Web creations, and so forth. Indeed, for that community the majority of the discussion is about the technical features of various hardware and software. CIOs gather together to share best practices through various "CIO Councils" that have emerged in many industries and firms, so they are on their way toward learning about the issues discussed in this book and sharing those with non-IT management, although they yet are not organized in some association in the way IT professionals used to be through the Data Processing Management Association (DPMA).

But what about other segments of the IT club, specifically, for example, computer scientists and those developing new hardware and software products? Leaving aside such high-profile members of that community as Bill Gates, Michael Dell, and Steve Jobs, as they are truly exceptions, what about the many hundreds of thousands of other members? Their voices are rarely heard on the issues addressed in this book, and their views hardly sought, particularly by senior management. Yet there is a role for them to play, either in direct dialogue with line management or through their CIO's organization, as discussed in previous chapters.

To reiterate a few basic points, for one thing, since technologies can be shaped to meet the values and needs of society and its users, inventors and computer scientists should participate more in the conversations held outside the IT world about the implications and uses of computing. Now that IT is such an integral part of so many lives and so many forms of work, it is imperative that these professors, software engineers, and product developers comment and consult on the implications and uses of the technology with respect to education, health, global trade, environmental concerns, and social and political stability. Open-source ways of doing work, identity management, data privacy, military robotics, Internet censorship, patent and copyright issues, and pornography and children's exposure to it are just a handfull of issues the technologists need to discuss and engage in with non-IT parts of their societies. Why? Because they can shape the future forms of various technologies to reflect the values, needs, and concerns of the end users. Put another way, IT does not evolve largely due to some immutable laws of science and, specifically, physics, but at least more so as a reflection of some social or nonscientific need, such as the creation of ATMs for banking or smaller cell phones because humans like to talk to each other.

It is no accident that every year a group of IBM scientists sit down with the firm's CEO to discuss trends and to suggest lines of research that they want to pursue, priorities that are as much byproducts of their personal values and needs of the business as they are of the physics and science of the technologies themselves. More computer scientists should be sitting down with leaders of various organizations to have similar dialogues, or participate in or even host managerial retreats that last a couple of days, to expose them to emerging technologies and trends so that, collectively, line management can set priorities for their institutions and for the research of their computer scientists.

The implied IT militancy I am suggesting should extend deep into any organization, with programmers and systems analysts learning more about the business issues of their employer's firm or agency and about those of the industry in which those organizations reside. Then they should turn around and apply that knowledge to their IT work and, conversely, take their understanding of IT and influence the work of others in their organizations. Thus, it is not simply good enough to be a good programmer of banking applications for a bank, for instance. Increasingly, programmers need to understand the role of IT in the banking industry and appreciate the implications of their own work, ultimately advising management about the possibilities, opportunities, and threats posed by the IT work they do.

Then there are the formal computer science and engineering societies, such as those of the IEEE and ACM, and computer science departments at universities. They can use their voice and numbers of members to take stands on issues affecting the use of IT, such as those listed a couple of paragraphs above. Today, this remains a role yet to be effectively played by such institutions.

Before we leave this discussion, there still remains the question to answer of how to execute the kinds of suggestions just made. It is a matter of leadership, one that historical experience would suggest is fraught with noble attempts and intentions on the part of the technical and scientific communities engaged in IT that never achieved significant results. We will leave it to historians to sort out why that was the case because we have several circumstances today that make it possible for the IT community to weigh in more forcefully and effectively with its points of view than might have been the case even ten or twenty years ago. To begin with, the IT community has within it a wide range of skills at the individual level: CIOs and line management with IT skills, major IT vendors that have enormous influence in today's societies around the world, and technical societies that are bulging with large memberships of well-educated, voting citizens embedded in almost every community in the industrialized world and increasingly in developing economies. This world of IT is no longer made up of isolated academics, IT professionals locked up in glass houses, and teenagers inventing the next great thing in college dorms and garages. Recognize that today IT is big and visible, with millions of members in positions of power and with potential influence.

Second, as I have demonstrated in this book, this vast, partially organized community has the capability of changing the very nature of many of society's actions and agendas. The environmental scientists have recently demonstrated that power of science and leadership. The IT community also has opinions about what should be done in society, expressed at the individual and organizational levels through the writings and actions of single people and of industry associations and professional societies. IT firms and industry associations are busily at work lobbying governments and influencing profoundly the work and play of modern societies. But the professional associations have not played a strong role yet, and it is to that community that I want to suggest some recommendations with respect to their way forward. How best should we proceed with good leadership?

Rather than relying just on heroic leadership by individuals, academics, and technologists who personally may or may not have the skills or time to provide such voice, their professional associations should lead. In other words, embed the responsibility for leadership in organizations, making it part of the fabric of their culture and operations. They have the economic resources to hire consultants, media specialists, and lawyers, if needed, to help frame issues and articulate them. They can begin by framing cogent points of view on matters of interest to their membership, initially defined through surveys and polished with roundtables and existing committees. Those committees already exist and tend to attract leaders who, in time, become senior officials of the professional societies and, thus, know how to manage organizations, understand many of the key issues of the day, have the personal prestige and credentials to command respect, and a proven record of being able to lead colleagues.

Armed with an agenda of issues that deal with technical issues, role of IT in government, society, health, and economic well-being, for example, these organizations can then begin a two-track campaign to communicate their points of view. The first track is public relations, a campaign of communicating to the public through advertisements, editorials, articles, and television programs and talk radio. The public must become aware of issues, such as how IT can help citizens, firms, and public agencies clean up the environment or reduce automobile accidents, with recommendations for specific actions these audiences can take. The second track involves the leaders of these organizations forming alliances among themselves, which they know how to do today, and with new partners, such as professional organizations in other academic technical disciplines or industries, to go forth with common agendas. For example, there is near silence on the part of IT organizations about the use of electronic health records, yet governments in North America and Europe are implementing programs to spread this use of IT while small groups of citizen organizations are expressing concerns about privacy and data security issues. Where do the professional IT associations stand on this issue? They do not seem to engage in the debate, but could in a highly facilitative manner because they know that technology today can protect privacy and data security and, thus, how to implement these tools, but they do not share their insights and knowledge with the public. They could alleviate a great deal of anxiety and counsel public officials on how best to shape laws and practices to protect privacy and leverage the efficiencies of digitized records, and they could do this in collaboration with medical and insurance associations.

Armed with a network of alliances with various other organizations, a professional association can then move forward to influence the views and actions of those who shape a nation's practices, such as legislators, regulators, cabinet officials, and whole companies. Models exist for how to do this. In the United States, for example, the interests of senior citizens are addressed through this two-pronged leadership strategy by the AARP, whereas those of the medical profession are addressed by various associations that are often aligned with the largest in their industry, the American Medical Association (AMA). The IT industry has literally dozens of similar associations, lobbyists, and affiliated institutions that have the staffing and skills to execute a leadership plan. If the rising technology of the age were railroads, steam, electricity, nuclear energy or some other technology, we would not have to advocate a more overt and public role for IT professional associations. But those other technologies are not the rising ones of our time, as are computer science and information technologies and, in time, probably biotechnologies. Because it is IT, going back to part of the reason for thinking about the Information Age discussion, its community must act if for no other reason than to advocate in the best interests of its members.

THE ULTIMATE TREND

I have been looking at the role of IT as it has unfolded around the world for over three decades. Leaving aside the rapid and extensive diffusion of those technologies seemingly to everywhere, there is one pattern of behavior that so transcends any time, place, or technology that I believe it is the ultimate activity that will manifest itself in the years to come, for both good and bad purposes. In a word, it is collaboration. The technology has made it easier for the world's people to become more intimate with each other. This is not a new message, as it was delivered by futurists decades ago and most recently even in the widely read book by Thomas L. Friedman, *The World Is Flat*. What is new is that collaborative behavior, rather than just adversarial actions, has been increasing thanks to the nature of IT; indeed, the technology itself has conversely been molded in service to make collaboration more possible than in any time in human history, to the extent that today it involves billions of people. When 17 million people can come together on the first day that a new video game is put on the Internet, or a political candidate can raise millions of dollars over a weekend from hundreds of thousands of people, or a home video is seen by tens of millions of people in a few days, we have to conclude that something new is happening and happening quickly.

It is collaboration extended beyond anything we have seen in the past. It is collaboration among businesses (usually large firms with many smaller business partners in a supply chain), public institutions (such as the EU, UN, WHO, WTO, NATO), nonprofits (for instance Bill Gates' foundation with local health organizations), social movements (environmental groups, political parties), individuals (with social networks over the Internet). The list is long and, indeed, nearly endless. The technologist Chris Anderson recently posited a notion that he calls the Long Tail, in which people interested in one product who are scattered all over the world can become a viable market thanks to the ability of the Internet to bring them together such that a vendor can justify offering a product to them. This stands in sharp contrast to an earlier time, which is still very much with us, in which a merchant had to have a certain number of customers in a particular community in order to justify stocking his or her shelves in that community with a specific product. Anderson has argued that thanks to the Internet, we do not need that store or to all be physically living in that one community in order to acquire a product. As a result, one can make a profit selling goods and services that appeal to a very discrete group [26]. For example, a book on a very narrow issue, for sake of argument, say about political nationalism in the Iberian Peninsula during the Middle Ages, would never sell many copies in the United States and, indeed, probably not even in Spain, as there just are not enough historians and others interested in the topic to make it worthwhile to write, let alone publish. However, if one could get the word out about the book, in theory every person around the world interested in the topic would constitute a big enough market to warrant its publication [27].

Individuals and groups have already started to implement social and political versions of the Long Tail. It began with business and economic purposes, which Anderson and others have amply described, but has now begun moving more broadly to all manner of human activity. That trend mirrors the patterns of deployment discussed early in this book. We are only at the tip of that new version of deployment and, more to the point, it is at least as dependent on proactive collaboration as upon the technology with which to make it happen. It is at the heart of viral marketing, for example, whereby people collaborate consciously or subconsciously with vendors by passing on information about a product or service to others in their e-mail network.

Managers and public officials need to understand the dynamics of these modern forms of collaboration because some of these will become the defining new managerial practices that they will have to master. If they fail, their institutions will too. The Chinese government understands this so well that its officials aggressively limit (censor) what comes into China via the Internet, even forcing the mighty Google Empire to conform to its wishes. Internet-based stock trading in the 1990s was a very early example of what could happen to companies that ignore the Internet and new forms of business interactions. Many American firms were caught flatfooted and had to scramble to create new business models and, in the process, fundamentally altered how brokers were paid while driving down the costs of transactions in many cases by over 75% in a matter of a couple of years. The point is, we cannot ignore this new form of what one can characterize as perpetual collaboration [28].

This form of collaboration is also becoming pervasive. That development makes it easier for businesses, for example, to leverage social networking behaviors to sell their products. Governments could do the same, and political parties are already doing that in some countries, as, for example, in the United States during the 2008 presidential elections. If we step back and look at the managerial practices of governments over the past several centuries and compare those to the private sector, we would quickly conclude that the way public institutions operated mirrored those practices evident in the private sector. In some instances, governments led on a new practice; on other occasions it was the private sector or individuals that charged forward with new ways. Given that long-standing pattern of behavior, it is easy to conclude that public officials will increase dramatically their use of pervasive collaborative practices in their management of public affairs. That will mean delegating tasks, responsibilities, and accountabilities to individuals, companies, and nonprofit organizations, an uncomfortable notion to be sure for many public officials. The same thing is beginning to happen in business as well, with firms integrating more closely in a collaborative fashion with government agencies (e.g., in regional economic development initiatives) or with nonprofit organizations.

Although information technologies of the type we use today—computers and telecommunications—may seem pervasive, they are still relatively new and, as suggested earlier in this chapter, are expected to continue evolving over the next several decades. That means we have much to learn about how these technologies will unfold and influence human society. This book does not provide all the answers but, hopefully, has demonstrated the value of stepping back and observing what is happening before our eyes.

NOTES AND REFERENCES

1. I personally am not convinced that managers act upon good knowledge about the future because they are more motivated to take actions in response to current conditions than to future possibilities, even though many have acknowledged to me that they really needed to act differently to prepare for a future they believed would come. Business managers are intensely focused on the current quarter or year, and public officials on the current year's budget year, or they may want to wait until the next election is behind them.

2. There is a substantial collection of such reports focused on changes in business and on the role of IT, published between the 1930s and the 1980s, at the Charles Babbage Institute at the University of Minnesota, Minneapolis.

3. I documented over 8700 examples of this literature in James W. Cortada, *A Bibliographic Guide to the History of Computing, Computers, and the Infor-*

mation Processing Industry, Westport, CT: Greenwood Press, 1990; *A Second Bibliographic Guide to the History of Computing, Computers, and the Information Processing Industry,* Westport, CT: Greenwood Press, 1996; *A Bibliographic Guide to the History of Computer Applications, 1950–1990,* Westport, CT: Greenwood Press, 1996.

4. Two excellent surveys tell the story: Martin Campbell-Kelly and William Aspray, *Computer: A History of the Information Machine,* Boulder, CO: Westview, 2004; and Paul E. Ceruzzi, *A History of Modern Computing,* Cambridge, MA: MIT Press, 1998.

5. Based on mid-sized IBM 370 computers sold in 1976.

6. M. M. Waldrop, *Complexity: The Emerging Science at the Edge of Chaos,* New York: Simon & Schuster, 1991, p. 140; D.J. Watts, *Six Degrees: The Science of a Connected Age,* New York: W.W. Norton, 2003.

7. Michael E. Porter, *Competitive Strategy: Techniques for Analyzing Industries and Competitors,* New York: Free Press, 1980; Clayton M. Christensen, *The Innovator's Dilemma: When New Technologies Cause Great Firms to Fail,* Boston, MA: Harvard Business School Press, 1997, pp. 187–206; James W. Cortada, *The Digital Hand: How Computers Changed the Work of American Manufacturing, Transportation, and Retail Industries,* New York: Oxford University Press, 2004.

8. Political, economic, social and technological factors. The facets of public policy discussed in Chapter 3 are examples of PEST models.

9. For an example, see the approach taken by one futurist organization: Institute for Alternative Futures, http://www.altfutures.com (last accessed 3/4/2008).

10. Alvin Toffler, *Future Shock,* New York: Random House, 1970, p. 1; John Naisbitt, *Megatrends: Ten New Directions Transforming Our Lives,* New York: Warner Books, 1982, p. 1.

11. James W. Cortada and Heather E. Fraser, "Mapping the Future in Science-Intensive Industries: Lessons from the Pharmaceutical Industry," *IBM Systems Journal* 44, no. 1 (2005): 163–183.

12. Richard E. Neustadt and Ernest R. May, *Thinking in Time: The Uses of History for Decision Makers,* New York: Free Press, 1986.

13. For example, see "U.S. Congress Scraps Cotton Subsidy," *BBC News,* February 2, 2006, http://news.bbc.co.uk/2/hi/americas/4672786.stm (last accessed 3/8/2008).

14. Reference to "subcellular" alludes to systems biology, protein folding, and, for some readers, might also include protein structure prediction. The first is often quite limited by the lack of sufficient experimental data to produce predictive models of the cell. Protein dynamics are only just now being subjected to computational analysis, but more will occur over the next decade.

15. A. Murray, *The Lisbon Scorecard: The Status of Economic Reform in the Enlarging EU,* London: Centre for European Reform, March 2004.

16. David C. Mowery and Nathan Rosenberg, *Paths of Innovation: Technological Changes in 20th-Century America,* Cambridge, UK: Cambridge University Press, 1998, pp. 123–179.

17. Gordon Moore, pioneer developer of the transistor, observed in 1965 that the number of transistors one could put on a chip or integrated circuit quadru-

pled every three years due to innovations in the technology. The "Law" varied over the years as an observation of a general trend, such that today one normally thinks of the quadrupulating occurring roughly every two years. See William Aspray (Ed.), *Chasing Moore's Law: Information Technology Policy in the United States*, Raleigh, NC: SciTech, 2004, p. 23.

18. Brain power is only one of many important issues about the future of IT drawing the attention of computer scientists. See Peter J. Denning and Robert M. Metcalfe (Eds.), *Beyond Calculation: The Next Fifty Years of Computing*, New York: Copernicus, 1997.

19. Richard Silberglitt, Philip S. Antón, David R. Howell, and Anny Wong, *The Global Technology 2020, In-Depth Analyses*, Santa Monica, CA: RAND National Security Research Division, 2006.

20. Viral marketing techniques are those used on the Internet that cause websites or users to spread a marketing message to other websites and users.

21. "100,000,000th Account," MySpace, 2007-02-25 (last accessed 3/8/2008)

22. For a fuller explanation of the logic behind his statement and for the quote, see Samuel J. Palmisano, "The Globally Integrated Enterprise," *Foreign Affairs* 85, no. 3 (May–June 2006): 127–136.

23. IBM Corporation, *Balancing Risk and Performance with an Integrated Financial Organization: The Global CFO Study 2008*, Somers, NY: IBM Corporation, 2007.

24. Ibid.

25. Recent examples include, Peter Weill and Jeanne W. Ross, *IT Governance: How Top Performers Manage IT Decision Rights for Superior Results*, Boston, MA: Harvard Business School Press, 2004; Marianne Broadbent and Ellen S. Kitzis, *The New CIO Leader: Setting the Agenda and Delivering Results*, Boston, MA: Harvard Business School Press, 2005; George Westerman and Richard Hunter, *IT Risk: Turning Business Threats into Competitive Advantage*, Boston, MA: Harvard Business School Press, 2007.

26. Chris Anderson, *The Long Tail: Why the Future of Business Is Selling Less of More*, New York: Hyperion, 2006.

27. In fact, I personally tested this concept by publishing a book on precisely that topic and selling it over the Internet, with the result that there were sales from countries one never would have thought about and exchanges of e-mail with people from multiple countries regarding concepts discussed in the book. It was also self-published as part of the experiment, using modern IT and Internet facilities, which slashed time to produce the book by 75% when compared to how a traditional publisher does it, lowered production costs by over 50%, and returned higher levels of revenues than a publisher would have. The book is *Origins of Nation Building in the Iberian Peninsula*, 2008, available from any online book dealer, such as Amazon.com.

28. The phrase "pervasive collaboration" was the brainchild of a writer at IBM, Joni McDonald, who was trying to make sense of some of my research on public administration. It captured exactly what I was attempting to describe in a succinct way.

8

KEEPING UP: BIBLIOGRAPHIC ESSAY

The publications discussed below are those that helped to support the discussions in each chapter and are not intended to represent a definitive list of references, merely those that proved useful to me. They will be of interest to those who work in the general field of information technology and want to keep up with interesting reading materials. I have organized them by chapter theme.

THE BIG PICTURE

The most prolific writer in recent years on the features of an information society has been sociologist Manuel Castells. His *The Internet Galaxy: Reflections on the Internet, Business, and Society* (Oxford: Oxford University Press, 2001), a short, tightly written volume, focuses on the Internet and its impact on society. This book should also be read in conjunction with a series by Richard Florida. His two most recent ones are, *The Flight of the Creative Class* (New York: HarperBusiness, 2005), which discusses how high-tech and other creative workers are global citizens living around the world, and how they work, and, *Who's Your City?* (New York: Basic Books, 2008), which demonstrates that this class of workers are clustering in a number of cities where they can be the most creative; it is a fascinating study. Clay Shirky has described how groups of people come together using information technology in *Here Comes Everybody* (New York: Penguin, 2008). Recently, two excellent studies have appeared on the digital habits of young people: John Palfrey and Urs Gasser, *Born Digital: Understanding the First Generation of Digital Natives* (New York: Basic Books, 2008), and Don Tapscott, *Grown Up Digital: How the Net Generation Is Changing the World* (New York: McGraw-Hill, 2009).

Technology continues to affect economics and public policy and books and articles on these themes are appearing at the rate of one or two each week. However, it is a complicated, yet important set of themes that we need to understand, and some of the best literature takes time and effort to digest. Begin with Yochai Benkler, *The Wealth of Networks* (New Haven, CT: Yale University Press, 2006), which looks at social networking in the context of economics and public policy. Jonathan E. Nuechterlein and Philip J. Weiser have written a major book on American telecommunications policy for our times, *Digital Crossroads* (Cambridge, MA: MIT Press, 2005), while Amar Bhidé has explored how innovations sustain economic prosperity in a world linked by the Internet and other forms of communication, *The Venturesome Economy* (Princeton, N.J.: Princeton University Press, 2008). An older book that is extremely informative and easy to read is by Robert Gilpin, *The Challenge of Global Capitalism: The World Economy in the 21st Century* (Princeton, N.J.: Princeton University Press, 2000). One recent book that has received good reviews for explaining how technology is affecting social and economic relations was written by Nicholas Carr: *The Big Switch: Rewiring the World, From Edison to Google* (New York: W.W. Norton, 2008). Focus on the chapters dealing with the Internet, as his comments on Edison do not strike me as particularly informative for today's reader. Finally, two books approaching the digital age from different perspectives are both important and well informed: Stephen Baker, *The Numerati* (Boston, MA: Houghton Mifflin, 2008), in which he discusses how modeling and forecasting are being used to understand today's world; and Jonathan Zittrain, *The Future of the Internet and How to Stop It* (New Haven, CT: Yale University Press, 2008), who cautions us on our enthusiasm for the connected world.

Many readers will already know of Thomas L. Friedman's column in the *New York Times,* and his popular book, *The World Is Flat* (New York: Farrar, Straus and Giroux, 2nd ed., 2006), should not be ignored. He argues that the economies and societies of the world are highly integrated today, thanks to various technologies. However, geographers and area specialists have argued that he overstated the case; rather, they argue that local conditions still are important. For an excellent view contrary to Friedman's, see Harm De Blij, *The Power of Place* (New York: Oxford University Press, 2009). Finally, I would humbly offer up my three-volume study of how three dozen American industries embraced computing over the past six decades, because many of their practices continue and are diffusing around the world: *The Digital Hand,* 3 vols. (New York: Oxford University Press, 2004–2008).

HOW COMPUTERS SPREAD AROUND THE WORLD

Conversations about the spread of computing, or any technology, for that matter, must begin with discussions about innovation and what causes such transformations and the emergence of new tools. The literature is vast, but everyone seems to begin with one book first, that by Everett M. Rogers, *Diffusion of Innovations* (New York: Free Press, 5th ed., 2003), which for a long time has catalogued the basic forms of innovation and is an excellent source for other publications. How governments have encouraged the use of IT is still the subject of much study, but a good place to begin, since it has historical context, is a set of papers written on a country-by-country basis by a group of contributors: Richard Coopey (Ed.), *Information Technology Policy: An International History* (Oxford: Oxford University Pres, 2004). Looking at the subject of innovation from the perspective of how technologists, organizations, and industries share knowledge of a technology, one cannot go wrong in reading Eric von Hippel's newest book, *Democratizing Innovation* (Cambridge, MA: MIT Press, 2005). For specific examples, see Linsu Kim and Richard R. Nelson (Eds.), *Technology, Learning, and Innovation: Experiences of Newly Industrializing Economies* (Cambridge, UK: Cambridge University Press, 2000). The great business historian, Alfred D. Chandler, Jr., has looked carefully at the computer industry and explained in very clear language how it evolved and spread in *Inventing the Electronic Cen-*

tury: The Epic Story of the Consumer Electronics and Computer Industries (Cambridge, MA: Harvard University Press, 2005).

China, India, and Asia as a whole continue to receive constant attention, with the result that there are whole bookshelves of materials on each. Two recent publications, however, present excellent discussions of the interactions among technology, economics, and public and private practices. The first is by Ernest J. Wilson, III: *The Information Revolution and Developing Countries* (Cambridge, MA: MIT Press, 2004). The second is by James M. Popkin and Partha Lyengar: *IT and the East: How China and India Are Altering the Future of Technology and Innovation* (Boston, MA: Harvard Business School Press, 2007). For open-source computing, my favorite book is still Steven Weber's, *The Success of Open Source* (Cambridge, MA: Harvard University Press, 2004). Just read it.

Many think tanks, government agencies, and banks publish extensively on these general themes. I find that the World Bank produces excellent economic analysis on a country-by-country basis that is quite readable and posts a great deal of this material on its website (http://publications.worldbank.org/ecommerce). It is also easy to navigate. Both the OECD (http://oecd.org.publications) and the European Union (http://publications.europa.eu) post similar material to their websites, although navigating them can sometimes be challenging, but worth the effort. Professor Hal Varian of the University of California-Berkeley has a great website that points to many other websites for information about technology, economics, social factors, and business (http://people.ischool.berkeley.edu/~hal/). The U.S. Department of Commerce and the U.S. Bureau of the Census routinely publish useful data and studies on the diffusion of IT as well.

GOVERNMENTS LEVERAGING IT FOR ECONOMIC DEVELOPMENT

I have mentioned a number of publications on this theme already, but I want to add several other recommendations on materials that are tactical and well informed. The United Nations, World Economic Forum, and the Economist Intelligence Unit routinely publish world-wide rankings of the deployment of IT by nations, in which they include information about national economic and technological public policies and programs. These are excellent sources for staying current. Monographic studies on various countries and regions appear continuously as well. Two recent publications in particular are useful. Dan Breznitz looked at three countries that are routinely showcased as leading examples of how governments leverage technology to improve local economies: *Innovation and the State: Political Choice and Strategies for Growth in Israel, Taiwan, and Ireland* (New Haven, CT: Yale University Press, 2007). Three very experienced and highly regarded economists wrote a most readable book: William J. Baumol, Robert E. Litan, and Carl J. Schramm, *Good Capitalism, Bad Capitalism, and the Economics of Growth and Prosperity* (New Haven, CT: Yale University Press, 2007). Open standards is looming as a technological strategy being embraced by public officials. To understand this angle of the topic, consult Rishab A. Ghosh, *An Economic Basis for Open Standards* (Maastricht: University of Maastricht, 2005), and the Committee for Economic Development, *Open Standards, Open Source, and Open Innovation: Harnessing the Benefits of Oppenness* (Washington, DC: Committee for Economic Development, 2006). A wonderful good read is Espen Moe, *Governance, Growth and Global Leadership: The Role of the State in Technological Progress, 1750–2000* (Burlington, VT: Ashgate, 2007), but if you are going to read that book, then take the time to also enjoy Carlotta Perez, *Technological Revolutions and Financial Capital: The Dynamics of Bubbles and Golden Ages* (Cheltenham, UK: Edward Elgar, 2002). There is also the short minor classic by Angus Maddison: *Growth and Interaction in the World Economy: The Roots of Modernity* (Washington, DC: American Enterprise Institute, 2005). A practical volume that I find useful is Richard H. K. Vietor, *How Countries Compete: Strategy, Structure, and Government in the Global Economy* (Boston, MA: Harvard Business School Press, 2007).

DECIDING WHAT TECHNOLOGY TO USE

There are two sides to this conversation: one is the "how do you do it" aspect and the other is the economic observations about managerial behavior. For the first issue, begin with Peter Weill and Jeanne W. Ross, *IT Governance: How Top Performers Manage IT Decisions for Superior Results* (Boston, MA: Harvard Business School Press, 2004). Every year it seems, there is a new crop of books advising CIOs how best to do their jobs. Some of the more useful ones to consult include Marianne Broadbent and Ellen Kitzis, *The New CIO Leader: Setting the Agenda and Delivering Results* (Boston, MA: Harvard Business School Press, 2004) which is a good primer on the basics. George Tillmann, *The Business-Oriented CIO: A Guide to Market-Driven Management* (New York: Wiley, 2008) was written by an ex-CIO; Mark D. Lutchen: *Managing IT as a Business: A Survival Guide for CEOs* (New York: Wiley, 2004) broadens the decision-making process to general management. Jan De Sutter's *The Power of IT: Survival Guide for the CIO* (North Charleston, SC: BookSurge, 2004) I mention because it is less about the role of CIOs as decision makers on what to acquire and more a large anthology about the technologies and general IT managerial issues they face. Phillip A. Lapante and Thomas Costello have written a "how to" book for CIOs and other IT managers, *CIO Wisdom II: More Best Practices* (Upper Saddle River, N.J.: Prentice Hall/PTR, 2006), although a better read is a book on the same subject by Karl D. Schubert, *CIO Survival Guide: The Roles and Responsibilities of the Chief Information Officer* (New York: Wiley, 2004). Finally, for a more strategic discussion of the role, there is Wayne L. Anderson, *Unwrapping the CIO: Demystifying the Chief Information Officer Position* (New York: iUniverse, 2006).

Economic discussions about how companies and whole industries acquire IT and their impact can be quite interesting and also esoteric. It is not a highly accessible literature because it is written largely by economists for other economists. For an introduction, however, begin with an older short book by Daniel E. Sichel, *The Computer Revolution: An Economic Perspective* (Washington, DC: Brookings Institution Press, 1997). If you can find a copy, one of the most interesting and clear-thinking books on how digital technologies affect economies and societies is by Graham Tanaka, *Digital Deflation: The Productivity Revolution and How It Will Ignite the Economy* (New York: McGraw-Hill, 2004). A very dry but highly authoritative set of essays by economists is Erik Brynjolfsson and Brian Kahin (Eds.), *Understanding the Digital Economy: Data, Tools, and Research* (Cambridge, MA: MIT Press, 2000). The first major book to appear on the implications of the Internet and what its economic impact would be remains the classic on the subject: Carl L. Shapiro and Hal R. Varian, *Information Rules: A Strategic Guide to the Network Economy* (Boston, MA: Harvard Business School Press, 1999). It became a best selling business book. The other book to read along with the Shapiro-Varian tome is an edited book of papers prepared by the Brookings Task Force on the Internet: Robert E. Litan and Alice M. Rivlin (Eds.), *The Economic Payoff from the Internet Revolution* (Washington, DC: Brookings Institution Press, 2001).

LIVING IN THE INFORMATION AGE

Many of the books listed above speak directly to life in a world in which IT plays an extensive role. I believe strongly that one useful way to understand contemporary circumstances is to read about their recent history. There are now a couple of hundred good books on this topic, but here are some basic works that one can begin with. Start with Martin Campbell-Kelly and William Aspray, *Computer: A History of the Information Machine* (New York: Basic Books, 1996), which provides a general, very accessible history, then follow it up with Paul E. Ceruzzi, *A History of Modern Computing* (Cambridge, MA: MIT Press, 2nd ed., 2003), which is more technical in its discussion of the technology. For a study of the role of information in American society, taking the story back to the 1700s, see Alfred D. Chandler, Jr. and James W. Cortada (Eds.), *A Nation Transformed by Information: How Information Has Shaped the United States from Colonial Times to the Present* (New York: Oxford University Press, 2000), and then for a general history of the Internet and business, see William Aspray and Paul E. Ceruzzi (Eds.), *The Internet and American Business* (Cambridge, MA: MIT Press, 2008). There are some hidden gems in the literature. One is by Jorge Reina Schement and Terry Curtis: *Tendencies and Tensions of the Information Age: The Production and Distribution of Information in the United States* (New Brunswick, NJ: Transaction Publishers, 1995). Its title tells it all. Another, though quite the academic monograph, that is well executed was written by Joel Mokyr: *The Gifts of Athena: Historical Origins of the Knowledge Economy* (Princeton, NJ; Princeton University Press, 2002). There are scores of histories of specific technologies, machines, software, and telecommunications, including some on the Internet. *The IEEE Annals of the History of Computing* is the journal of record for histories of the technologies and their uses, users, inventors, and for bibliographic discussions and reviews.

The sociological literature on contemporary affairs is also useful; many of the key works have already been introduced above. However, there are several other important publications. The monumental work done by Manuel Castells remains essential: *The Information Age: Economy, Society and Culture,* 3 vols (Oxford: Blackwell, 1996–1998). It is one of the few publications that is global in scope; most sociological studies focus on the experience of the United States, or are articles in academic journals on very narrow themes. Part of the reason I questioned whether we lived in the Information Age is because the sociologists have yet do the serious work of documenting the contemporary period's use of IT and its consequences; the economists and media experts are the ones who have done the most work and their evidence is insufficient so far to be persuasive. Despite the good work of Castells and Florida, and to a lesser extent Tapscott and a few others, there is much remaining to be done. But even in this space, there are some useful materials. For example, Christopher M. Kelty has taken on the difficult task of attempting to look at technology from essentially an anthropological perspective, succeeding nicely with *Two Bits: The Cultural Significance of Free Software* (Durham, NC: Duke University Press, 2008). Examples worth reading that deal with the Internet are essays in a contributed volume, David Porter (Ed.), *Internet Culture* (New York: Routledge, 1996). There is a growing body of research on the role of technology on language, primarily about English. A recent example of a well-done study by a professor of linguistics is Naomi S. Baron, *Always On: Language in an Online and Mobile World* (New York: Oxford University Press, 2008). Then there is Ray Kurzweil, who no serious student of the role of technology in modern society should ever ignore. He is an inventor, social commentator, and author of important books on technology and modern society. I suggest you begin with his latest book, the very long and substantive volume, *The Singularity Is Near: When Humans Transcend Biology* (New York: Viking, 2005), which argues forcefully what the future of society will look like in large part thanks to the evolving nature of information technology and biology.

ROLE OF TECHNOLOGISTS

Computer scientists have been commenting on technology, their role in it, and the nature of society for decades. One of the first important collections of such writings was collected into a volume by Michael Dertouzos and Joel Moses (Eds.), *The Computer Age: A*

Twenty-Five Year View (Cambridge, MA: MIT Press, 1979). Nicholas Negreponte, of MIT, wrote *Being Digital* (New York: Alfred A. Knopf, 1995), in which he describes the kind of future for society that he envisions. Whole IT corporations are embracing more socially aggressive agendas. Google is the most obvious because of its aspiration to organize all the information in the world into a digital form. Its role is described by Randall Stross, *Planet Google: One Company's Audacious Plan to Organize Everything We Know* (New York: Free Press, 2008). Finally, there is the most famous computer technologist of them all, Bill Gates, who has taken what he has learned and set up the world's largest nonprofit foundation to address the educational and medical needs of the planet. He has also published two books that speak to the role people, including computer experts, should play as members of the larger society: *The Road Ahead* (New York: Viking, 1995) and *Business @ The Speed of Thought: Using A Digital Nervous System* (New York: Warner Books, 1999).

INTO THE TWENTY-FIRST CENTURY

To understand how computing is evolving, we need to appreciate some of the scientific and engineering trends at large. A good introduction to chaos theory is M. M. Waldrop, *Complexity: The Emerging Science at the Edge of Chaos* (New York: Simon & Schuster, 1991), and on the parallel developments of connections and interactions among atoms and digits, see, for example, D. J. Watts, *Six Degrees: The Science of a Connected Age* (New York: W.W. Norton, 2003). Both are highly accessible in the way they present complex scientific ideas. With respect to IT itself, much continues to appear about its future. A thoughtful analysis is provided by Richard Silberglitt, Philip S. Antón, David R. Howell, and Anny Wong, *The Global Technology 2020. In-Depth Analyses* (Santa Monica, CA: RAND National Security Research Division, 2006). With respect to nanotechnologies, there is Serge Luryi, Jimmy Xu, and Alex Zaslavsky (Eds.), *Future Trends in Microelectronics: The Nano Millennium* (New York: IEEE/Wiley, 2002), but see also David M. Berube, *Nano-Hype: The Truth Behind the Nanotechnology Buzz* (Amherst, NY: Prometheus Books, 2006). A more populist view is provided by Stanley Schmidt, *The Coming Convergence: Surprising Ways Diverse Technologies Interact to*

Shape Our World and Change the Future (Amherst, NY: Prometheus Book, 2008). But not all is blue skies and open highways for technology ahead. For a discussion of the implications and possible constraints on unbridled adoption of technologies, see Tarleton Gillepsie's excellent book, *Wired Shut: Copyright and the Shape of Digital Culture* (Cambridge, MA: MIT Press, 2007).

INDEX

ABOUT THE AUTHOR

James W. Cortada is a 35-year veteran of IBM, where he has held various sales, consulting, and managerial positions. He currently is a member of the IBM Institute for Business Value, leading teams that do research, publish, and work with clients on issues of importance to management in public sector industries around the world. He is the author or editor of more than 50 books on business and the management and history of Information Technology. Some of Cortada's most recent publications include the three-volume history of Information Technology in American industries, *The Digital Hand* (Oxford University Press, 2004–2008) and with Pulitzer Prize-winning historian Alfred D. Chandler, Jr., co-edited *A Nation Transformed by Information* (Oxford University Press, 2000). He is currently writing a history of how computers spread around the world. Cortada serves on the editorial board of the *IEEE Annals of the History of Computing*, the Museum Prize Committee of The Society for the History of Technology (SHOT), the IEEE Computer Society Press Operations Committee, and on the board of directors of the IT History Society. He holds a B.A., M.A., and Ph.D. in History.